The Irish Policeman, 1822–1922

The Irish Policeman
1822–1922

A Life

Elizabeth Malcolm

FOUR COURTS PRESS

Set in 12.5 on 14.5 point Centaur for
FOUR COURTS PRESS LTD
7 Malpas Street, Dublin 8, Ireland
e-mail: info@four-courts-press.ie
http://www.four-courts-press.ie
and in North America for
FOUR COURTS PRESS
c/o ISBS, 920 N.E. 58th Avenue, Suite 300, Portland, OR 97213.

A catalogue record for this title
is available from the British Library.

ISBN (10 digit) 1–85182–920–2
ISBN (13 digit) 978–1–85182–920–0

Printed in England
by MPG Books, Bodmin, Cornwall

Contents

Illustrations
appearing between pages 128 and 129

Acknowledgments and apologies

This book has been so long in the making as to have become, frankly, something of an embarrassment to me. I have been researching and writing it seriously – on and off – for more than fifteen years, and the topic has interested me for nearly thirty. There are certainly many tales of historians – Irish historians included – taking ten, twenty or even thirty years to produce books, so I am aware that my experience is far from unusual. But does such an extended gestation period actually improve the end product? I confess that I do not know. Yet, I fear, I am rather enamoured of the romantic notion of a brilliant book rushed off in a matter of weeks or months that changes perceptions of the subject forever. Well, this book has certainly not been rushed off, and whether it changes perceptions, or not, remains to be seen. Perhaps all I can say to my readers is that, had I published the book ten years ago, it would have been very different from what it is today.

As I explain in Chapter 2, the historiography of policing, and of Irish policing in particular, has developed substantially in recent years. This has had a profound influence on my work. Originally I was thinking in terms of writing a political history of policing, devoted to exploring the role that the police played in maintaining British rule in Ireland during the nineteenth and early twentieth centuries. The police were a crucial arm of British government: the 'eyes and ears' of Dublin Castle, as their critics liked to claim. But a great deal has now appeared on the politics of policing, and, being myself basically a social historian, I decided – with a degree of relief – some years ago that I would write instead a social history of policing.

Of course policemen worked for political masters and so politics inevitably shaped their lives profoundly, and, by extension, the lives of their families. The book therefore has a substantial political content. But what I have essentially tried to do is to offer a collective biography of the Irish police from about 1822 to about 1922. In others words, I have structured the book as a chronological life history, tracing lives from birth to death

— and beyond, in terms of descendants. However, instead of only dealing with one life or a handful of lives, I have dealt with tens of thousands of lives. Obviously my collective portrait will not accurately reflect the lives of all policemen who served during this one-hundred-year period, but I confidently believe it does reflect the lives of many of them. I suspect that if any pre-1922 policemen were able to read it — and I think there are none now alive — they would find much of what I describe to be familiar.

Readers I hope will gain a better understanding of why so many Irishmen served the British state for so many years. They were bitterly condemned by some at the time for doing so, and have been condemned subsequently. My aim is not to justify their choice of career or the actions they took as policemen. I leave judgments on that score up to my readers. My aim is simply to identify who they were and re-create what their lives were like. I hope readers will finish the book knowing these men rather better than they did before — and perhaps also feeling a degree of empathy with them in the very difficult choices that many of them were forced to make.

I cannot possibly thank all the people who have helped with and contributed to the making of this book. There have simply been too many people over too many years. But there are a number of individuals and institutions I would like especially to acknowledge.

I began work on this project with Professor W.J. Lowe, who has gone on to publish a series of important articles about policing. I am very grateful to him for his assistance and advice. Richard Hawkins, who has also produced a number of key studies, has always been extraordinarily generous with his knowledge.

At the Institute of Irish Studies, University of Liverpool, where I worked during the 1990s, the directors — first Professor Patrick Buckland and later Professor Marianne Elliott — were extremely supportive. Professor Elliott, like a number of Irish scholars, has police ancestry and she urged me on more than one occasion to finish this book. I am grateful for her much-needed confidence and encouragement. Others whose ancestors served in the police and who assisted me include, Professor Tom Garvin, Professor Roy Foster, Professor Nicholas Grene, Dr Stephen Lalor, Dr Margaret MacCurtain and the late Professor Patrick O'Farrell.

At the Institute, I would also especially like to thank Linda Christiansen, Dorothy Lynch and Dr Ian McKeane, who all helped make my years in Liverpool very pleasant indeed. Dr Mark Radford and Dr

Michael Huggins were postgraduate students of mine researching theses connected with crime and policing. I benefited a great deal from discussions with them both. Dr Radford in particular worked for me as a research assistant, while I was in Liverpool and later in Melbourne, and has made a huge contribution to this book. I am deeply in his debt.

The publicity given to my work by a number of Irish journalists was invaluable in the collection of family policing histories. Chapter 9 is largely based on material acquired by means of newspaper appeals. I am grateful to Kevin Myers of the *Irish Times* for his support, and especially to the over 200 policemen and their descendants who wrote to me during the early 1990s. Many were elderly and the physical act of writing was a struggle; some were recalling painful childhood experiences and disclosing family secrets. A number wrote to me regularly, enclosing important documents and photographs. In most cases I have respected their privacy by not naming them; others I have acknowledged in footnotes. I was very moved by their willingness to share difficult and complex memories with me. Although the book has taken far longer to produce than I expected when I corresponded with them ten to fifteen years ago, their contribution remains immense.

At various times over many years I have also benefited from discussions and correspondence with the late Professor T.W. Moody, Professor John Belchem, Professor Clive Emsley, Dr Ian Bridgeman, Professor Mark Finnane, Associate Professor David Philips, Professor John D. Brewer, Professor Maria Luddy, Professor James S. Donnelly, Jr, Dr Angela Bourke, Dr Pauline Prior, Dr Patrick O'Sullivan, Jim Herlihy and the late Gregory Allen.

The staff of the Garda Síochána Museum and Archives, first based at Garda Headquarters in Phoenix Park and later in Dublin Castle, helped me find many important sources. I cannot speak too highly of the enthusiastic assistance and hospitality I received from Inspector John Duffy, former curator of the archives, and from his staff. The Royal Ulster Constabulary Museum and Archives at Knock Road in Belfast also allowed me access to many vital sources. The former curator, Superintendent Robin Sinclair, was always remarkably generous with advice and information and the current curator, Hugh Forrester, has assisted on numerous occasions.

Staff of the National Library of Ireland, the Irish National Archives, the Library of Trinity College, Dublin, the Folklore Archives at University

College, Dublin, the Public Record Office of Northern Ireland and the Linenhall Library in Belfast, the Public Record Office in London, the John Rylands Library at the University of Manchester and the Baillieu Library at the University of Melbourne, were all extremely helpful at different times.

Funding to help support this project came from various sources. I would like to acknowledge the support, in the UK, of the Economic and Social Research Council, the Wellcome Trust, the Leverhulme Trust, the British Academy and the British Council, and, in Australia, of the Australian Research Council. In recent years visiting fellowships at Queen's University, Belfast, Trinity College, Dublin, and the University of Liverpool have afforded me valuable further opportunities for research and writing.

I came to Melbourne in 2000 to take up a new and demanding position. I would like to thank all those who welcomed me then and have supported me since, especially Dr Val Noone, Mary Doyle, Dr Philip Bull, Associate Professor Frances Devlin-Glass, Dr Lindsay Proudfoot, Fr Peter L'Estrange SJ, Dr Brad Patterson, Dr Peter Kuch, Dr Pamela O'Neill, Dr Nicola Nixon, Dr Rosemary Sheehan, Mary Kenneally and Rod Quantock. The Higgins and Myers families have been extraordinarily generous in supporting Irish Studies in Melbourne, as was Professor Alan Gilbert, the former vice chancellor of Melbourne University.

Finally, my old friends, Professor Ruth Sherry, Dr Christina Hunt Mahony and Tonie van Marle, and newer friends, Ria Hayward and Robyn Bradbury, have sustained me in ways I could not possibly explain. As both colleague and friend, Dr Dianne Hall has been a joy to work with in Melbourne, and I look forward to our continuing collaboration in the future on projects related to this one. In the early stages of the project Dr Robert Stevens challenged me with difficult questions and helped me struggle to overcome my congenital technological deficiencies. Aside from Bill Lowe, I owe many of the statistics in this book to Rob Stevens.

My brother, Robert Johnston, and my son, Hartley Stevens, have endeavoured, in different ways, to convince me that there is life outside academic research and writing. I fear that, for better or worse, I remain unpersuaded.

ELM
17 March 2005

Abbreviations

CSORP	Chief Secretary's Office, Registered Papers
DI	District Inspector (before 1883 Sub Inspector)
DMP	Dublin Metropolitan Police
ELM	The Author
HO	Home Office
IRA	Irish Republican Army
JP	Justice of the Peace
MS	Manuscript
NAI	National Archives of Ireland
NLI	National Library of Ireland
OP	Outrage Papers
PMG	Paymaster General
PRO(L)	Public Record Office, London
PRONI	Public Record Office of Northern Ireland
RIC	Royal Irish Constabulary
RM	Resident Magistrate
RUC	Royal Ulster Constabulary
TCD	Trinity College, Dublin
UCD	University College, Dublin
USC	Ulster Special Constabulary

CHAPTER ONE

Policing Ireland before 1836:
from kin to constables

> In spite of the absence of a State system of law-enforcement in pre-Norman Ireland ... it is likely that in most cases the prestige of the law and the judge's office – combined with the system of pledges and sureties [by the defendant's kin] – would have ensured that the fines imposed by judges in court were actually paid.[1]

> ... when thieves or robbers come into any district to take plunder or do any other evil, all the people of the district ... shall rise together and effectually pursue them ...[2]

> In order to maintain a regular Police a constant and uniform support is necessary which can be had from the principal inhabitants alone. The occasional interference of the superior government may quell an insurrection and repress a temporary violence, but will contribute nothing towards establishing habitual obedience to the law ...[3]

Policing in Ireland has a long and complex history – and one not yet adequately explored. This book is far from a comprehensive study of that history, as it deals with only one force – the Irish county constabulary, which in 1867 became the Royal Irish Constabulary (RIC) – and it covers only one century – 1822 to 1922. Moreover, it does not even aspire to be a definitive history of the constabulary; rather it is an attempt to re-create the lives of those who served in that force.

Yet, Ireland has been policed for many centuries, in various ways, by different groups. In order therefore to situate the constabulary in a broad Irish policing context and to highlight some of the force's novel features, this chapter offers a brief survey of policing before 1822–1922 and an

1 Fergus Kelly, *A guide to early Irish law* (Dublin, 1988), p. 214. 2 Philomena Connolly, 'The enactments of the 1297 parliament: translation' in James Lydon (ed.), *Law and disorder in thirteenth-century Ireland: the Dublin parliament of 1297* (Dublin, 1997), p. 153. 3 Lord Carysfort to Chief Secretary Thomas Orde, 31 Jan. 1787, quoted in Stanley Palmer, *Police and protest in England and Ireland, 1780–1850* (Cambridge, 1988), p. 109.

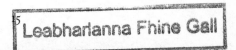

account of the consolidation of the constabulary in 1836. For convenience
the history of Irish policing can be divided into four chronological periods: pre-1780s, 1786–1822, 1822–1922 and 1922 to 1968.[4] This chapter will
survey the first two periods, extending the discussion up to 1836; Chapters
2 to 8 will largely deal with the third period; and the final period will be
examined in Chapter 9.

THE PRE-HISTORY OF IRISH POLICING BEFORE THE 1780S

The years before the 1780s are perhaps most appropriately characterised
as the pre-history of Irish policing in the sense that state-controlled,
highly organised, professional forces did not exist. It is vital to recognise
that modern police forces were largely a nineteenth-century innovation
in Ireland, as they were in many other countries as well. In Ireland before
the nineteenth century policing was essentially community based and
locally regulated, and was generally a part-time occupation.

. Medieval Ireland certainly had full-time, professional judges whose
job it was to interpret the laws and to use them to resolve disputes and
punish malefactors. Before the arrival of the Anglo-Normans in the late
twelfth century, Irish brehon law operated throughout the country.[5]
Thereafter brehon law was restricted to Irish lordships, while English
common law operated in the English lordship[6] and a mixture of the two,
known as 'march law', developed in frontier areas.[7] Medieval Ireland was
thus far from a lawless society; in fact, it was a society with several competing, and sometimes conflicting, law codes, which meant that enforcing the laws was often difficult.[8]

Under traditional Irish brehon law, crimes were mostly punished by
an elaborate system of fines. The brehons, or judges, investigated cases,

---

4 Seamus Breathnach proposed three chronological periods defined by nomenclature: 'garda' covering both the pre-
Norman and the post-1922 periods; 'constable' covering the twelfth to the eighteenth centuries; and 'police' covering the late eighteenth century down to 1922, plus 'in a general modern sense thereafter'. Breathnach was right to
stress that changing terminology is important, but his loose use of different names and his jumbling of quite
diverse periods is decidedly confusing. My periodisation, although certainly not unproblematic, is at least clearer
and more straightforward. Seamus Breathnach, *The Irish police from the earliest times to the present day* (Dublin, 1974), p. 8.
5 For a compendium and general discussion of brehon law, see Kelly, *A guide to early Irish law*. 6 G.J. Hand, *English
law in Ireland, 1290–1324* (Cambridge, 1967); A.J. Otway-Ruthven, 'The native Irish and English law in medieval
Ireland', *Irish Historical Studies*, vii, 25 (March 1950), pp 1–16. 7 Brendan Smith, 'The concept of the march in
Medieval Ireland: the case of Uriel', *Proceedings of the Royal Irish Academy*, 88 C, 8 (1988), pp 257–69. 8 Some of the
problems of law enforcement, from an English perspective, are discussed in Lydon (ed.), *Law and disorder*.

determined guilt or innocence and levied fines accordingly. But it was up to kinship groups to enforce these penalties. There were no specialised constables, policemen or guards to carry out the decisions of the judges and there were no prisons in which the guilty parties could be confined for punishment. Within Irish kingdoms or lordships kinship groups appear to have cooperated reasonably effectively to enforce brehon law, as Fergus Kelly suggests in the quotation at the beginning of this chapter. But when crimes crossed the boundaries of individual lordships, then enforcement of penalties became much more problematic.[9]

From the beginning of the fourteenth century, copying recent developments in England,[10] a system of keepers or justices of the peace (JPs), petty or parish constables and night watchmen was introduced into the English lordship in Ireland.[11] But such officials were few and operated only on a part-time basis.[12] Watchmen were restricted to towns and constables had extensive administrative functions, in addition to their peace-keeping role. So, despite significant differences between Irish brehon law and English common law, in both parts of Ireland policing was essentially community-based. In Gaelic Ireland the onus for enforcement fell upon the kin; in the Pale and the English towns it was householders who were obliged to keep arms and, if called upon by justices, constables or watchmen, to participate in the 'hue and cry'. All property-holding males were expected to play an active role in maintaining peace and order in their localities, as the statutes of the 1297 Dublin parliament, quoted at the beginning of the chapter, make very plain.[13]

As English rule expanded in the sixteenth and seventeenth centuries so this system of part-time magistrates, constables and watchmen slowly spread throughout the country.[14] Yet the notion that communities and kin

---

9 For a valuable account of the operation of brehon law in terms of the crime of homicide, see Neil McLeod, 'The blood-feud in medieval Ireland' in Pamela O'Neill (ed.), *Between intrusions: Britain and Ireland between the Romans and the Normans* (Sydney, 2004), pp 114–33. 10 Clive Emsley, *The English police: a political and social history* (Hemel Hempstead, 1991), pp 8–9. 11 The Statute of Winchester, passed by an English parliament in 1285, was extended to Ireland in 1308. It and subsequent acts of 1360 (34 Edw. III, c.1), 1465 (5 Edw. IV, c.5) and 1495 (10 Hen. VII, c.9) empowered local justices of the peace to have criminals arrested and to hear cases, ordered the appointment of parish constables and regulated the duties of night watchmen in towns. Breathnach, *The Irish police*, pp 13–15. 12 Robin Frame, 'The judicial powers of the medieval Irish keepers of the peace', *Irish Jurist*, new series, 2 (1967), pp 308–26. 13 In Ireland keeping the peace involved justices and householders in both military and policing duties, while in England these duties tended to become separated during the fourteenth century. Robin Frame, 'Military service in the Lordship of Ireland, 1290–1360' in Robert Bartlett and Angus Mackay (eds), *Medieval frontier societies* (Oxford, 1989), pp 108–9. 14 For a description of the system of law enforcement at the end of the seventeenth century and during the early eighteenth century, see Neal Garnham, *The courts, crime and the criminal law*

had a right to enforce laws lingered on. Most of the enforcers of the law up to the early nineteenth century were still not professionals, in the sense of being full-time, trained officers; thus community policing did not disappear even with the English conquest. Undoubtedly also, the fact that judges, magistrates, lawyers and constables were Protestants – Catholics having been excluded from these offices under the Penal Laws[15] – helped strengthen, among Catholics at least, a belief in the greater efficacy of local methods of justice. It is surely no coincidence that secret societies, which flourished between the 1760s and the 1840s, often adopted quasi-legal modes of expression when inflicting punishment.[16] They saw themselves as enforcing community laws in opposition to the official English code, which was firmly under the control of their Protestant rulers.[17] And, in a certain sense, they were correct when they regarded their methods as more traditional and therefore, by extension, as more legitimate.

THE IRISH POLICE EXPERIMENTS, 1786–1822

In the twenty-first century we tend to take the need for state police forces as self-evident. Yet, not only are they a relatively recent phenomenon in many countries, but their introduction was often slow and highly contentious. In Ireland it took nearly half a century of experimentation with various types of police force, in the face of a great deal of opposition from all sections of society, before a national constabulary finally emerged in 1836.

This 'experiment', as Stanley Palmer has termed it,[18] began in Dublin in 1786. Policing in eighteenth-century Dublin was organised on the basis of Protestant parishes, with churchwardens assembled at vestry meetings empowered to appoint part-time constables, who were then responsible for

in Ireland, 1692–1720 (Dublin, 1996), pp 27–47. 15 Catholics were not excluded, however, from serving as night watchmen, except in Dublin. But they were excluded explicitly from filling the office of constable, although this ban does not appear to have been enforced rigorously. Ibid., pp 28–9. 16 Michael Beames, *Peasants and power: the Whiteboy movements and their control in pre-Famine Ireland* (Brighton, 1983), pp 75–7. There are many examples of such modes in the letters reproduced in S.R. Gibbons, *Captain Rock, Night Errant: the threatening letters of pre-Famine Ireland, 1801–45* (Dublin, 2004). 17 The operation of communal law was by no means restricted to Ireland. As E.P. Thompson demonstrated in his seminal article on the 'moral economy' of the English crowd, so-called riots were often expressions of a popular set of policing norms. E.P. Thompson, *Customs in common* (London, 1991), pp 185–351. For early modern English attitudes to the law, see John Brewer and John Styles (eds), *An ungovernable people: the English and their law in the seventeenth and eighteenth centuries* (London, 1980), pp 11–20. 18 Stanley Palmer, 'The Irish police experiment: the beginnings of modern police in the British Isles, 1785–95' in Ian O'Donnell and Finbarr McAuley (eds), *Criminal justice history: themes and controversies from pre-Independence Ireland* (Dublin, 2003), pp 98–112.

the recruitment of night watchmen.[19] In rural Ireland part-time magistrates controlled the appointment of parish constables and watchmen. Policing was largely seen as an after dark activity and watchmen were householders who were obliged to serve from sunset to sunrise on a rotating basis. Originally they were not paid, but as Irish cities and towns grew in the eighteenth century, some introduced payment for night watch duties. Yet constables were often incompetent or corrupt and watchmen frequently failed to fulfil their duties, while the Irish magistracy was notoriously negligent.[20]

In Ireland, as in England[21] during the final decades of the eighteenth century, there was growing concern over the maintenance of law and order and a perception that the existing policing system was outdated and ineffective. In Ireland the government was faced with large-scale outbreaks of popular unrest from the 1760s led by secret societies; with the spread of the Volunteer movement during the 1770s and 1780s; and, in the 1790s, with the emergence of a substantial Republican agitation represented by the United Irishmen. At the same time the army was overstretched by a succession of major wars in America, Europe and India. Government responded to unrest in Ireland by introducing new military and policing bodies, notably a militia in 1793,[22] a yeomanry in 1796[23] and several different types of police force beginning in the late 1780s. The first of these new and innovative forces was established in Dublin in 1786.

The act that set up a Dublin police force (26 Geo. III, c.24) was mainly intended to curb the activities of the Volunteer movement, which was growing increasingly radical and had even claimed for itself the right to police law and order in the city.[24] Under the act, Dublin was divided into four districts, each with a chief constable, 10 petty constables and 100 night watchmen, who were obliged to patrol day and night on a full-time basis. The men were salaried, armed and uniformed; and they had to be young, healthy and Protestant. The whole force was under the control of three

19 Brian Henry, *Dublin hanged: crime, law enforcement and punishment in late eighteenth-century Dublin* (Dublin, 1994), p. 118.
20 The question of how lawless and violent eighteenth-century Ireland was has generated debate and disagreement among historians. For differing views, see S.J. Connolly, 'Violence and order in the eighteenth century' in P. O'Flanagan, P. Ferguson and K. Whelan (eds), *Rural Ireland: modernisation and change* (Cork, 1995), pp 42–61; Neal Garnham, 'How violent was eighteenth-century Ireland?', *Irish Historical Studies*, xxx, 119 (May, 1997), pp 377–92.
21 For handy surveys of late eighteenth- and early nineteenth-century English policing, see Clive Emsley, *Crime and society in England, 1750–1900* (London and New York, 1987), pp 171–200; David Taylor, *Crime, policing and punishment in England, 1750–1914* (London and New York, 1998), pp 71–87. 22 Thomas Bartlett, 'An end to moral economy: the Irish militia disturbances of 1793', *Past and Present*, 99 (1983), pp 41–64. 23 Allan Blackstock, *An ascendancy army: the Irish yeomanry, 1796–1834* (Dublin, 1998). 24 Henry, *Dublin hanged*, pp 119–36.

police commissioners appointed by the lord lieutenant from among the Dublin magistracy; and it was paid for by a levy on householders. Thus a government-controlled, professional police force was abruptly introduced into the third largest city in the British Isles. Nowhere else in Britain or Ireland did such a force exist at this time – nor had one ever existed.[25]

Not surprisingly perhaps, the MPs, aldermen and householders of Dublin fiercely opposed this innovation, which involved them paying much more for a police force that they no longer had any control over, and which many of them saw as representing an oppressive government. And they were quickly joined in this opposition to police reform by landlords, MPs and justices throughout the country, for the government followed its Dublin police act of 1786 with a new bill in 1787 intended to establish an Irish rural constabulary, somewhat along the lines of the French *maréchausée*.[26] But this time the strength of opposition forced the government into major concessions. Thus the county constabulary established in 1787, by 27 Geo. III, c.40, was not a large, permanent, national force, as dictated by the French model; instead it was a small, temporary force that would only be deployed in parts of Munster in support of the existing JPs and constables in times of crisis. Also county grand juries, which had to bear much of the cost of the force, were permitted to appoint its sub constables. Nevertheless, the lord lieutenant had control over where and when it should be used and appointed the stipendiary magistrates and chief constables who were in charge.

But local opposition to the new Dublin and county police remained widespread and neither force was a success. The views of Lord Carysfort, the Co. Wicklow landlord quoted at the beginning of the chapter, were typical: Ireland's 'principal inhabitants' should control the enforcement of the law, not the government. A ferocious campaign against the Dublin police, led by Henry Grattan, one of the city's MPs, succeeded in having the force abolished in 1795 and replaced by an unarmed 'civic guard', under the control of the mayor and corporation. The county force was little used and in 1792 control of it was turned over totally to the grand juries.[27] In the crisis years of the mid and late 1790s the government relied

25 In the wake of the Gordon riots of 1780 attempts were made to establish a government-controlled police force in London as well, but popular opposition was too strong and a police bill introduced in parliament in 1785 had to be withdrawn. Palmer, *Police and protest*, pp 84–92.   26 For a discussion of this force, see Chapter 2.   27 Palmer, *Police and protest*, pp 119–40.

primarily on the army, the militia and the yeomanry to maintain or restore order, not on the police.

Despite these initial failures, the British government's impulse to experiment with policing in Ireland did not abate. Popular unrest and threats of rebellion persisted after 1800, the army and militia were heavily occupied abroad fighting the French and the yeomanry was considered unreliable. Thus, in 1808, the chief secretary, Arthur Wellesley, later duke of Wellington, re-organised the Dublin police along lines very similar to the 1786–95 force,[28] while in 1814 another young, ambitious chief secretary – and future British prime minister – Robert Peel, introduced what was called the Peace Preservation Force, which was modelled on the 1787–92 county constabulary.[29] Again the Protestant Ascendancy bitterly opposed these renewed attempts to impose state police forces, but having surrendered its own parliament in 1800, the Ascendancy's power to frustrate them was much diminished. Nevertheless, many landlords and JPs continued to resist the gradual development of a national constabulary throughout the pre-Famine era and even beyond.

The Peace Preservation Force,[30] which was established by Peel in 1814 and finally absorbed by the constabulary in 1836, was a temporary body to be raised from ex-soldiers, most of whom were Catholics, and despatched quickly, under the command of a stipendiary magistrate, to areas proclaimed as disturbed by the lord lieutenant. These first 'peelers' were essentially 'flying squads', intended to suppress outbreaks of civil disorder rather than to investigate and prosecute crime. Twenty-one peelers, under a magistrate, were first deployed in Co. Tipperary in September 1814. By December 1817 the force was nearly 400 strong and stationed in parts of seven counties. Under Peel's successor as chief secretary, Charles Grant, the peelers were used more extensively and by October 1822 numbered over 2,300 men stationed in sixteen counties, mainly in north Munster and east Connacht. As much of the cost of the force had to be met by local taxpayers, the peelers were extremely unpopular. Landlords and magistrates protested, not only at the cost, but also at the usurpation of their traditional law enforcement duties by stipendiary magistrates, paid and controlled by Dublin Castle.

28 Ibid., pp 152–9. 29 Ibid., pp 195–203. 30 The following discussion of the Peace Preservation Force draws heavily upon Palmer, *Police and protest*, pp 195–236, supplemented by Galen Broeker, *Rural disorder and police reform in Ireland, 1812–36* (London and Toronto, 1970), pp 55–127.

The Peace Preservation Force certainly was expensive and Stanley Palmer, who studied its activities most closely, concluded that it was not particularly effective either. If there was substantial disorder, the peelers were too few in number of handle it and had to call upon the army for support. Nor did their presence in an area appear to have much impact on rates of prosecution or conviction. After eight years of this experiment, even Dublin Castle and Peel, who was by now home secretary, were ready to acknowledge that the Peace Preservation Force was not the answer to unrest in Ireland.

THE COUNTY CONSTABULARY, 1822–36

In the summer of 1822 the British parliament passed an Irish constabulary act (3 Geo. IV, c.103), introduced by Grant's successor as chief secretary, Henry Goulburn. Under the terms of the act, the lord lieutenant was empowered to appoint an inspector general in each of Ireland's four provinces and a chief constable in each of the country's 250 baronies. Local magistrates had the right to select sixteen constables and sub constables per barony to serve under the chief constable, but the lord lieutenant could dismiss these men or transfer up to two-thirds of them. Half the cost of the force, which numbered around 4,800, was to be met by Irish taxpayers and the rest by the government. From 1822 Ireland thus had, for the first time, a national police force.

To appreciate the extent of this innovation, it is worth noting that the bill was opposed in parliament, not only by most of the leading Irish Whig MPs, including Thomas Spring Rice, Sir John Newport and Sir Henry Parnell, but more surprisingly by the Charles Grant, who as chief secretary (1818–21) had made extensive use of Peel's Peace Preservation Force. Peel himself strongly supported the 1822 constabulary act, but Grant denounced it as placing Ireland 'under an armed police … subject … to a species of *gendarmerie*', which would 'render the whole magistracy of the country liable to the control of the lord lieutenant'.[31] And, indeed, Grant was right: the new constabulary was like the French *gendarmerie* and its creation did undermine the magistracy, while significantly strengthening the power of Dublin Castle.

But, the new force, faced with widespread unrest during Daniel O'Connell's emancipation campaign of the 1820s and the Tithe War of

---

31 Quoted in Broeker, *Rural disorder and police reform*, p. 145; see also Palmer, *Police and protest*, pp 242–3.

the early 1830s, was quickly deemed to be inadequate and it underwent a series of reforms and a major re-structuring in 1836. The main effect of the changes made between 1822 and 1836 was to tighten central control. The 1822 act had left the issue of control unclear, with chief constables, for instance, meant to obey both local magistrates *and* stipendiary magistrates appointed by Dublin Castle. Appointments too, as we have seen, remained shared between local magistrates and the Castle. But by the early 1830s appointment and control had been taken into government hands and provincial inspectors general, assisted from 1828 by new county inspectors, were establishing strict recruitment standards.

The 1836 Irish Constabulary Act (6 Wm. IV, c.13) gave legal sanction to these developments. At the same time, it amalgamated the Peace Preservation Force and the constabulary to form one body totalling around 7,700 men; it did away with provincial inspectors general and brought the new force under the control of a single inspector general based in a constabulary office in Dublin Castle; it created the rank of head constable; and it divided all ranks into classes in order to facilitate promotion. Ironically, the act to create this much more centrally-controlled police force was supported by English and Irish Whigs, including Daniel O'Connell and Henry Grattan's son – in some cases, by the very men who had opposed the 1822 act. And it was opposed by some who had played a significant role in earlier police reform, notably the duke of Wellington. O'Connell justified his stance on the basis that it was better for Dublin Castle to control this powerful new body than local magistrates, most of whom O'Connell claimed were Orangemen.[32]

From 1836 until 1922 the majority of Ireland was policed by the one force.[33] Known at first as the county constabulary or Irish constabulary, in 1867 it became the Royal Irish Constabulary (RIC), in recognition of its success that year in putting down a Fenian rebellion.

Although attempts to establish a national Irish police force had been going on for half a century, it is important not to overlook what a rad-

32 Palmer, *Police and protest*, pp 356–60.   33 Other police forces did continue to exist alongside the constabulary, notably the Dublin Metropolitan Police or DMP (until 1925); the Revenue Police (until 1857); the Belfast police (until 1865); and the Londonderry police (until 1869). The latter forces were superseded by the constabulary, while the DMP was absorbed by the Garda Síochána. For short accounts of these forces, see Jim Herlihy, *The Dublin Metropolitan Police: a short history and genealogical guide* (Dublin, 2001); N.W. Dawson, 'Illicit distillation and the revenue police', *Irish Jurist*, xii (1977), pp 282–94; Brian Griffin, *The Bulkies: police and crime in Belfast, 1800–65* (Dublin, 1997); Mark Radford, 'The borough policemen of Londonderry, c.1832–70', *Proceedings of the Royal Ulster Constabulary Historical Society* (winter 1998), pp 6–7.

ical innovation a centrally controlled, armed, constabulary was in Ireland during the early nineteenth century. It was a major departure from centuries of locally based policing, and communities naturally resented the state taking over their traditional right to discipline their members. Moreover, such a force was not introduced in England at the time, nor subsequently.[34] And, as we shall see in the next chapter, no British colony overseas ever boasted a police force quite like the Irish constabulary. Contemporaries almost invariably compared the force to European *gendarmeries* – and such a comparison was certainly apt.

Opposition to the force in Ireland was intense and this opposition came from both ends of the social and political spectrums. Some of the fiercest opponents of the constabulary, especially before the Famine, were Tory landlords and magistrates, who saw it as usurping their ancient right to maintain law and order among the lower orders. Most landlords were magistrates.[35] Their power and status certainly derived primarily from their ownership of land, but their ability to use the law to further their own ends was crucial to their standing. Thus they strongly resisted attempts by government to replace them with paid magistrates and policemen. Farmers and labourers also resented the intrusion of strangers seeking to dictate how they should behave, suppressing traditional customs and celebrations and interfering in their relations with each other and with their landlords.

There is little doubt that both landlords and tenants were right in perceiving the constabulary as a major threat to their traditional ways of doing things. British governments used the police from the 1820s onwards to regulate and control everyday life in Ireland to an unprecedented degree. As we shall see, apprehending and prosecuting those who broke the law formed only a part of police duties – and, arguably, the lesser part. The Irish constabulary became during the century of its existence essential to the maintenance of British rule in Ireland. If, under the Union, successive British governments ruled Ireland through Dublin Castle, Dublin Castle ruled Ireland through the Irish constabulary.

---

34 England was policed by a number of independent, unarmed county and borough forces – as it largely still is today. But their introduction, facilitated by important acts in 1839 and 1856, was met with fierce opposition and even riots, especially in working class areas of the north. R.D. Storch, 'The plague of blue locusts: police reform and popular resistance in northern England, 1840–57', *International Review of Social History*, xx (1975), pp 61–90.   35 It is impossible to obtain accurate figures for the numbers of Irish magistrates, but it would seem that in 1816 there were around 3,600 on the rolls, while in 1832 there were 2,600. Governments purged the magistracy in 1822–3 and again in 1832, attempting to get rid of absentees and incompetents – and also the dead. Palmer, *Police and protest*, p. 681, n. 35.

CHAPTER TWO

Men in the middle: the historiography and contexts of Irish policing

> ... smeller of rot
> in the state, infused
> with its poisons,
> pinioned by ghosts
> and affections,
> murders and pieties ...[1]

> ... recruited as body-servants of privilege and property [police-men] were given, as servants must be, access to privileged information, took away with them secrets, an understanding of how the social machinery was kept working, and often, miserably, an understanding of their own role in that process ...[2]

In the early autumn of 1990 a man's body was recovered by the Garda Síochána from a bog on a hillside at Turaheen near Rossmore in Co. Tipperary. Elderly local people, who had long known of the existence of the burial, alerted the county council when plans were afoot to restore graveyards in the area. Apparently there was a feeling in the community that the man in the bog should at long last be given a Christian burial. Yet this was no Iron Age pagan bog sacrifice, as famously chronicled by the Danish archaeologist, P.V. Glob, and celebrated by the Irish poet, Seamus Heaney.[3] The corpse was reputed in the district to be that of Thomas Kirby, a member of the Royal Irish Constabulary (RIC), who had been tried by a Sinn Féin court and executed early in 1921.[4]

---

1 Seamus Heaney, 'Viking Dublin: trial pieces', *North* (London, 1975), p. 23. 2 Carolyn Steedman, *The radical soldier's tale: John Pearman, 1819–1908* (London and New York, 1988), pp 1–3. 3 P.V. Glob, *The bog people: Iron-Age man preserved*, trans. by R. Bruce-Mitford (London, 1969). While Glob makes only brief reference to Irish bog burials, his book was influential in inspiring a number of poems in Heaney's important 1975 collection *North*. 4 *Irish Times*, 27 Sept. 1990. Who this man was has not been conclusively established. There is no Thomas Kirby recorded in the RIC General Register serving in Tipperary and disappearing in 1921. In addition, newspaper reports suggested the well-preserved body was wearing a British army uniform without any police insignia. Even a Black-and-Tan would have worn an RIC cap badge. Thus the identity of the Turaheen bog body remains something of a mystery. Richard Abbott, *Police casualties in Ireland, 1919–22* (Cork, 2000), p. 314.

When these human remains were exhumed in Tipperary there were a handful of former members of the RIC still alive, although during the 1990s their numbers swiftly dwindled.[5] It was doubtless no coincidence that, just as the last members of Britain's Irish police force were disappearing, public hostility towards them was waning. Physically the final survivors of the RIC were being buried, but at the same time, metaphorically, they were being recovered. The RIC, some seventy years after its disbandment, was finally and irrevocably passing from contemporary experience into history. And, belatedly, historians were beginning the task of dissecting the remains.

HISTORIOGRAPHY

Why did it take so long for this police force to become a legitimate object of academic study? Twentieth-century Irish historiography was in fact characterised by some startling gaps.[6] It was not easy for a country that had fought long and hard, on both political and military fronts, to secure its independence to acknowledge that many, perhaps even most,

---

5 When John Brewer published his oral history of the RIC in 1990, he calculated, based on pension records, that about a dozen former RIC men were then alive. My researches in the early 1990s uncovered two others, both of whom have since died. J.D. Brewer, *The Royal Irish Constabulary: an oral history* (Belfast, 1990), p. vii. In 1999 Gerard O'Brien found that the Paymaster General's Office was paying forty-seven RIC pensions – all to widows. Gerard O'Brien, 'The missing personnel records of the R.I.C.', *Irish Historical Studies*, xxxi, 124 (Nov. 1999), p. 511.   6 Perhaps the most notable gap in the historiography of nineteenth-century Ireland before the 1990s was the Famine. For important discussions of the shortcomings of its historiography, see Brendan Bradshaw, 'Nationalism and historical scholarship in modern Ireland', *Irish Historical Studies*, xxvi, 104 (Nov. 1989), pp 329–51; M.E. Daly, 'Review article: historians and the Famine: a beleaguered species', *Irish Historical Studies*, xxx, 120 (Nov. 1997), pp 591–601.
7 For resident magistrates, see Penny Bonsall, *The Irish RMs: the resident magistrates in the British administration in Ireland* (Dublin, [1997]). For lawyers, see Daire Hogan, *The legal profession in Ireland, 1798–1922* (Dublin, 1986); John McEldowney and Paul O'Higgins (eds), *The common law tradition: essays in Irish legal history* (Dublin, 1990). For civil servants, see Lawrence McBride, *The greening of Dublin Castle: the transformation of bureaucratic and judicial personnel in Ireland, 1892–1922* (Washington, D.C., 1991); Eunan O'Halpin, *The decline of the Union: British government in Ireland, 1892–1920* (Dublin, 1988). For doctors, see Peter Froggatt, 'Competing philosophies: the "preparatory" medical schools of the Royal Belfast Academical Institution and the Catholic University of Ireland, 1835–1909' in Elizabeth Malcolm and Greta Jones (eds), *Medicine, disease and the state in Ireland, 1650–1940* (Cork, 1999), pp 59–84. For teachers, see D.H. Akenson, *The Irish education experiment: the National system of education in the nineteenth century* (London and Toronto, 1970); T.J. McElligott, *Secondary education in Ireland, 1870–1921* (Dublin, 1981); Tom Garvin, *Nationalist revolutionaries in Ireland, 1858–1928* (Oxford, 1987), pp 24–48. For the yeomanry, see Allan Blackstock, *An ascendancy army*. For the army, see Thomas Bartlett and Keith Jeffery (eds), *A military history of Ireland* (Cambridge, 1996); E.A. Muenger, *The British military dilemma in Ireland: occupation politics, 1886–1914* (Lawrence, KS, 1991); Philip Orr, *The road to the Somme: men of the Ulster Division tell their story* (Belfast, 1987); Terence Denman, *Ireland's unknown soldiers: the 16th (Irish) Division in the Great War* (Dublin, 1991); Keith Jeffery, *Ireland and the Great War* (Cambridge, 2000).

of its citizens accepted, worked for and even supported the 'occupying' power. The Irish Republic was not unusual among post-colonial societies in that it was only from the 1980s, sixty years after independence, that scholars began to look closely – and, moreover, sympathetically – at those Irish men and women who had served the British state. Studies of magistrates and lawyers, of landlords and their agents, of civil servants, of teachers and doctors, of the yeomanry and, especially, of the army and police have proliferated since.[7]

Given the very different circumstances of Ireland and England during the nineteenth century, the historiography of Irish policing that has developed is distinctive and markedly unlike the historiography of English policing.

Much was written during the early and mid twentieth century about the origins of English policing and what was written was generally admiring.[8] As Robert Reiner has said of this literature:

> The police were seen as an inevitable and unequivocally beneficent institution, a cornerstone of national pride, which had been developed by English pragmatic genius as a response to fearsome threats to social order and civilised existence. There was initial opposition to the police, but it arose from vested interest, malevolence or blinkered obscurantism, and was rapidly dissipated when the benefits of a benign police institution became apparent to all.[9]

During the 1970s, however, a more critical note emerged, with some historians arguing that in nineteenth-century England the police were essentially introduced to uphold the interests of the ruling classes, often in the face of bitter and prolonged opposition from sections of the industrial working class.[10] Yet even this critique was challenged in later

---

8 For leading examples of this 'Whig' interpretation, see Charles Reith, *A short history of the British police* (London and New York, 1948); T.A. Critchley, *A history of police in England and Wales* (London, 1967). 9 Robert Reiner, *The politics of the police* (New York and London, 1985), p. 9. 10 The revisionist interpretation of English policing was pioneered by Robert Storch in two important articles: 'The plague of blue locusts' (1975), and 'The policeman as domestic missionary: urban discipline and popular culture in northern England, 1850–80', *Journal of Social History*, ix, 4 (summer 1976), pp 481–509. Storch also contributed an article on efforts to regulate working-class leisure to an important book promoting the social control thesis: A.P. Donajgrodzki (ed.), *Social control in nineteenth century Britain* (London, 1977). For a recent detailed study of the political debate behind the introduction of new police forces in rural England, see David Philips and R.D. Storch, *Policing provincial England, 1829–56: the politics of reform* (London and New York, 1999).

writings, which reverted to a more flattering view of the role of the new police.[11]

But whereas English writings about the police were in the main complimentary, in Ireland the reverse was true. Critical assessments by Nationalist politicians, writers and newspapers were frequent throughout the late nineteenth century and up to 1922. And Conservatives and Unionists too were often equivocal and sometimes even openly hostile.[12]

Visitors to Ireland, depending upon their political inclinations, expressed divergent views. The English soldier and colonial administrator, Sir Francis Head, during his 'fortnight in Ireland' in 1852 inspected the constabulary's depot in Phoenix Park, Dublin. Commenting upon the recruits in training, Head wrote:

> I certainly have never seen assembled a more intellectual force; indeed there was an intelligence in their countenances, a supple activity in their movements, and a lightness in their tread, that was very remarkable ... Without reference to religion, almost all had been selected as being the sons of deserving small farmers. They were, generally speaking, fine, handsome, intelligent lads of from 18 to 20; well dressed ... There was nothing clownish or cloddish in their appearance; and the progress which the more advanced had made during the very short period of their probation exemplified what I believe is an old remark, namely, the natural aptitude of the Irish to be soldiers ...[13]

Head obviously intended this passage as a compliment to the Irish constabulary, but his evident surprise that the recruits he saw were intelligent and not 'clownish or cloddish in their appearance' is hardly flatter-

11 Reiner, Emsley and Palmer rejected both extremes, with Reiner arguing in favour of the middle ground, or what he terms a 'neo-Reithian synthesis'. Reiner, *The politics of the police*, p. 47; Clive Emsley, *The English police*, pp 1–7; Palmer, *Police and protest*, pp 7–8. For some of the 'myths' associated with the English policeman, see Clive Emsley, 'The English Bobby: an indulgent tradition' in Roy Porter (ed.), *Myths of the English* (Cambridge, 1992), pp 114–35. 12 The paramilitary character of the RIC often attracted criticism from Irish magistrates and Tory MPs, as well as from Nationalists. During debates over police reform in England from the 1830s to the 1850s, some prominent English politicians championed the Irish constabulary model, but the majority did not. As the most recent historians of these debates comment: 'the Irish Constabulary hovered in the background largely as an example to be shunned'. Philips and Storch, *Policing provincial England*, pp 63, 68–9, 127–8, 227. For a defence of the constabulary's paramilitary character from its then inspector general, see H.J. Brownrigg, *Examination of some recent allegations concerning the Constabulary Force of Ireland, in a report to his excellency, the lord lieutenant* (Dublin, 1864).   13 Francis Head, *A fortnight in Ireland* (London, 1852), pp 60–1.

ing. And his opinion that the Irish had a 'natural aptitude' for soldiering and, moreover, that such soldier-policemen were necessary in Ireland, further highlights his stereotyped anti-Irish views.

Visiting the country just four years later in 1856, the German Marxist Frederich Engels expressed more straightforwardly critical views of Irish policemen. Ireland, according to Engels, was 'in ruins', without any industry, yet supporting such 'parasitic growths' as [g]*endarmes*, priests, lawyers, bureaucrats and country squires in pleasing profusion'. Engels had 'never seen so many *gendarmes* in any country, and the sodden look of the bibulous Prussian *gendarme* is developed to its highest perfection here among the constabulary, who are armed with carbines, bayonets and handcuffs'.[14]

Perhaps partly because outsiders' assessments were frequently so hostile, from an early date former RIC men exhibited a marked tendency to write, and sometimes publish, memoirs. Some of these accounts, especially those written by Protestant officers, lauded the RIC and offered stout defences against the force's critics. But accounts written by Catholic constables tended to be far more ambivalent: still mainly laudatory, yet at the same time defensive, uneasy and full of self justification. The first attempt at a history of the RIC appeared as early as 1869 and was written by a recently retired inspector, Robert Curtis. Although purporting to be an account of the establishment and development of the constabulary since the 1810s, the book was in fact a defence of the force's paramilitary character and a celebration of its recent successes against Fenianism.

If studies of the RIC before disbandment were generally negative, leavened occasionally by defences from former members, during the half-century after 1922 hostile accounts went virtually unchallenged.

Two large works of early twentieth-century Irish Nationalist historiography set the tone for most treatments of the RIC up to the 1980s. In her popular history *The Irish Republic*, published in 1937, Dorothy Macardle noted that the RIC was composed 'entirely of Irishmen'. This was evidence, she argued, of 'the extremities to which the Irish people had been reduced' by British rule. The 'smallest village had its R.I.C. barracks', manned by constables 'possessing the most intimate knowledge of the

---

14 Karl Marx and Frederick Engels, *Ireland and the Irish question* (Moscow, 1971), p. 83. Novels and plays that treated the RIC very occasionally offered rather more sympathetic representations. See, as examples, Tighe Hopkins, *The Nugents of Carriconna* (4th ed., London, 1890); Robert Thynne, *Story of a campaign estate; or, The turn of the tide* (London, 1896); Lady Gregory, *The rising of the moon* (Dublin and London, n.d.).

daily lives of their fellow countrymen'. Thus the British administration in
Ireland 'placed its chief reliance, and rightly, on the almost flawless system
of espionage carried out by the R.I.C.' The failure of the 1916 Rising in
the provinces was 'chiefly due' to the espionage work of the RIC.
Macardle summed up the RIC thus: 'They served England for pay with
a courage and loyalty which, had it been given to their own country, would
have made its history a tale less filled with suffering and defeat'.[15]

Even more scathing was P.S. O'Hegarty in his influential 1952 book,
A history of Ireland under the Union, 1801–1922. O'Hegarty devoted a short
chapter to the RIC. Like Macardle, he acknowledged that most members
were Irish-born Catholics and like her he also stressed that they 'found
no great difficulty in keeping accurately in touch with what was going
on amongst the people'.

> But it was, in fact, not a police force at all, but a Janissary force.
> The Turkish Janissary, used to keep down his own people, is the
> only parallel in history to the Royal Irish Constabulary man. His
> duties were military duties, and not police duties ... The first duty
> inculcated on them was loyalty, loyalty not Ireland, but to England
> and they were loyal to England. By virtue of this loyalty, they bul-
> lied, terrorized, and when ordered, murdered their own people
> without compunction for nearly a hundred years ... What they
> were in 1847, and what they were in 1907, they were in the between
> and in the after years. It is difficult to convey to modern minds
> what they were like. With their black uniforms, their carbines, their
> batons ... They manufactured crime when it suited their purpose
> and they condoned crime ... Children fled at their approach ...
> England had every reason to be grateful to them ... But when they
> were broken her grip on Ireland was broken with them.[16]

That RIC men were mercenaries and traitors, who spied upon their own
people, and petty tyrants, who played a crucial role in maintaining British
rule, were commonplaces of early and mid twentieth-century Nationalist
historiography.

15 Dorothy Macardle, *The Irish Republic* (4th ed., London, 1951), pp 40, 134, 167. Yet Macardle displayed an 'under-
lying disquiet' over the killings of some RIC men during the Anglo-Irish War. Eunan O'Halpin, 'Historical revisit:
Dorothy Macardle, *The Irish Republic* (1937)', *Irish Historical Studies*, xxxi, 123 (May 1999), pp 389–94. 16 P.S.
O'Hegarty, *A history of Ireland under the Union, 1801–1922* (London, 1952), pp 401–4.

Signs of the beginnings of a shift in views, among academics at least, were not apparent until the 1960s when two ground-breaking articles appeared. One dealt with the early years of policing in Ireland and the other with the final years of the RIC a century later. Tadhg Ó Ceallaigh examined in some detail the law-and-order problems of the period marking the end of the Napoleonic Wars, 1814–18, and described how Robert Peel, the then Irish chief secretary, responded by establishing a Peace Preservation Force. Ó Ceallaigh rejected a polemical approach and treated the introduction of the first 'peelers' fairly dispassionately. Indeed, he argued, on pragmatic grounds, that policemen were probably preferable to soldiers in dealing with civil unrest.[17] In an even more important article, written, somewhat ironically, in connection with the fiftieth anniversary of the 1916 Rising, Richard Hawkins[18] set out the problems that Ireland's police faced in 1916–22, almost exactly a century after Peel's time. Describing the force as having been in 'suspended animation' since the turn of the century, if not since the Land War years of the early 1880s, Hawkins quoted tellingly from the *Constabulary Gazette* of September 1916:

> The R.I.C. may be likened unto a noble mansion of the early Victorian era, still occupied but showing visible signs of decay ... Over the door, in dim but discernible letters, is printed 'Ichabod' – 'the glory has departed'.[19]

Hawkins' tone verged on the elegiac at times as he described an ill-trained and inadequately-equipped force of Irishmen, constantly criticised by their own government, struggling during the early 1920s to cope with military problems that were clearly beyond them. This valedictory tone was to inform a good deal of the subsequent historiography of the RIC, especially that chronicling the force's final years. Perhaps the tone was dictated by the fact that numbers of elderly members of the force were slowly dying off during the last third of the twentieth century. A similar tone can be found in some works published during the same period dealing with Republicans of the years 1916–22.[20]

---

17 Tadhg Ó Ceallaigh, 'Peel and police reform in Ireland, 1814–18', *Studia Hibernica*, 6 (1966), pp 25–48. For a critique of some of Ó Ceallaigh's interpretations, see Palmer, *Police and protest*, p. 200. 18 I would like to thank Richard Hawkins for his help and encouragement over many years. 19 *Constabulary Gazette*, xxxix, 7 (4 Sept. 1916) quoted in Richard Hawkins, 'Dublin Castle and the Royal Irish Constabulary (1916–22)' in Desmond Williams (ed.), *The Irish struggle, 1916–26* (London, 1966), p. 170, n. 1. 20 A number of books and television programmes sought to

Even after the publication of these 1966 articles interest in Irish policing remained only fitful. The early 1970s saw several significant works, some at least inspired by the then controversy surrounding policing in Northern Ireland. Galen Broeker's *Rural disorder and police reform in Ireland, 1812–36*, which appeared in 1970, was a very detailed and scholarly account of the politics of Irish police reform prior to the consolidation of the constabulary in 1836. But it was largely based on English sources and thus its viewpoint was an English one. It was admiring, claiming that the constabulary 'had proved itself an effective instrument to be used in the "civilization" of Ireland'. At the same time Broeker argued, incorrectly, that even after 1837 'violence and crime remained at what was undoubtedly a higher level than in any other area of western Europe'.[21]

Both the early and the later years of British policing in Ireland continued to attract most attention. In a series of articles in 1972–3 Kevin Boyle went back beyond Peel to demonstrate that modern policing in Ireland actually originated in the late eighteenth century. He singled out the Dublin Police Act of 1786, which created a short-lived, centrally controlled force, as a crucial innovation and described further government efforts in the late 1780s to reform rural policing.[22] Boyle's stress on the late eighteenth century was reinforced by Stanley Palmer in 1975 in an article entitled 'The Irish Police Experiment: the Beginnings of Modern Police in the British Isles, 1785–95'.[23] Both Boyle and Palmer recognised that, thirty years before Peel, British ministers were experimenting with new methods of policing in Ireland that were subsequently to have an important impact on England.

The scholarship of Broeker, Boyle and Palmer certainly added much to our understanding of the origins of modern Irish policing and made clear the significant influence that developments in Ireland had on the evolution of policing in England, but such work was hardly calculated to improve the popular image of the RIC in Ireland. This was especially

---

interview elderly Nationalists and Republicans and preserve their memories. See, for example, Uinseann MacEoin (ed.), *Survivors: the story of Ireland's struggle as told through some of her outstanding living people* (Dublin, 1980); Kenneth Griffith and T.E. O'Grady, *Curious journey: an oral history of Ireland's unfinished revolution* (London, 1982). 21 Galen Broeker, *Rural disorder and police reform in Ireland, 1812–36* (London and Toronto, 1970), p. 239. For a critique of Broeker's work, see Palmer, *Police and protest*, pp 30, 200. 22 Kevin Boyle, 'Police in Ireland before the Union: I; II; III', *Irish Jurist*, new series, vii (1972), pp 115–37; viii (1973), pp 90–116; viii (1973), pp 323–48. 23 Palmer, 'The Irish police experiment', *Social Science Quarterly*, 56 (Dec. 1975), pp 410–24; reprinted in Ian O'Donnell and Finbarr McAuley (eds), *Criminal justice history*, pp 98–112. This experiment is discussed at greater length in Chapter 1.

so given that the outbreak of the Troubles in Northern Ireland in the late 1960s was widely blamed in the Republic on the tactics of the Royal Ulster Constabulary (RUC), supported by members of the Ulster Special Constabulary, known as the B Specials. To many in the south the RUC was simply the modern embodiment of the RIC.

Two books on Irish police forces published in 1974, both the work of journalists, were obviously influenced by the Troubles. Conor Brady wrote a history of the Garda Síochána, while Seamus Breathnach produced a more general account of Irish policing, although with a large section also devoted to the Garda. Both authors expressed admiration for the concept of an unarmed police force in the context of Ireland's, and especially Northern Ireland's, history of paramilitary policing. For Brady the Garda were 'perhaps the most daring experiment to be undertaken by the first government of the Irish Free State'. For a time, he claimed, 'Ireland was leading Europe, and indeed the world, in the development of a positive and coherent police philosophy'.[24]

In comparison, both the RIC and the RUC were found seriously wanting. Echoing earlier Nationalist writers, Brady characterised the disbandment of the RIC in 1922 as the 'inglorious end ... of the force which had embodied the strength of alien power'. The RIC had been the 'eyes and ears of the Castle, and where necessary ... its strong right hand ... which had enabled Britain to hold Ireland in a condition of relative tranquility in the previous hundred years'.[25] Breathnach's interpretation was similar. He regretted that the study of the police had been so neglected in Ireland, but attributed this to what he termed the 'inscrutable political background'. Irish policemen were under enormous 'strain' for 'they knew the Castle to be rotten and the public which they served to hate them on that account'. While expressing admiration for individual policemen, Breathnach nevertheless took the view that the RIC helped 'keep the nation in chains'.[26]

It was not until the 1980s that a substantial body of literature on Irish policing began to accumulate; and this was expanded and consolidated during the 1990s. A number of studies of nineteenth-century British ruling

---

24 Conor Brady, *Guardians of the peace* (Dublin, 1974), p. x. For more recent and scholarly histories of the guards, see Liam McNiffe, *A history of the Garda Síochána* (Dublin, 1997); Gregory Allen, *The Garda Síochána: policing independent Ireland, 1922–82* (Dublin, 1999). 25 Brady, *Guardians of the peace*, pp 1–2. 26 Breathnach, *The Irish police*, pp 27, 57.

institutions appeared at this time and many of these included sections on the police.[27] As the Troubles continued, apparently with no hope of resolution, the RUC and its history too gained increasing attention particularly from journalists and sociologists.[28] In 1988 Stanley Palmer published his monumental work on policing in both England and Ireland during the late eighteenth and early nineteenth centuries. In this influential book Palmer laid particular emphasis upon Ireland and took English police historians to task for refusing to acknowledge that innovations in Ireland had helped shape the character of early English policing. 'The reluctance of modern English police historians to cross the Irish Sea', he chided, 'would have surprised Robert Peel, who made the crossing many times. The Irish connection was clearer to some Victorian Englishmen.'[29]

Research on Irish policing over the last ten or fifteen years has been pursued by a variety of specialists: by historians, by sociologists, by policemen, by genealogists and by journalists. Instead of just examining the early years of Irish policing before 1840 or the ordeal of the RIC after 1916, historians have begun to dissect the force at its peak in the second half of the nineteenth century.[30] Other Irish police forces, such as those of Dublin, Belfast and Derry, have also attracted attention.[31] The estab-

27 See, for example, Charles Townshend, *Political violence in Ireland: government and resistance since 1848* (Oxford, 1983), pp 67–88; K.T. Hoppen, *Elections, politics and society in Ireland, 1832–85* (Oxford, 1984), pp 408–23; David Fitzpatrick, *Politics and Irish life, 1913–21: provincial experience of war and revolution* (Dublin, 1977), pp 1–45. 28 Chris Ryder, *The RUC: a force under fire* (rev. ed., London, 1997); J.D. Brewer and Kathleen Magee, *Inside the RUC: routine policing in a divided society* (Oxford, 1991); Michael Farrell, *Arming the Protestants: the formation of the Ulster Special Constabulary and the Royal Ulster Constabulary, 1920–7* (London and Sydney, 1983); Arthur Hezlet, *The 'B' Specials: a history of the Ulster Special Constabulary* (London, 1972). 29 Palmer, *Police and protest*, pp 27–8. 30 Brian Griffin, 'The Irish police, 1836–1914: a social history', unpublished PhD thesis, Loyola University of Chicago, 1990; idem, 'Religion and opportunity in the Irish police forces, 1836–1914' in R.V. Comerford et. al (eds), *Religion, conflict and coexistence in Ireland: essays presented to Monsignor Patrick J. Corish* (Dublin, 1990), pp 219–34; idem, 'The Irish police: love, sex and marriage in the nineteenth and early twentieth centuries' in Margaret Kelleher and James Murphy (eds), *Gender perspectives in nineteenth-century Ireland: public and private spheres* (Dublin, 1997), pp 168–78; W.J. Lowe and E.L. Malcolm, 'The domestication of the Royal Irish Constabulary, 1836–1922', *Irish Economic and Social History*, xix (1992), pp 27–48; W.J. Lowe, 'The constabulary agitation of 1882', *Irish Historical Studies*, xxxi, 121 (May 1998), pp 37–59; Ian Bridgeman, 'Policing rural Ireland: a study of the origins, development and role of the Irish Constabulary, and its impact on crime prevention and detection in the nineteenth century', unpublished PhD thesis, Open University, 1993; Virginia Crossman, *Politics, law and order in nineteenth-century Ireland* (Dublin, 1996). 31 For the DMP, see Nigel Cochrane, 'The policing of Dublin, 1830–46: a study in administration', unpublished MA thesis, University College, Dublin, 1984; idem, 'Public reaction to the introduction of a new police force: Dublin, 1838–45', *Eire-Ireland*, xxii, 1 (spring 1987), pp 72–85; idem, 'The policeman's lot is not a happy one: duty, discipline, pay and conditions in the DMP, c.1833–45', *Saothar*, 12 (1987), pp 9–20; Fergus D'Arcy, 'The Dublin police strike of 1882', *Saothar*, 23 (1998), pp 33–44; for the Belfast borough police, see Brian Griffin, *The Bulkies*; for the Londonderry borough police, see Radford, 'The borough policemen of Londonderry, c.1832–70'; for the revenue police, see N.M. Dawson, 'Illicit distillation and the revenue police'.

lishment of police archives and museums in both Dublin and Belfast during the 1970s helped spur research.[32] Efforts were also hurriedly made to collect the oral testimony of the last survivors of the RIC.[33]

Genealogy has undoubtedly played an important part in the recent growth of interest in Irish policemen. The personnel registers of the RIC and of the Dublin Metropolitan Police (DMP) provide a wealth of information on the lives of tens of thousands of Irishmen over a period of more than a century. Family historians have been eager to exploit these remarkable records and to make them more readily available to the public.[34] Also some of the children of RIC men began in the 1980s to publish autobiographies in which they reflected upon their fathers' controversial occupation and how it had shaped their lives.[35] As more and more Irish people have recognised that they had a 'peeler' in the family, so interest has grown and attitudes towards the RIC have softened.[36]

CONTEXTS

Chapter 1 looked briefly at the history of policing in Ireland before 1836 in order to demonstrate that community-based policing had been the norm for centuries, and that the establishment during the 1820s and 1830s of a centrally-control national force was thus a major break with tradition.

32 A Garda Síochána Museum was established in 1975 in the Phoenix Park headquarters (the former RIC depot) and twenty years later moved to Dublin Castle. A Police Museum is located at the Knock headquarters of the Police Service of Northern Ireland (PSNI) in Belfast. For the background to the establishment of the Dublin museum, see the letter of Sergeant Gregory Allen, the museum's first curator, in the *Irish Times*, 11 Aug. 1978. For some of the material held by the Belfast museum, see R.J.K. Sinclair and F.J.M. Scully, *Arresting memories: captured moments in constabulary life* (Belfast, 1982). There is also a Garda Síochána Historical Society and an RUC Historical Society. The *Proceedings* of the latter contain a good deal of material on the RIC and other Irish forces. I would like to thank Inspector John Duffy, the former curator of the Garda Museum, and Chief Superintendent Robin Sinclair, the former curator of the RUC Museum, for their generous assistance over a number of years. 33 In the late 1980s John Brewer interviewed fifteen former members of the RIC and recorded their recollections in *The Royal Irish Constabulary: an oral history*. Since 1989 I have corresponded with over 200 people, most of whom are the children and grandchildren of RIC members. 34 See, for example, the guides produced by Jim Herlihy: *The Royal Irish Constabulary: a short history and genealogical guide* (Dublin, 1997); *The Royal Irish Constabulary: a complete alphabetical list of officers and men, 1816–1922* (Dublin, 1999); *The Dublin Metropolitan Police: a short history and genealogical guide* (Dublin, 1999). 35 Patrick Shea, *Voices and the sound of drums: an Irish autobiography* (Belfast, 1981); Denis Donoghue, *Warrenpoint* (London, 1991). See also Sean O'Faolain, *Vive moi!: an autobiography*, ed. Julia O'Faolain (London, 1993), pp 22–34. All are discussed in Chapters 7 and 9. 36 During the 1980s popular historical novels began to appear that presented a largely sympathetic view of the RIC: see, for example, David Marcus, *A land in flames* (London, 1987). During the 1990s Sebastian Barry produced a major play and also a novel whose main characters were policemen: see *The steward of Christendom* (1995) and *The whereabouts of Eneas McNulty* (London, 1998). For an interesting discussion of Barry's work, which touches upon issues raised in this book, see Elizabeth Cullingford, 'Colonial policing: *The steward of Christendom* and *The whereabouts of Eneas McNulty*', *Eire-Ireland*, xxxix, 3/4 (2004), pp 11–37.

In Ireland the police were never accepted as an 'inevitable and unequivocally beneficent institution' the way some police historians claim that English forces were. Thus comparisons with England, while enlightening in certain respects, have their limitations. In attempting to identify the contexts in which Irish policing can be most usefully discussed, it is necessary therefore to look further afield, in particular to colonial societies and to Europe. Comparisons with English colonial policing and its historiography are certainly valuable, but even here there are significant differences. Again, a favourable view of English colonial policing tended to prevail up until the 1970s and 1980s, with laudatory accounts provided by novelists, former civil servants and ex-policemen.[37] Since then interpretations have become far more sophisticated and critical, especially under the influence of post-colonial theory. The classic imperialist critiques of Albert Memmi and Frantz Fanon, which initially focused on French North Africa, have begun to inform the examination of the policing of the far-flung British Empire, and even of England itself.

There is a Latin word 'limen' meaning a threshold, from which is derived the English adjective 'liminal'. This term was first used at the end of the nineteenth century by psychologists in a neurological context, to identify the point beyond which sensation could not be perceived, but more recently it is a word that has been employed in post-colonial theory to signify individuals and groups caught between colonisers and colonised. Typically these were 'natives' who worked for and were to some extent assimilated by the foreign ruling elite. As liminal figures they had a foot in two camps and acted as a bridge between often mutually hostile groups. In 1988 Carolyn Steedman took the concept, interpreted it in terms of class, and applied it to nineteenth-century English policemen. According to her, the police authorities put constables in a situation that could be described as liminal: they were 'in an awkward position between two ways of life, two belief-systems'.

> [W]orking-class recruits were cut off from the communities of
> their birth and stationed at a geographical distance from them;

37 See, for example, Charles Jeffries, *The colonial police* (London, 1952); James Cramer, *The world's police* (London, 1964) pp 109–243; J.C. Curry, *The Indian police* (London, 1932); G.K. Pippet, *History of the Ceylon police, 1795–1870* (Colombo, 1938); G.M. O'Brien, *The police forces of Australia* (Melbourne, 1961); R.C. Fetherstonhaugh, *The Royal Canadian Mounted Police* (New York, 1940); W.H. Gillespie, *The Gold Coast police, 1844–1938* (Accra, 1955); W.R. Foran, *The Kenya police, 1887–1960* (London, 1962); Lenno van Onselen, *A rhapsody in blue* (Cape Town, 1960); Edward Horne, *A job well done: a history of the Palestine Police Force, 1920–48* (Leigh-on-Sea, Essex, 1982).

they were dressed in uniform, and expected to live by the rules of sobriety and self-discipline; and possessed of these attributes were sent out to watch a society from which they had but recently been removed.[38]

While Steedman treated the dilemmas of working-class English constables sympathetically, the critics of colonialism had adopted a very different attitude towards policemen. In his seminal 1957 study of colonialism, based on Tunisia where he was born, Memmi claimed that 'representatives of the authorities', such as policemen, 'form a category of the colonized which attempts to escape from its political and social' oppression by adopting the ideology of the coloniser. But to Memmi's mind this strategy offered no solution. Even though he may at times profit 'from this unjust system, the colonized still finds his situation more of a burden than anything else'.[39] Memmi saw complete assimilation as an impossibility and characterised those like 'native' colonial policemen, as caught in a permanent and crippling duality.[40] Fanon, shaped by the brutal experience of the Algerian War of 1954–62, was if anything even more negative about the role of liminal figures such as policemen.

> In the colonial countries … the policeman and the soldier, by their immediate presence and their frequent and direct action maintain contact with the native and advise him by means of rifle-butts and napalm not to budge. It is obvious here that the agents of government speak the language of pure force. The intermediary does not lighten the oppression; nor seek to hide the domination; he shows them up and puts them into practice with the clear conscience of an upholder of the peace; yet he is the bringer of violence into the home and into the mind of the native.[41]

The concept of policemen as liminal figures, whether in a colonial or a class context, is a valuable one and certainly has resonance in Ireland. As we shall see in later chapters, RIC men were not only called upon to

---

38 Steedman, *The radical soldier's tale*, pp 56–7. 39 Albert Memmi, *The colonizer and the colonized*, trans. by Howard Greenfield (London, 1974), p. 82. 40 Ibid., pp 172, 187. 41 Yet Fanon, a psychiatrist, in a chapter on colonial war and mental illness, recounted sympathetically the case histories of two policemen deeply traumatized by their duties. Both, however, were European. Frantz Fanon, *The wretched of the earth*, trans. by Constance Farrington (London, 1965), pp 29, 212–17.

uphold the authority of the state, but, through their training and discipline, they were imbued with middle-class English values and were
expected to impart – if not impose – these values to their fellow countrymen and women. Thrift, honesty, sobriety, reliability, loyalty and, above
all, the great nineteenth-century middle-class virtue of respectability, were
demanded of Irish policemen. Not only would such qualities make them
better policemen, but these qualities would it was hoped turn RIC men
into role models for the farming and labouring classes from which most
constables came.

If post-colonial theory can inform our analysis of Irish policemen,
it is also important to note that Irish police forces, in particular the RIC,
have been seen as major influences shaping the character of English colonial policing generally. James Cramer claimed in 1964 that the RIC 'was
for many years the pattern on which many Colonial Police Forces were
modelled'.[42] Although this view has been challenged, two important collections of essays on British colonial policing published in the early 1990s
were full of references to the employment throughout the empire of RIC
practices, regulations, training and even personnel, from the 1840s right
up until the 1940s.[43]

In the 1880s, for instance, the Queensland police were using the *Irish
Constable's Manual* written by RIC Inspector General Sir Andrew Reed.[44]
When a paramilitary police force was established in New Zealand in the
late 1840s to counter Maori unrest, the RIC was 'perceived as the major
model', particularly in rural areas.[45] The withdrawal of the army from
police-keeping duties in Trinidad prompted the local authorities to recruit
four RIC sergeants in 1884 and a further twelve in 1890 to boost the military efficiency of the constabulary.[46] The 'model' for the North West
Mounted Police, later the Royal Canadian Mounted Police, was the
RIC.[47] Students of African colonial policing have also found plenty of
evidence of Irish influence. The RIC was the 'structural model' for the

---

42 Cramer, *The world's police*, p. 81. For a similar claim, see Jeffries, *The colonial police*, pp 30–1. 43 See D.M.
Anderson and David Killingray (eds), *Policing the empire: government, authority and control, 1830–1940* (Manchester, 1991)
and idem, *Policing and decolonization: nationalism, politics and the police, 1917–65* (Manchester, 1992). 44 Mark Finnane,
'The varieties of policing: colonial Queensland, 1860–1900' in Anderson and Killingray (eds), *Policing the empire*, p.
38. 45 R.S. Hill, 'The policing of colonial New Zealand: from informal to formal control, 1840–1907' in ibid.,
pp 56–7. 46 Howard Johnson, 'Patterns of policing in the post-emancipation British Caribbean, 1835–95' in ibid.,
pp 81, 84. 47 W.R. Morrison, 'Imposing the British way: the Canadian Mounted Police and the Klondike gold
rush' in ibid., p. 94.

Gold Coast (Ghana) police force and from 1907 officers were trained at the RIC Depot in Dublin.[48] The Egyptian *gendarmerie* was 'modelled after' the RIC,[49] while in 1905 and 1906 the Kenya police attempted to recruit RIC men.[50] Between 1900 and 1903 a number of RIC constables were also recruited for the Cape Town police, and for decades thereafter the force was noted for its Irish character.[51] When the RIC was disbanded in 1922 its influence by no means ceased. Significant numbers of men sought and found employment in colonial constabularies, most notably in Palestine where ex-RIC officers were still running policing in the 1940s. 'RIC men "stiffened" the ranks of many colonial forces' during the inter-war years.[52]

Yet in one of these collections Richard Hawkins struck a discordant note by questioning the 'nebulous assumption' of a 'protean "Irish model"' and calling for a more thorough examination of the influence of RIC practices in individual colonies. Hawkins conceded that from '1907, when all officers of colonial police forces had to undergo instruction at the Dublin depot, the RIC undoubtedly held primacy among the police forces of the empire', but he went on to ask: 'has there perhaps been a tendency to read the pattern set up in 1907 back into the previous forty or sixty years?' The Irish police offered ideas and 'precedents', but Hawkins argued that the force was never deliberately nor wholly replicated abroad.[53]

In trying to identify the distinctive features of the RIC that might have influenced colonial forces, Hawkins noted its centralised control, its paramilitary character and the separation of police from people – all factors that reinforced each other.[54] RIC men were not under the control of local magistrates; most lived apart from the community in barracks; they were forbidden to serve in their home counties and were automatically transferred if they married a local woman; they could not vote, own land or engage in business. Colonial forces also frequently relied on outsiders to undertake policing. As the editors of these volumes, Anderson

48 David Killingray, 'Guarding the extending frontier: policing the Gold Coast, 1865–1913' in ibid., p. 112. 49 D.H. Johnson, 'From military to tribal police: policing the Upper Nile Province of the Sudan' in ibid., p. 164. 50 D.M. Anderson, 'Policing, prosecution and the law in colonial Kenya, *c*.1905–39' in ibid., p. 184. 51 Bill Nasson, 'Bobbies to Boers: police, people and social control in Cape Town' in ibid., pp 240, 247. 52 David Killingray and D.M. Anderson, 'An orderly retreat? Policing the end of empire' in Killingray and Anderson (eds), *Policing and decolonization*, p. 8; Charles Smith, 'Communal conflict and insurrection in Palestine, 1936–48' in ibid., pp 72–3. 53 Richard Hawkins, 'The "Irish model" and the empire: a case for reassessment' in Anderson and Killingray (eds), *Policing the empire*, pp 19, 24. 54 Ibid., pp 25–9.

and Killingray, wrote: 'the trustworthy stranger to police other strangers was the man required'. Certain ethnic groups, often considered by the English 'martial races', were favoured for police recruitment. Indians and Sikhs especially, were employed as police in Mauritius, Hong Kong and Fiji. In the West Indies the policy was to use 'other islanders', as for instance Barbadians in Trinidad.[55]

Nevertheless, RIC men, even if not serving in their counties of birth, were still Irishmen. Moreover, as we shall see, during the post-Famine period membership of constabulary came increasingly to reflect accurately the social, economic and religious structure of rural Ireland. In this respect, policemen were not strangers, even if their life-styles and duties tended to cut them off from the communities they policed. Contemporaries recognised the representative nature of the RIC and were sometimes puzzled by it. Writing of the Land War period, the staunchly anti-Nationalist Resident Magistrate (RM) Clifford Lloyd, who had previously served in the Burma police, asked:

> Can any one suggest why one-half of the sons of farmers in Ireland, who have been or are members of the Royal Irish Constabulary, represent a body of men unequalled for their respectability, loyalty and courage, while a large portion of the other half, during the last five years, have made up the ignoble army of moonlighters, cattle-maimers, and crouching assassins of whom we have all unfortunately heard so much?[56]

More than a century later, this question remains a pertinent one. Why did some Irish Catholic farmers and labourers loyally serve in the RIC, while men from exactly the same background – indeed, on occasion from the same families – swelled the ranks of Nationalist and Republican movements, which railed against the constabulary? This is one of the many issues upon which this book seeks to throw light.

In attempting an initial elucidation of Lloyd's conundrum, it is helpful to place Irish policing in a European context. European police forces grew out of long-established state agencies and were seen as servants of

---

55 D.M. Anderson and David Killingray, 'Consent, coercion and colonial control: policing the empire, 1830–1940' in ibid., p. 7. 56 Clifford Lloyd, *Ireland under the Land League: a narrative of personal experiences* (Edinburgh and London, 1892), p. 137.

the crown rather than of the people. Their primary goal was to ensure order on behalf of the ruler and thus their model was a military one. In addition, their duties were much wider than those of most English forces.[57] The centrally controlled, paramilitary RIC, with its wide-ranging responsibilities, was far more like a European-style *gendarmerie* than it was a locally regulated, unarmed English borough or county constabulary, primarily concerned with the prevention and detection of non-political crime. In Europe the French had the longest and best-developed tradition of policing and thus provided the most influential model.[58]

The French policeman, as Tom Bowden has written, was definitely 'not a friendly guardian of the *status quo* or a crime fighter'; he was 'a paramilitary political agent. Likewise the force of which he was a member was a unit designed not just to *admonish* but to *crush* opposition and dissidence from whatever source it emanated.'[59] During the eighteenth century Paris was heavily policed by a guard that in the 1770s numbered some 2,000.[60] In the rest of the country the *maréchaussée*, a mounted force, patrolled the roads, supervised public gatherings, apprehended vagrants and criminals and monitored foreigners. There are striking similarities between the eighteenth-century French *maréchaussée* and the nineteenth-century Irish constabulary. Like the RIC, the *maréchausséé* was housed in barracks; the force was uniformed and equipped like the military; men were forbidden to serve in their places of birth; and sons were encouraged to follow fathers into the service. However, the *maréchaussée* had an even more pronounced military character than the RIC: its men had to

57 There is an extensive literature on European policing, of which the following is only a small English-language selection. For general studies, see R.B. Fosdick, *European police systems* (New York, 1915); D.H. Bayley, 'The police and political development in Europe' in Charles Tilly (ed.), *The formation of national states in Western Europe* (Princeton, NJ, 1975), pp 328–79; idem, *Patterns of policing: a comparative international analysis* (New Brunswick, NJ, 1985); R.I. Mawby, *Comparative policing issues: the British and American experience in international perspective* (London, 1990). For national studies, excluding France, see E.G. Spencer, *Police and the social order in German cities: the Dusseldorf district, 1848–1914* (Dekalb, Ill., 1992); R.J. Evans (ed.), *Rereading German history: from unification to reunification, 1880–1996* (London, 1997); idem, *Tales from the German underworld: crime and punishment in the nineteenth century* (New Haven, CT, 1998); Alf Ludtke, *Police and state in Prussia, 1815–50* (Cambridge, 1989); Marc Raeff, *The well-ordered police state: social and institutional change through law in the Germanies and Russia, 1600–1800* (New Haven, CT, 1983); J.A. Davis, *Conflict and control: law and order in nineteenth-century Italy* (London, 1988); Jonathan Dunnage, *The Italian police and the rise of Fascism: a case study of the province of Bologna, 1897–1925* (Westport, CT, 1997). 58 For the history of French police forces, see Clive Emsley, *Policing and its context, 1750–1870* (London, 1983); P.J. Stead, *The police of Paris* (London, 1957); idem, *The police of France* (London, 1983); Alan Williams, *The police of Paris, 1718–89* (Baton Rouge, LA, 1979); Richard Cobb, *The police and the people: French popular protest, 1789–1820* (London, 1970); Peter de Polnay, *Napoleon's police* (London, 1970); E.A. Arnold Jr., *Fouché, Napoleon and the general police* (Washington, DC, 1979); H.C. Payne, *The police state of Louis Napoleon Bonaparte, 1851–60* (Seattle, WG, 1966); J.R.J. Jammes, *The French gendarmerie* (Bradford, 1982). 59 Tom Bowden, *Beyond the limits of the law: a comparative study of the police in crisis politics* (London, 1978), p. 144. 60 Stead, *The police of Paris*, p. 46.

be ex-soldiers and it was controlled by the Ministry of War.[61] When a national *gendarmerie* was established during the Revolution, it was 'the direct descendant of the *maréchaussée*': again staffed by military veterans and responsible to the Ministry of War.[62]

Early nineteenth-century English critics of the introduction of police forces looked across the Channel and saw French *gendarmes*, not as citizens in uniform protecting local communities or as neutral upholders of the law, but as soldiers and spies charged with enforcing repressive and authoritarian forms of government.[63] Irish critics of British rule were later to view the RIC similarly. One of the most forceful statements – not to say over-statements – of the ubiquity of the French police comes from the philosopher Michel Foucault, as an aside in his study of the growth of prisons.

> The organisation of a centralized police had long been regarded … as the most direct expression of royal absolutism … although the police as an institution were certainly organized in the form of a state apparatus … It is an apparatus that must be coextensive with the entire social body and not only by the extreme limits that it embraces, but by the minuteness of the details it is concerned with … With the police, one is in the indefinite world of a supervision that seeks ideally to reach the most elementary particle, the most passing phenomenon of the social body … It had to be like a faceless gaze that transformed the whole social body into a field of perception: thousands of eyes posted everywhere …[64]

As we have seen, Irish nationalist critics of the RIC also highlighted its preoccupation with the minutiae of everyday life and its 'thousands of eyes posted everywhere'.

While some of those who were instrumental in the establishment of Irish police forces were probably influenced by the French model,[65] there

61 Emsley, *Policing and its contexts*, pp 13–18. 62 Ibid., pp 40–1. 63 Palmer, *Police and protest*, pp 71–3. 64 Michel Foucault, *Discipline and punish: the birth of the prison*, trans. by Alan Sheridan (London, 1977), pp 213–14. 65 To what extent Robert Peel was influenced by the French model has never been established. But he certainly visited France in 1814 and talked to Fouché, Napoleon's notorious police minister. In 1822 he admitted that he 'was more inclined to the establishment of a Body of Gendarmerie (to be called by some less starting name)' than to the Peace Preservation Force, the temporary body that he introduced into parts of Ireland beginning in 1814. Palmer, *Police and protest*, p. 216.

was one important factor that they tended to overlook — as did Foucault. Although boasting the most sophisticated policing system in Europe, with large forces drawn from the working-class population, French governments were repeatedly overthrown in uprisings supported by exactly those classes from which the *gendarmerie* came. In 1919–21 the British were to learn what the French had known since 1789: that a large, tightly controlled, paramilitary police force, even if representative of the general population, was no guarantee of the survival of the regime.

Strict military discipline and isolation from the community helped foster a potent *esprit de corps* in both Irish and European *gendarmeries*. As one sociologist of policing has remarked: 'Police group solidarity increases in direct proportion to their isolation from the rest of society.'[66] We shall see later that, in addition to isolation, a significant influence on the development of this sense of solidarity among the RIC was the fact that, like French forces, large numbers of policemen had relatives who had served or were serving in the constabulary. There are many examples of two and even three generations of the same family serving consecutively or of four and five members of the one family serving concurrently. Thus an Irish policeman may well have conceived of his loyalty as owing primarily to his family, his comrades and the policing culture of which he was a part, rather than to distant political entities or abstract concepts. Such personal connections are inevitably intense and simple *camaraderie* is a factor that should not be underestimated. The RIC's Nationalist critics perhaps missed the point somewhat when they accused its Catholic members of being disloyal to Ireland; Catholic policemen may just have had a more personal and less abstract notion of what constituted the Irish nation.

How we portray the RIC depends to some extent on what we choose to measure it against: seventeenth- or eighteenth-century Irish parish constables, nineteenth-century English constabularies, colonial police forces or Continental *gendarmeries*. Compared to earlier Irish forces and to contemporary English forces, the RIC appears large, militaristic and intrusive. The same to some extent can be said of it in relation to many colonial forces. Although the RIC's influence in shaping such forces is obvious, Hawkins was right to stress that no colonial constabulary was

66 Bowden, *Beyond the limits of the law*, p. 30.

ever an exact replica of the RIC. The colonial context also highlights the unenviable position of policemen as liminal figures, mediating between two very different and often hostile worlds. The European comparison, on the other hand, emphasises the highly political nature of much Irish policing and, in so doing, explains why successive British governments felt a large, isolated, loyal, paramilitary force was necessary rather than an English-style civilian constabulary. In truth, all these contexts help reveal the complex character of the RIC and point to the fact that in many respects it was a unique institution. While comparable to all these other forces and, especially to a European paramilitary *gendarmerie*, the RIC was, at the same time, exactly like none of them.

This study aims to explore the Irish constabulary in some detail, and specifically to explore it through an examination of the men who composed the force from the 1820s to the 1920s. The book is structured as a collective biography. Beginning with the socio-economic origins of policemen, it charts their recruitment and training, their duties and conditions of service, their family and personal lives, what happened to them after they left the force and some of the experiences of their descendants.

Foucault claimed that the French police sought to reach even the 'most elementary particle' in society. By focusing on the elementary particle of the RIC – that is, the individual policeman – hopefully we can build up a clear picture of this group of men whom friend and foe alike agreed were absolutely essential to the maintenance of British rule in Ireland for a century.

CHAPTER THREE

Portrait of a peeler: a man on the make

I was born on 10 October 1896 in Tuam, County Galway. I was
the eighth child of a family of nine children consisting of four
boys and five girls. I was a farmer's son and I worked on a farm
after leaving school ... Times were hard and labour[ing work]
was scarce, and of course money was scarce; there was no other
employment. All the family went off, most of them, to America
and I decided with a chum of mine to join the RIC ... in that
locality a big crowd of fellows joined. I think eight of us joined
the police in that townland.[1]

My father, whose name was Denis Whelan, was a police constable in the Royal Irish Constabulary. He came from a small farm
near the hamlet of Stradbally, about fifty miles southeast of
Dublin ... He was a modest, pious, trusting man, upright, honest
as daylight, and absolutely loyal to the Empire as only a born
hero-worshipper can be ... In his dark bottle-green uniform,
black leather belt with brass buckle, black helmet or peaked cap,
black truncheon case and black boots, my father embodied the
Law. What was far more important, he embodied all the accepted
and respected values and conventions of what we would nowa-
days call the Establishment. In simple language, his language, he
considered that the highest state in life that anyone could achieve
was to be a Gentleman ...[2]

This chapter aims to offer a general picture of the backgrounds of
Irish policemen and thus of the socio-economic composition of the
force. It seeks to answer an apparently simple question: who were the
Irish police? The straightforwardness of the question is deceptive, however. The Irish constabulary operated for a century and during that time
more than 86,000 men served in its ranks. Given the lengthy period and

1 Constable William Dunne, RIC 1917–22, quoted in Brewer, *The Royal Irish Constabulary*, pp 37–8. 2 O'Faolain,
Viva moi!, pp 22–3.

the large number of individuals involved, describing the membership of the force is a complex task.

In order to create a socio-economic portrait of the Irish police, a series of subsidiary questions about the backgrounds of both constables and officers must be addressed. These include: where were policemen born; what were their family backgrounds; what religious denominations did they belong to; what, if any, previous occupations had they had; what ages were they on recruitment; and what was their marital status? Recruitment remained consistent to a considerable extent, yet the composition of the constabulary nevertheless changed significantly over time. These changes need to be explained and evaluated. An analysis of who the police were enables us to assess the attractions, and also some of the drawbacks, of policing as a career. In addition, it allows consideration of how representative the constabulary was of the community that it policed. It may seem reasonable to assume that the more representative policemen were the more acceptable they became, but, as we shall see, this was not necessarily the case.

NUMBERS AND STRUCTURE

Before analysing the composition of the constabulary, however, its size needs to be established because simple numbers can be revealing as to the character of a police force. Numbers also entail a consideration of the structure of the constabulary. In the force's General or Personnel Register, which covers the period from August 1816 to August 1922, nearly 84,000 constables are listed, as well as nearly 1,500 officers. This register was created from earlier ones during the late 1840s. After that date it is essentially complete, but men who served for short periods before the late 1840s appear not have been included. So the figure of around 86,000 for the membership of the constabulary is almost certainly an under estimate. Taking into account the various police forces that operated in Ireland between the establishment of Robert Peel's Peace Preservation Force in 1814 and the disbandment of the RIC in 1922, it is likely that well over 100,000 Irishmen served as policemen during the Union with Britain.[3]

3 It would appear that in 1848 a collection of earlier personnel registers dating back to 1816 was consolidated into one single general register that thereafter listed all members of the constabulary, no matter how brief their

The act that consolidated the Irish constabulary in 1836 and continued to govern the force throughout its existence (6 Wm. IV, c.13) specified numbers of policemen for each borough and barony. But, as the following table demonstrates, constabulary numbers varied significantly during subsequent decades.

Actual numbers of the RIC at ten-year intervals
on 1 January 1837–1907 and during 1917–18 and 1921–2[4]

	County inspector	District inspector	Head Constable	Sergeants & Constables	Total
1837	35	210	–	7,388	7,633
1847	35	219	285	10,446	10,985
1857	35	249	326	11,420	12,030
1867	36[a]	268	351	11,415	12,070
1877	36	203[b]	239	10,648	11,126
1887	37	224	260	12,119	12,640
1897	37	221	247	11,365	11,870
1907	37	202	225	9,459	9,923
1917–18	37	164	231	9,500[c]	9,932
1921–2	37	256	276	12,650	13,219

a From 1867 includes one Belfast town inspector
b From 1877 includes one private secretary to the inspector general
c Does not include upwards of 650 men absent on military service

The complement of the RIC was generally boosted during times of social and political unrest. As the above table demonstrates, the Famine of the late 1840s, the Land War of the early 1880s and the Anglo-Irish War of the early 1920s, all precipitated increased recruitment. Outside crisis times, expanded duties also often necessitated extra men. However,

service. But the compilers of the single register only included men serving in 1848 and those who had received a pension prior to 1848. We know that there was a high turnover of policemen in pre-Famine Ireland, so hundreds, and perhaps even thousands, of men who had served for short periods in the thirty years before 1848 were omitted from the consolidated register. Ian Bridgeman, 'Policing rural Ireland, p. 111. For a list of constables' service numbers, which offers a guide to the volume of rank-and-file recruitment between 1816 and 1922, see Herlihy, *The Royal Irish Constabulary: a short history and genealogical guide*, pp 232–3. 4 Treasury Blue Notes. Civil Services. Class III, 19: 1922–3 Royal Irish Constabulary (PRO(L), T.165/49, p. 5). I would to thank Richard Hawkins for providing me with a copy of this valuable source.

maximum numbers for the various ranks were regulated by statute and this meant that enlargement was a cumbersome process.

By the last quarter of the nineteenth century the RIC was composed of four elements, although they were regulated as one body. The size of the main element of the force, sometimes referred to as the 'free quota', was fixed by statute (11 & 12 Vic., c.72) in 1848 at a maximum of 10,678 men, but by 1909 had been revised down to 9,837. Men of the 'free quota' formed the core of the force and they were deployed throughout the country in numbers deemed necessary for day-to-day policing. Until 1846 half their cost was met by taxes levied on counties, but thereafter, under 9 & 10 Vic., c.97, the whole cost of the 'free quota' was met by the British Treasury out of central taxation revenue.

The second component of the RIC was termed the 'extra force'. This was composed of men recruited to police Belfast from 1865 and Derry from 1870. Initially 450 men were required for Belfast and 45 for Derry, but by 1914 these figures stood at 733 and 14 respectively. The 'extra force' also included men authorised under Sections 12 and 13 of the 1836 Constabulary Act, who could be deployed at the request of local magistrates or in counties proclaimed as disturbed by the lord lieutenant. Their total cost was borne by the county taxpayers. They were not a permanent force and their numbers varied considerably depending upon circumstances: in 1882 during the Land War there were 3,379 of them, but by 1914 they were down to 329 men.[5]

The third element of the RIC was the 'reserve force' established by statute (2 & 3 Vic., c.75) in 1839 and based at the Phoenix Park depot, but capable of being deployed in any part of the country where extra men were urgently required. Originally 200 men, plus 12 district inspectors and head constables, the reserve was boosted during the Famine to 400 in 1846 and 600 in 1847, before being reduced to 400 again after the end of the Land War in 1882. The reserve, a permanent force under the direct control of the inspector general, was paid for centrally. It could be deployed rapidly, without the prior approval of either Dublin Castle or of local magistrates. Men from the counties and the depot were posted to the reserve for varying periods and in it they gained experience of policing major outbreaks of public disorder.[6]

5 Bridgeman, 'Policing rural Ireland', p. 163. 6 Ibid., pp 164–5.

The fourth component of the RIC was the revenue force. This was created in 1857, by 17 & 18 Vic., c.89, when the old Revenue Police were abolished and many of the members were absorbed by the constabulary. It officially numbered 400 men, but was often below strength and in 1896 it was decided no longer to recruit especially for revenue service. There was also in essence a fifth component of the constabulary, for, during periods of unrest, constabulary pensioners could be called upon for support. They constituted a substantial group, numbering 4,408 in 1876/7, 6,603 in 1896/7 and 8,370 in 1916/17.[7]

As well as the size of the force being augmented, at times it could be reduced. Often, as in 1870 when the numbers of district inspectors and head constables were cut, this accompanied pay rises and was in fact an attempt by the Treasury to off-set additional expense.[8] The 1870 reduction required an act of parliament, but numbers could also be kept down by simply not filling positions. In addition, the constabulary was sometimes unable to find enough suitable recruits. In December 1913, for instance, the RIC was under strength by 756 sergeants and constables, 40 head constables and 37 district inspectors.[9]

To a large extent the way the RIC was organised and deployed helped boost its numbers. Men were scattered in small groups of generally less than ten, and often only four, based in barracks in nearly 1,400 stations throughout Ireland, excluding Dublin. Each station was run by a head constable or sergeant, and stations were grouped into nearly 250 districts commanded by sub, later termed district, inspectors. But the county was also crucial to the structuring of the constabulary, for districts were organised by counties under the command of a county inspector, directly answerable to the inspector general based in Dublin Castle. The RIC had a passion for standardisation, so it operated often without much consideration to local circumstances. All counties, regardless of size, were commanded by a county inspector – and in the cases of Cork and Tipperary by two – and these men were paid the same basic salary. This produced rather startling anomalies. In 1907, for instance, the county inspector of East Cork was in charge of 97 stations, including those in Cork city, while

7 A large number of these men would no longer have been fit for duty due to advanced age or ill health. But in 1914 it was noted that 57 per cent of pensioners were in employment, which would suggest that around half of pensioners may have been available for service if called upon. *Report of Committee of Inquiry into the RIC and DMP*, [Cd 7421], H.C. 1914, xliv, pp 10, 25–6. 8 Ibid., pp 2, 11; Treasury Blue Notes. Constabulary of Ireland, 1891–2 (PRO(L), T.165/9, p. 3). 9 *Report of Inquiry into RIC and DMP*, 1914, p. 26.

the county inspector of Carlow commanded a mere 15 stations – yet both received a gross salary, depending upon length of service, of between £350 and £450 per annum, plus £173 5s. 0d. in allowances.[10]

The combination of a large number of small stations and a county-based structure produced a 'top heavy' force in terms of staffing. In 1864, for instance, there was one sergeant to every four constables. Head constables, the most senior and experienced members of the rank-and-file, were less numerous, with one head constable to every 33 sergeants and constables.[11] Despite attempts to reduce senior staff, these ratios did not change greatly over time. In 1913 there was one RIC sergeant to every 3.88 constables and one officer to every 3.1 men. From at least the 1850s the Treasury considered that the Irish constabulary was over manned and sought a reduction in numbers of the order of 2,000: that is a massive cut of about one-quarter to one-fifth of the force. But this drastic measure was successfully resisted by Dublin Castle, and circumstances also contrived to prevent it ever being implemented.[12]

A report in 1914 by the Treasury Remembrancer, Maurice Headlam, whose job entailed monitoring and, if at all possible, reducing Irish government expenditure, was extremely critical of the constabulary's organisation. Pointing out that the army allowed more responsibility to be assumed by the rank-and-file than did the Irish constabulary, Headlam argued that the RIC should 'require less supervision than the rank and file of the army rather than more'. As well as proposing that some counties be amalgamated and the thirty-six county inspectors reduced in number, Headlam also suggested a huge cut in the number of district inspectors, to two for every county inspector. Cadet recruitment should therefore stop, and most of the duties of district inspectors should be assumed by head constables. The numbers of sergeants and constables required reduction as well. Headlam noted that with a population a little under seven million in 1849 the constabulary was 12,212 strong, while in 1914 with a population of around 4.4 million the RIC still numbered 10,712.[13] But with the outbreak of World War One Headlam's major reforms were shelved.

10 This allowance does not include mileage and subsistence allowances. The inspector of a large county like East Cork would certainly have drawn upon these allowances far more heavily than the inspector in charge of a small county, like Carlow, Longford or Louth. The editor of the *Constabulary Gazette* [William Harding], *The R.I.C.: a plea for reform* (Dublin, [1907]), pp 10–12. 11 Bridgeman, 'Policing rural Ireland', p. 141. 12 Ibid., pp 261–2. 13 *Report of Inquiry into RIC and DMP*, 1914, pp 33–5. Headlam was certainly not the first to notice this discrepancy. As early as 1880, the prime minister, William Gladstone, was writing to the then chief secretary, W.E. Forster, querying

After the end of the war, in 1919, the issue of the size of the RIC was revisited. Headlam was a member of a vice-regal commission which recommended that twelve counties be amalgamated into five; that the ratio of sergeants to constables be 1:5; and also that the mounted section of the force be abolished. In a minority report, Headlam and several others went even further, proposing in addition the amalgamation of the RIC and the DMP.[14] But again Headlam's proposed reductions in numbers were forestalled by events. During the Anglo-Irish War there were substantial increases rather than reductions in the membership of the RIC.

Headlam was certainly correct when he questioned whether the RIC's structure was efficient, either financially or operationally. It almost certainly wasn't: in peaceful times the constabulary had too many men and was excessively expensive, while during periods of unrest, as for instance during the Land War and the Anglo-Irish War, the county-based structure did not allow the necessary coordination of effort required. During both outbreaks new divisional commissioners had to be introduced over the heads of the county inspectors.[15]

Headlam was also correct in noting that this structure meant Ireland was a heavily policed country, especially in comparison with England and most of the empire. Stanley Palmer has pointed out that in 1851 Ireland and England had approximately the same number of policemen, but, while Ireland's population was 6.5 million, England's was 18 million. By 1901, in proportion to population, Ireland was twice as heavily policed as England.[16] Theodore Hoppen offered somewhat different figures, but he reached the same conclusion as Palmer. According to him, Ireland had one policeman for every 791 inhabitants in 1842, while England had one for every 1,611 inhabitants. In 1881 the comparable figure for Ireland was 374 inhabitants and for England 833.[17] Most colonies were even more lightly policed than England. 'Single European officers frequently presided over huge tracts of territory and large, if scattered, populations, with only a handful of locally recruited and often untrained constables under their charge.'[18]

why Ireland in the 1830s, with a population of around eight million and being a more lawless country, could be policed by 8,000 men, when at the present time, with two-thirds of that population, it required 12,000 policemen. Quoted in Margaret O'Callaghan, *British high politics and a nationalist Ireland: criminality, land and the law under Forster and Balfour* (Cork, 1994), p. 54. 14 *Report of the Vice-Regal Commission on Re-Organisation and Pay of the Irish Police Forces*, [Cmd 603], H.C. 1920, xxii, pp 11, 16–17. 15 Hawkins, 'Dublin Castle and the Royal Irish Constabulary (1916–22)' in Desmond (ed.), *The Irish struggle, 1916–26*, p. 170. 16 Palmer, *Police and protest*, pp 529–30. 17 Hoppen, *Elections, politics and society*. 18 Anderson and Killingray, 'Consent, coercion and colonial control', p. 4. For a comparison of

Clearly Ireland's police force was a very large one indeed in terms of the country's population.[19] In this regard it resembled most closely some European *gendarmeries*. In the 1870s, for instance, Italy had approximately one policeman for every 530 inhabitants and 2 per cent of gross public expenditure was devoted to the cost of policing.[20] Paris in the late 1860s was even more heavily policed, with around one paramilitary policeman for every 140 inhabitants.[21] These ratios highlight a point made by Richard Hawkins, that 'the Irish constabulary was an example of a *gendarmerie*, a system common in continental Europe'. Thus, as suggested in Chapter 2, while comparisons with England and the empire are helpful, comparisons between Ireland and countries like France, Italy, Germany and Spain may in some cases be more apposite.[22] Certainly in terms of sheer numbers, the RIC resembled a European *gendarmerie* rather than an English constabulary.

The size of the Irish constabulary had another important implication, which will be discussed in later chapters, but is worth noting here briefly. Both constables and officers were well aware that the schemes put forward at various times aimed at major reform almost inevitably involved a drastic reduction in numbers. This made many policemen resistant to change. In particular, sergeants and both district and county inspectors knew that a re-structuring of the RIC would almost certainly have meant the loss of their jobs.

ORIGINS

Numbers, while establishing useful parameters and allowing interesting comparisons, tell us very little about who the RIC were. In terms of where in Ireland constables came from, a distinct pattern emerged over time. With regard to provinces, in the years up to 1871, a disproportionate number came from Leinster; after then Munster emerged as more sig-

police numbers in London, Sydney, Calcutta and also Stockholm during the nineteenth and twentieth centuries, see T.R. Gurr, *Rogues, rebels and reformers: a political history of urban crime and conflict* (Beverly Hills, CA, and London, 1976), pp 124–30. 19 A comparison with large American urban centres, which were more heavily policed than other parts of the country, also highlights the size of the RIC. In 1880 Chicago had one policeman for every 1,390 inhabitants, while Philadelphia had one for every 705 inhabitants. D.R. Johnson, *Policing the urban underworld: the impact of crime on the development of the American police, 1800–87* (Philadelphia, 1979), p. 104. 20 Davis, *Conflict and control: law and order in nineteenth-century Italy*, pp 232–3. 21 Stead, *The police of Paris*, pp 120–1. 22 Hawkins, 'The "Irish model" and the empire', p. 24.

nificant. But, after 1851 and right through until 1920, Connacht supplied an excess number of recruits to the constabulary in terms of its general population. Only in the decade 1900–10 did the percentage of recruits from Ulster exceed that province's proportion of Ireland's population. Thus during the second half of the nineteenth century and the first two decades of the twentieth, Munster and Connacht consistently provided more than half of RIC constables, although together they had only about 40 per cent of the total Irish population.

Within the provinces recruitment also exhibited patterns in terms of the counties from which policemen came. In the 1830s counties in the south and west, such as Limerick, Kerry, Tipperary and Galway in Munster, and in the south and east, such as Queen's (Laois) and Kilkenny in Leinster, produced disproportionate numbers of recruits. But by the 1890s policemen were coming disproportionately from the midlands and the Ulster/Connacht border counties. Cavan, Fermanagh, Roscommon, Leitrim, Monaghan and Westmeath, all provided the RIC with large numbers of recruits.[23] Thus, over time, the focus of recruitment shifted from the south and west more towards the midlands and the north west.[24]

Yet, despite this shift, recruitment remained consistent in the sense that few policemen came from cities or from the counties containing cities. The overwhelming majority were born in rural counties and even those with trades tended to come from small towns rather than large urban areas.[25] Presumably cities offered more varied opportunities for employment, but, as we shall see in the next section, the constabulary authorities also preferred to recruit constables from rural areas.

OCCUPATION AND CLASS

If most constabulary recruits were born in rural areas then their back-grounds, as well as being agricultural, were also likely to have been work-

---

23 Bridgeman, 'Policing rural Ireland', pp 115–16. 24 Unless otherwise stated, the following analysis of the composition of the RIC rank-and-file is based upon a 10 per cent stratified random sample, amounting to a little over 7,000 men, drawn from constables recruited between January 1837 and August 1920, who were recorded in the RIC's General Register, 1816–1922 (PRO(L), HO 184/1–44). I would like to thank Professor W.J. Lowe, who undertook this analysis, for allowing me to make use of it. For a more detailed account of the analysis, see Lowe and Malcolm, 'Domestication' (1992), pp 27–48. 25 For a discussion of the tradesmen who joined the constabulary, see Bridgeman, 'Policing rural Ireland', pp 124–7.

ing class and unskilled. And an analysis of their previous occupations confirms this assumption. Until 1871 the largest occupational group listed in the RIC register were labourers; thereafter, until the final years of the force's existence, the predominant group were farmers. Palmer in his study of occupations between 1816 and 1840 found that around 55 per cent of recruits were described as labourers and 26 per cent as farmers.[26] By 1882 this balance had been exactly reversed.[27] In 1901 61 per cent of recruits were being classed as farmers' sons and only 5 per cent as labourers; the latter being outnumbered by those with no previous employment (12 per cent) and by shop assistants (6 per cent), and closely followed by clerks and teachers (4 per cent each).[28]

These categories of farmer, farmer's son and labourer are not precise, however, nor necessarily mutually exclusive. The number of rural labourers in Ireland certainly declined drastically during and after the Famine.[29] Yet, given the ages of constabulary recruits, some of the labourers of the earlier years were probably small farmers' sons, while most of the farmers of the latter period almost certainly belonged to this same category. A Cork head constable informed the 1872 enquiry into the RIC that most recruits were farmers' sons and that: 'A small farmer's son sometimes calls himself a labourer'.[30] Thus the switch from labourer to farmer in the previous occupations of RIC recruits did not in fact reflect as major a change in socio-economic origins as might appear. Throughout its existence the Irish constabulary found most of its rank-and-file recruits among the sons, and especially the younger sons, of small-farming families in the south, west and midlands of Ireland. The farmers' sons of the post-Famine era were undoubtedly more prosperous and better educated than the rural labourers of the pre-Famine years, but they all came from very similar backgrounds.

In England too during the 1860s and 1870s Carolyn Steedman noticed a tendency for both county constabularies and urban watch committees to recruit policemen from rural backgrounds. 'What was bought', she argued, 'when a rural labourer signed a police recruitment form was not

26 Palmer, *Police and protest*, pp 564–6. Palmer offers a statistical analysis of a sample of recruits from the RIC General Register between 1816 and 1850. He also provides a helpful discussion of the shortcomings of the early register.   27 Hoppen, *Elections, politics and society*, p. 412.   28 *Report of Inquiry into the RIC and DMP*, 1914, p. 182.   29 David Fitzpatrick, 'The disappearance of the Irish agricultural labourer, 1841–1912', *Irish Economic and Social History*, vii (1980), pp 66–92.   30 *Report of the Commissioners appointed...to enquire into the Condition of the Civil Service in Ireland on the RIC*, [C 831], HC 1873, xxii, p. 18.

just his willingness to work for low wages, but his understanding and acceptance of a set of social relationships.' Sons of the landed gentry tended to become chief constables in the new English police forces; farmers, land agents, bailiffs and clerks became officers; while rural labourers became constables. Social relationships based on traditional divisions and forms of deference were thus preserved and, indeed, reinforced.[31]

In Ireland the recruitment of rural labourers as constables and the separate recruitment of middle- and upper-class young men for the officer corps reflected a similar desire to maintain existing class divisions. But, in adopting this recruitment strategy, the Irish constabulary was far from embarking upon a novel course; it was in fact simply following in the footsteps of the British army.

In 1852, as we have seen, Sir Francis Head was impressed by constabulary recruits training in Phoenix Park and concluded that they 'exemplified ... the natural aptitude of the Irish to be soldiers'.[32] The Irish, like the Scots, the Sikhs and the Gurkhas, were often viewed by the English as a 'martial race'. When the right to enlist and bear arms was restored to Catholics in the early 1790s, recruitment of Irish Catholics into the British army increased dramatically, with some 130,000 Irishmen serving between 1800 and 1815.[33] By 1830 42 per cent of the rank-and-file of the army, totalling some 43,000 soldiers, were Irish-born and the majority of these men had come from rural-labouring backgrounds. After the Famine the proportion of the Irish fell to 28 per cent in 1870, 15 per cent in 1890 and 9 per cent in 1912, but, in terms of the number of men of military age in Ireland's population, the Irish were still disproportionately represented in the army throughout the second half of the century.

Rural labourers were especially favoured by army recruiters because of their physical 'fitness and docility'.[34] Thus in recruiting rural labourers for police service, the Irish constabulary was simply copying what had already been done successfully by the British army. Irish recruits had proved themselves amenable to military discipline and capable of loyalty

31 Carolyn Steedman, *Policing the Victorian community: the formation of English provincial police forces, 1856–80* (London, 1984), pp 2–3. 32 Head, *A fortnight in Ireland*, p. 61. 33 E.M. Spiers, 'Army organisation and society in the nineteenth century' in Bartlett and Jeffery (ed.), *A military history of Ireland*, pp 335–7. 34 E.M. Spiers, *The army and society, 1815–1914* (London, 1980), pp 46–8; A.R. Skelley, *The Victorian army at home* (London and Montreal, 1977), pp 284–8. The Irish were also disproportionately represented in the officer ranks of the army, with 15 per cent of colonels and 12 per cent of generals being Irish-born in 1868. E.M. Spiers, *The late Victorian army, 1868–1902* (Manchester, 1992), p. 98.

and courage. If the army could turn the sons of Irish small farmers into worthwhile soldiers, then the constabulary was convinced it could do the same: use military training and discipline to create loyal and obedient paramilitary policemen.[35]

AGE, RELIGION AND MARRIAGE

Before the consolidation of the constabulary in the late 1830s, ages of recruits had varied considerably, with significant numbers of men over 28 years of age being appointed. Thereafter recruits tended to be in the age group 19–24 years; indeed most were below 21 years of age.[36] Not until the recruitment of the Black-and-Tans in 1920–21 did average age increase substantially and then it rose to 23 years. By 1900 the RIC's regulations specified that recruits had to be between 19 and 27 years of age, at least 5 feet 9 inches in height and with a chest measurement of 37 inches. However, slightly lower standards operated for the sons of RIC men who wished to follow in their fathers' footsteps.[37] So men joining the police were young, generally around 20 years of age, and many had had no previous occupation aside from working for their farming families as rural labourers.

Given that small-farming families in the south, west and midlands of Ireland were overwhelmingly Catholic, it is hardly a surprise to find that the rank-and-file of the constabulary was predominantly Catholic and that this Catholic bias increased over time. While recruits were 69 per cent Catholic in the years 1837–50, by 1901–10 they were 79 per cent Catholic. Only with the employment of ex-British soldiers in 1920–21 did the Catholic proportion of the force show some decline. Yet Catholics were not distributed evenly through all ranks. The Catholic preponderance was most obvious in the lower ranks of the force, among sub constables and constables. Among sergeants and head constables, it was less pronounced; and even less so among the officer corps.[38] The RIC

---

35 Before the mid 1830s the constabulary favoured recruits who had seen military service, especially in light infantry regiments. See Elizabeth Malcolm, 'From light infantry to constabulary: the military origins of the Irish police, 1798–1850', *Irish Sword*, xxi, 84 (winter 1998), pp 163–75.   36 Palmer, *Police and protest*, pp 572–4; Griffin, 'The Irish police', pp 27–8. In England police recruits tended to be older. Before the 1880s most were in their mid twenties and, though ages fell thereafter, it was rare for a recruit to be less than twenty years of age. Steedman, *Policing the Victorian community*, p. 80.   37 Herlihy, *The Royal Irish Constabulary*, p. 77.   38 Hoppen, *Elections, politics and society*,

denied that religion was a factor in recruitment. This may well have been true, particularly at the constable level after 1850, but in promotions and officer appointments, as we shall see in later chapters, it certainly appears to have been influential.

After consolidation in 1836 the constabulary did not accept married recruits and policemen had to serve satisfactorily for at least seven years before they could request permission to marry. Even then permission might not be forthcoming. The ban on accepting married recruits was introduced by the first inspector general, Colonel James Shaw Kennedy, who before his appointment had served for some forty years in the British army.[39] The ban reflected army practice; but also, as recruits became younger, fewer of them were likely to be married. Until the late 1860s the proportion of married constables was restricted to 20 per cent of the force. This was, however, more generous than the army which only allowed between 6 and 10 per cent of its complement to marry.[40] From the point of view of the constabulary authorities there were sound operational reasons for restricting marriage. Policemen lived in barracks and, as we shall see, accommodating wives and children posed significant problems. In addition policemen had to be mobile: they were transferred fairly regularly and even between transfers they might be required to serve in the reserve or in the extra force. Family ties were an obvious impediment to mobility. During the 1870s, however, the restriction on marriage was relaxed somewhat. Recruits were still required to be single, but the 20 per cent limit on married men was done away with and the proportion of the force allowed to marry rose significantly. We shall look in more detail at the married lives of policemen in Chapter 6.

As this survey of the backgrounds of policemen demonstrates, constabulary recruits did change to some extent over time, becoming in particular younger and more Catholic. Yet it is the continuity of police recruiting over the period of a century that is most striking. In the 1920s, as in the 1820s, recruits were mainly young, unmarried, Catholic, small farmers' sons. William Dunne, quoted at the beginning of this chapter, who joined in 1917 and recalled his experiences in the 1980s, was fairly

p. 410 n. 4. **39** For Shaw Kennedy's military background and his short, but influential, career as inspector general, see Elizabeth Malcolm, '"The reign of terror in Carlow": the politics of policing Ireland in the late 1830s', *Irish Historical Studies*, xxxii, 125 (May 2000), pp 59–74. **40** Myna Trustram, *Women of the regiment: marriage and the Victorian army* (Cambridge, 1984), p. 30.

typical of recruits throughout the period. Before the Famine many only served for relatively short periods, but increasingly thereafter recruits settled into lengthy police careers that saw them serving for twenty-five or thirty years and retiring on a modest pension in their fifties.

So, while the sorts of men who joined the force did not change drastically, the composition of the rank-and-file did undergo a process of evolution. From being a force of fairly young men with a high turnover rate before the 1860s, the constabulary developed in the last quarter of the nineteenth century into a force dominated by long-serving, middle-aged, married, career policemen. Denis Whelan, recalled somewhat wryly by his son Sean, in a quote at the beginning of the chapter, very much typifies the loyal and conscientious constable of the first decade of the twentieth century.

ATTRACTIONS OF POLICE SERVICE

In the public mind peelers were often stereotyped as stupid. The archives of the Irish Folklore Commission contain many stories of peelers being tricked by cunning locals.[41] A popular song of the nineteenth century, 'The Peeler and the Goat', satirised the RIC by having a peeler on patrol question a 'suspicious' goat, who protests: 'I am no rogue, no ribbonman,/No Croppy, Whig or Tory O/But I'm a goat that's fond of sport/And this is the rambling saison O.'[42] Yet the decision made by young rural labourers and farmers' sons to opt for police service, rather than life on a small farm or emigration, was actually a wise career choice during the bulk of the century from the 1820s to the 1920s. The advantages, and also the disadvantages, of RIC pay and conditions will be discussed in a later chapter, but it is perhaps appropriate to dwell briefly here upon the social gains that RIC service brought with it.

Jeremiah Mee, who served as an RIC constable between 1910 and 1920, offered in his memoirs an interesting account of how some men were encouraged to join the constabulary.[43] He was twenty years old and

41 Irish Folklore Archives, University College, Dublin, MS 1839, pp 226–30, 261–2. Townshend, *Political violence in Ireland*, pp 83–4. 42 Quoted in Patrick Logan, *The story of Irish fairs and markets* (Belfast, 1986), pp 128–9. I would like to thank Jim Madden for drawing my attention to this song. 43 For Mee's personnel record, which contains no indication of when or why he left the force, see RIC General Register (PRO(L), HO 184/34).

had been working for eight years as a labourer for his father on the family's small farm in Co. Galway. He was, he wrote, 'anxious to leave home, but there seemed to be no place to go to'. On one occasion when he went to the local police barracks to pay a dog-licence fee, he became involved in a game of cards with the sergeant and some of the constables. The sergeant suggested that he join the RIC and, with his father's permission, Mee applied. After several stringent medical exams, over a period of twelve months, Mee was finally called to the Dublin depot for training in August 1910.[44]

A Protestant, William Britton, the son of a small-farming family from Co. Donegal, who joined the RIC in 1918 and subsequently the RUC, recalled his reasons for doing so many years later.

> Once you got say about ten, you were out into the fields … You had about three months in the wintertime at school. It was a hard life because you were working all the time, you never got any money … I went in [the police] for a job, nothing else … Well, in Donegal there's nothing but farming and small farms at that, and a lot of them had big families and the only thing if you didn't join the police you went to America.[45]

Both Mee and Britton, like their contemporary William Dunne quoted earlier, were small farmers' younger sons who had spent most of their teenage years working as rural labourers. For young men like them an RIC career offered a way out of an impoverished and frustrating existence. Neither Mee nor Britton seems to have had any relatives already serving, nor is there evidence that they felt any great admiration for the constabulary, but both desperately wanted to escape the life of a labourer/farmer's son on a small west-of-Ireland farm. And, neither appears to have been attracted by the other main alternative route out of such a life, emigration. Discontented young rural labourers had few employment options. If they wanted to stay in Ireland, police service was an obvious path to explore.

---

44 J.A. Gaughan (ed.), *Memoirs of Constable Jeremiah Mee, R.I.C.* (Dublin, 1975), p. 11. The editor of this published version of the Mee memoirs has omitted substantial and significant sections of the MS without acknowledgment. Reference will therefore be made to the MS as well as the book. I would like to thank the Mee family for allowing me access to the MS and other related documents. 45 Brewer, *The Royal Irish Constabulary*, p. 33.

The constabulary, however, offered more than mere escape. It held out significant attractions for men from insecure backgrounds. In material terms, police service involved reliable employment; wages that, if not generous, were at least regular; allowances and paid leave; and, most importantly, a retirement pension.[46] Before the introduction of state old-age pensions in 1909, jobs that carried a pension with them were highly attractive. As we shall see when we come to discuss marriage, a constable was also generally considered a good marriage prospect by most rural women and their families. The same could not be said of the younger sons of small farmers, increasingly large numbers of whom remained unmarried in post-Famine Ireland. Somewhat more intangibly, the job was a varied and often interesting one. It allowed men to travel to different parts of the country; it gave them the opportunity to exercise some authority and also, as already indicated, to win some respect. None of these things was true of the life of a rural labourer. There was in addition a strong *camaraderie* among the RIC, a sense of self-respect, even, as David Fitzpatrick suggests, of self-importance.

> This was essentially a function of the degree of deference popularly accorded them and the social status assigned them by their betters. When the constable appeared at ceremonial occasions or riots splendid in his helmet, complemented sometimes by sword, boxspurs and silver crest, he could imagine that he had transcended his usually humble origins ... policemen touched their caps less often than other caps were touched to them, and they guarded their high position jealously.[47]

Others, particularly those with family members already in the force, probably regarded the RIC somewhat differently. Family connections were obviously important. For some recruits the encouragement of a policeman father, brother or uncle may well have been more decisive than anything else. Of the fifteen surviving RIC men who were interviewed by John Brewer in the 1980s, five had had fathers in the RIC, two had brothers and one an uncle. Another had joined with several friends who were the sons of RIC men. One had a father, brother, brother-in-law and

46 The conditions of service in the RIC are discussed at greater length in Chapter 5. 47 Fitzpatrick, *Politics and Irish life, 1913–21*, pp 4–5.

several uncles all in the force. In other words, eight out of the fifteen had relatives who had served or were serving in the RIC.[48] This group was of course not a representative sample, being defined solely by their longevity. But in 1901 a parliamentary inquiry into the RIC was told that 12 per cent of recruits during the period 1891–1900 were the sons of constables, while a later estimate for the years 1901–13 put the proportion at 17 per cent.[49] While it is impossible to quantify the number of men at any one time who came from families with traditions of RIC service, they undoubt-edly formed an influential nucleus within the constabulary from an early date. This core membership helped shape the culture of the RIC, with its emphasis on obedience, loyalty, respectability and *camaraderie*.

OFFICERS AND GENTLEMEN

The officers of the constabulary, like those of the army, were recruited separately from the rank-and-file and therefore generally have to be treated apart from their men.[50] A system of officer cadetship was insti-tuted in 1842 with cadets being nominated by the lord lieutenant, the chief secretary or the inspector general. But, by the end of the nineteenth century, promotion from the ranks also began to produce a significant number of officers who had started their police careers as constables.

During the whole period 1837 to 1921 the majority of officers were born in Leinster (27 per cent) and Munster (25 per cent). Munster contributed the largest group up to 1880, Leinster thereafter until 1900, when Munster again took the lead. Connacht supplied 19 per cent of officers, Ulster only 14 per cent and a further 15 per cent were classed as 'other'. This last cate-gory reflects the fact that the RIC always had a small but significant group of English- and Scottish-born officers. The largest group of Catholic offi-cers came from Connacht: indeed, 43 per cent of Connacht-born officers were Catholic. But Ulster, although it supplied the least number of offi-cers, also had a sizeable Catholic minority of 35 per cent. This exceeded the

48 Brewer, *The Royal Irish Constabulary*, pp 20–22. 49 Griffin, 'The Irish police', pp 86, 146; Lowe and Malcolm, 'Domestication', p. 34. 50 Unless otherwise stated, the following analysis of the composition of the RIC's offi-cer corps is based upon a 10 per cent stratified random sample, comprising 122 men, drawn from officers appointed between January 1837 and August 1921 as recorded in the RIC's General Register, 1816–1922 (PRO(L), HO 184/45–8). I would like to thank Dr Robert Stevens for assistance in the compiling of this data. For a new analy-sis of the officer corps, which appeared too late to include in this discussion, see W.J. Lowe, 'Irish Constabulary officers: profile of a profession', *Irish Economic and Social History*, xxxii (2005), pp 19–46.

proportions from Leinster (30 per cent), Munster (29 per cent) and 'other' (22 per cent). That a little over one-third of Ulster-born officers were Catholic highlights the fact that RIC officer service appears to have been least popular among the Protestants of Ulster. As we shall see, this fact had important implications for the policing of the province and especially for the policing of sectarian and political disorder.

Few inspectors or constables came from Ulster, but in other respects there were major differences between the backgrounds of officers and the men under their command. Officers were far more likely to be middle class, Protestant and from the east of the country, if not from urban backgrounds. As with the British army, the officers and men of the RIC really did not share much in common.

Between 1837 and 1921 exactly one-third of RIC officers were Catholic, but this aggregated figure masks significant changes over time. Up until 1891 the overwhelming majority – of the order of three-quarters – of officer recruits were Protestant. But thereafter there was a rough balance in appointments. Thus the 1890s saw a major change in the RIC officer corps with substantially greater numbers of Catholics being appointed as district inspectors. Analysis shows that most of these Catholics were in fact men promoted from the ranks.

Cadets had to be unmarried and under 30. In 1872 this was lowered to between 21 and 26 years of age, but the average age of officers appointed rose dramatically in the 1890s. This reflected the fact that increasing numbers of officers were former constables. In 1895 a regulation was introduced reserving one-half of district inspectorships for promoted head constables. In 1901–10 Protestant recruits had an average age of 28 years, while newly appointed Catholic officers had an average age of 40 years. This marked discrepancy is explained by the fact that most Protestants entered the RIC officer corps through cadetships, while increasing numbers of Catholic officers were constables promoted after usually 20 years' service. In the 1890s, for instance, while 77 per cent of cadets were Protestant, only 35 per cent of promoted head constables were.[51] So after the 1890s constabulary officers fell into two distinct groups: those who had joined as cadets in their early and mid-20s and were mainly Protestant and those who had been promoted from the ranks in their late 30s and early 40s and were mainly Catholic.

51 Griffin, 'The Irish police', p. 886.

Yet promoted Catholic officers were clearly at a disadvantage as regards their Protestant colleagues. Protestants, having entered the service as young cadets and served longer, were more likely to reach the higher ranks of the force. Between 1837 and 1921 of the RIC's first-class county inspectors 71 per cent were Protestant and only 29 per cent Catholic. As overall about one-third of officers were Catholic, this might seem a fairly representative figure. But of these Catholic county inspectors fully 80 per cent were appointed in 1920–21. In other words, there was a rush to appoint Catholics to senior positions only in the final days of the RIC's existence. Prior to then Protestants had been dominant.

Sons of RIC officers could be admitted as cadets aged 18 and those with army, navy or police experience up until 28.[52] These exceptions demonstrate that family service was encouraged among officers, as well as constables, and that a military or police background was considered an asset.

As with the constables, there are some striking examples of family service among the officers of the constabulary. William Waters, a Wicklow-born Protestant served in the Dublin police from 1810 until 1820 when he joined the newly established Irish constabulary. After postings in Cos Galway, Mayo and Down, he retired on a pension in 1840. His son, Abraham, born in Dublin in 1816, joined the constabulary as a sub constable in 1835. After postings in Cos Londonderry, Clare and Dublin, he was appointed a sub inspector. When he retired in 1872 Abraham Waters was the county inspector of Sligo. His son, Samuel Abraham Walker, rose even higher in the RIC. He joined as an officer cadet in 1866 and, after extensive service, including a period in the Crime Branch Special during the mid-1880s, he was appointed county inspector of Kerry in the early 1890s. In 1901 he became assistant inspector general and retired in 1906.[53] Thus three generations of the Waters' family served in various Irish police forces over a period of nearly a century. This family's long involvement in Irish policing is well documented because S.A.W. Waters wrote a memoir in 1924, but there were undoubtedly other families with similar lengthy police histories.

Palmer lamented that, up to 1850, the officers' register 'gives virtually no occupational data', although he concluded that many recruits would

52 Ibid., p. 265. 53 RIC General Register (PRO(L), HO 184/45, pp 3, 134 and 237).

have had military experience.[54] In fact it was during both the early and last years of the Irish constabulary that military service was most sought after. In 1837–50 17 per cent of officers appointed had military backgrounds, but in 1851–60 the figure fell to 7 per cent and it remained negligible until 1911–20 when it jumped to 30 per cent. In 1921 it was a huge 62.5 per cent, reflecting the recruitment of ex-British army officers to create the RIC Auxiliary Division.

Griffin has calculated that one-third of officers appointed between 1852 and 1914 had been previously employed. In order of significance, they had worked as clerks, teachers, revenue police officers and military or naval officers.[55] A large number of ex-revenue officers were appointed in the mid and late 1850s when the constabulary took over the duties of the Revenue Police. Many sons of Protestant clergy could also be found among RIC officers. All these backgrounds bespeak middle-class origins, although ones not notable for their wealth. A career as a police officer enabled such men to maintain their social status, without the expense, commitment or academic demands that careers in the army, the church, law or medicine would have entailed.

In a sense then, although constables and officers were recruited separately and came from different classes, both groups within their particular class backgrounds were marginalised. Constables, as we have seen, were rural labourers and the younger sons of small farmers. Their prospects of a fulfilling life on the land were bleak. But most officers too, lacking money or outstanding intellectual abilities, faced very limited career opportunities. Many appear to have aspired to the life of an army officer or a country gentlemen and, although an Irish police inspector was neither, officers could lead lives that at least approximated such ideals. Officers and constables also shared another important characteristic: both groups had turned their backs on emigration. Many others in their circumstances did emigrate. But presumably they wished to stay in Ireland and joining the police allowed them to do so.

Establishing the marital status of officers on the basis of the constabulary's Personnel Register is not altogether easy. Cadets had to be unmarried, but promoted officers usually were married. Details of marriage should have been entered in a cadet's file, as they were in the case of

54 Palmer, *Police and protest*, pp 576–7. 55 Griffin, 'The Irish police', pp 261–5.

constables, but it would appear that this was not always done. However, the surviving evidence suggests that officers tended to find their wives in rather more complex ways than did constables. It wasn't simply a matter of being stationed in the wife's neighbourhood, as it clearly was with the rank-and-file. For example, in 1882 one Catholic officer from Co. Roscommon at the age of thirty-five married a Dublin woman. But he had never been posted to Dublin, although in 1877–8 he had served in Galway where his future wife had relatives. Perhaps he met her through her relatives. Certainly a number of officers married women who did not live in the counties to which they were posted, but in adjoining ones. This may well reflect the simple fact that officers were more mobile than their subordinates and could seek social contacts within a wider geographical area.

RIC officers were considered 'gentlemen' and, as cadetships were much sought after, there was a certain amount of lobbying for them. In this they were similar to resident magistrate appointments – and, indeed, many officers went on to be appointed RMs.[56] Sir John Nott Bower, who, during a police career spanning more than fifty years, successively headed the Leeds (1878–81), Liverpool (1881–1902) and City of London (1902–25) forces, described in his memoirs his appointment as an RIC cadet, aged twenty-four, in 1873.

> My father's old friend – the Right Hon[ora]ble. W.E. Foster – at that time Minister for Education, gave me, towards the end of 1872, a letter of introduction to Lord Hartington, then Chief Secretary for Ireland. The result was to procure for me, in a very few weeks, a nomination to a Cadetship in the Royal Irish Constabulary, which seemed to offer the most likely, and sure, approach to a successful police career. These nominations were very eagerly sought after, and needed some influence for *an Englishman* to secure, so I was specially fortunate in receiving one so promptly.[57]

The superior social status that RIC officers aspired to made them rather dismissive of some of their less pleasant duties and also of their

---

56 For the lobbying connected with these appointments, some of it done by RIC officers, see Bonsall, *The Irish RMs*, pp 16–23.   57 Nott Bower's son, who shared his name, later headed the London Metropolitan Police (1953–8). J.W. Nott Bower, *Fifty-two years a policeman* (London, 1926), p. 5.

promoted colleagues. In 1871 a court official from Co. Westmeath, critical of the military character of the Irish police, told a select committee that 'they [RIC officers] assume all the airs and importance of officers of the line'.[58] In 1872 Sub Inspector Henry Blake argued before another enquiry that constabulary officers should be gentlemen and thus should not be promoted from the ranks. According to Blake: 'If you promote the men in Ireland, you would have the force officered and guided by a lower form of intelligence.'[59] RIC officers clearly regarded themselves as gentlemen, on a par with army officers, not as policemen on a par with the constables who served under them. Class distinctions were important to the officer corps of the RIC. Promoting officers from the ranks blurred these distinctions and so it is not surprising to find many officers strongly opposed to this policy.

In the main then, inspectors came from a higher social class than did constables. They were also far more likely to be Protestant and from urban backgrounds. But, as with rank-and-file recruits, there was a continuity in the origins of officer cadets, at least up until the advent of the Auxiliaries in 1920/1. Yet, despite consistency in recruitment, the officer corps, like the rank-and-file body of the constabulary, underwent significant change. And the changes in the officer corps were connected to changes among constables. As long-serving, experienced head constables emerged in significant numbers from about the 1860s, so pressure to promote such men into the officer ranks increased. Many officers resisted this pressure, but in the 1890s the RIC opened the inspectorate substantially to appointment by promotion. This marked a major move away from the military model upon which the Irish constabulary had been based, towards a civil model of policing.

In Chapter 2 we noted that policemen have been labelled 'liminal figures' in post-colonial theory. This chapter's brief examination of the socio-economic backgrounds of Irish policemen, whether officers or men, suggests that the situation was actually more complex than is sometimes realised. Even *before* they joined the police, many of these men had been marginalised in economic and social terms. As we have seen, the rank-and-file were overwhelmingly the sons of rural labouring and small farming families. Their prospects of secure employment, marriage and

58 *Report from the Select Committee on Westmeath, &c. (Unlawful Combinations)*, H.C. 1871 (147), xiii, 630.   59 *Report of the Commissioners*, 1873, p. 227.

family life were pretty bleak in Ireland. Ironically, although the officer corps was recruited separately and many officers strove to maintain a clear distinction between inspectors and constables, officers too came in the main from marginalised groups. As the sons of professional men, clergymen, small landlords or businessmen and junior army officers, their options were also limited. While constables were obviously attracted to police service initially by the prospect of secure employment, for officers status seems to have been almost as important. Thus they fought with great determination to exclude constables from their ranks.

As we shall see in later chapters, one characteristic that officers and men shared was social ambition. If officers wanted to maintain their class status, many constables, probably influenced by their training in the values and virtues of respectability, sought to improve the status of their families. Officers were obsessed with the trappings of army and gentry life: fine uniforms, mounted orderlies, unquestioning obedience from their inferiors, socialising with landlords and living in fine houses. Constables, on the other hand, were obsessed with educating their children and providing them with opportunities to secure good marriages and reliable employment. Whatever his rank, the peeler was undoubtedly 'a man on the make', and a career in the Irish constabulary offered, among many other things, an avenue for upward social mobility.

CHAPTER FOUR

Recruitment and training:
creating a 'highly efficient machine'

The Depot 'R.I.C. A.B.C.'

A is the Adjutant who struts on the square.
B is the Barrack room dreary and bare.
C is the Commandant whose word is our law.
D are the 'Drills' we wish we ne'er saw.
E is the Engine which on Tuesdays we pump.
F the Fatigues which give us the hump.
G's the Gymnasium reigned o'er by M'Gurgan.
H is the Hospital in which is the Surgeon.
I's for Instructions at morn, noon and night.
J is the Jump-sheet which shakes us with fright.
K are our Kits we clean without zest.
L is the Library our haven of rest.
M is the Musketry our ambition and aim.
N is the nose-cap we seldom have 'clane'.
O are the Orderlies watching the work.
P the Parades we seldom can shirk.
Q is the Question we ne'er heard before.
R the Regulations we learn by the score.
S is for Stevens [Steeven's], where we go when we're sickly.
T are the Tubes which teach shooting so quickly.
U is the Uniform which makes men of us youngsters.
V are the Voices of our many instructors.
W's the Whistle with which is the chain.
X is the Stout that's in the 'cantane'.
Y is the Yearning we feel for our home.
Z is the Zeal as recruits we have shown.

Llewdor[1]

1 *Royal Irish Constabulary Magazine*, ii, 2 (Dec. 1912), p. 67.

RECRUITMENT

The Irish constabulary had stringent admission criteria for constables. Essentially the force was looking for healthy, young men from rural backgrounds, with an elementary education and no obvious political affiliations, who could be moulded into hard-working and utterly loyal policemen. Under RIC regulations, as mentioned in the previous chapter, rank-and-file recruits had to be between 19 and 27 years of age, although sons of members and pensioners[2] of the force could be admitted at age 18 if they satisfied the other main selection requirements of good character and sound health. In addition recruits had to be single or widowers without children, at least 5 feet 7 inches – later raised to 5 feet 9 inches – in height, with corresponding chest measurements, and able to read and write to prescribed standards, as well as to solve basic arithmetical problems.[3]

Unlike the army, the constabulary did not have specialised recruiters. At first it was the task of magistrates and grand juries to recommend men for police service, but by the 1860s the constabulary was finding its own rank-and-file recruits. As one head constable from Galway explained in 1872: '[e]very constable is a recruiting sergeant'.[4] Sometimes men went to their local barracks looking for information about joining the police. In the main, however, head constables and sergeants took the initiative. They were expected always to be on the lookout for likely recruits and to recommend names to district inspectors, who in turn, after investigation, passed on names to county inspectors. County lists of candidates for recruitment were then compiled and held at the county inspector's headquarters. As vacancies occurred, men were 'called' to the depot in rotation from these lists, although sometimes this 'call' could take several years.[5] Such a cumbersome, bureaucratic procedure – supposedly neutral, but obviously open to favouritism and patronage – was very typical of the RIC.

---

2 In June 1891 Inspector General Andrew Reed issued a circular instructing that pensioners' sons could in future be admitted 'at the same age and height as the sons of men actually serving'. Circular on Code, 6 June 1891 (NLI, RIC Circulars, 1882–1900, IR3522R, p. 2).   3 A recruit of height 5 feet 11 inches had to have a chest measurement of at least 37 inches. Sons of members and pensioners of the force, as well as being admitted at 18, could be 5 feet 8 inches in height, when the minimum for other recruits was 5 feet 9 inches, but they had to have a chest measurement of at least 36 inches. *Royal Irish Constabulary Directory*, no. 124 (July 1903), p. 188; Brian Griffin, 'The Irish police', pp 27–8.   4 *Report of the Commissioners, 1873*, p. 27.   5 C.W. Leatham, *Sketches and stories of the Royal Irish Constabulary* (Dublin, 1909), p. 7.

At times when the constabulary was agitating for pay increases, constables and officers often complained that they had trouble getting recruits or that the recruits were of a lower calibre than in previous years. In 1914, with steeply declining recruitment, even the inspector general, Sir Neville Chamberlain,[6] made this excuse. Asserting that recruits were 'distinctly inferior' to what they had been and that this was due to inadequate pay, Chamberlain told an investigating committee that, if suitable men were to be found, 'the service must be made more attractive'.[7] Other witnesses before earlier enquiries recognised that police recruitment, and also retention, had to compete with emigration. In 1866 the commissioners enquiring into the constabulary reported that the class from which most recruits came – 'small farmers and their sons' – had been 'materially reduced in number' through emigration as 'better wages and an improved position' were sought 'on the other side of the Atlantic'. Those remaining in Ireland had 'less inducement to quit their ordinary pursuits for the life of a constable' due to the low rates of pay prevailing in the constabulary.[8] In 1872 the RIC's surgeon claimed that most recruits had relatives who had emigrated, while a sub constable added that many in the force received letters from family and friends overseas urging constables to join them.[9]

Potential candidates on county inspectors' lists were divided into two groups. The first combined the physical strength, education and 'superior moral character' required, while the second group included those who had only satisfied the RIC's basic physical requirements. The essential 'moral' characteristics had been laid down as early as 1837 in the constabulary's book of rules and regulations compiled by the first inspector general, James Shaw Kennedy, a Scottish-born light infantry officer with extensive military experience. These were 'honesty, sobriety, fidelity and activity'.[10] District inspectors were only to recommend a man for appoint-

6 Chamberlain (1856–1944), not to be confused with the later British prime minister of the same name, had served for many years with the army in India before his appointment in 1900 to head the RIC. He was censured for the failure of police intelligence to warn the government of plans for the 1916 Rising and forced to resign. Today he is best remembered for inventing a game, based on pool, while serving in India in 1875, which was known in military slang as, snooker. See *Dictionary of national biography*.   7 *Report of Committee of Inquiry into the RIC and DMP*, 1914, p. 182.   8 *Report of the Commissioners of Enquiry into the Irish Constabulary*, H.C. 1866 (3658), xxxiv, p. 11.   9 *Report of the Commissioners*, 1873, pp 45, 55. The army was having similar recruitment problems in these same years. Spiers, 'Army organisation and society in the nineteenth century', p. 340.   10 [James Shaw Kennedy,] *Standing rules and regulations for the government and guidance of the Constabulary Force of Ireland* (Dublin, 1837), p. 107. There had been an earlier

ment whom they knew personally and about whom they had made searching enquiries. Not only did the young man have to be of good conduct, but his relatives and associates also had to be 'respectable'. No one was to be recommended, declared Chamberlain in 1914, about whom 'there is any suspicion that he is in any way imbued with sectarian or strong political feelings'. In the event of an 'act of misconduct of a candidate, committed either before or subsequently to his name having been placed on any list', the district or county inspector was authorised to strike out the candidate's name.[11] While there were sufficient first-class young men, second-class candidates would not be considered for appointment. However, they could attempt to improve themselves and apply again at a later date.[12]

But even first-class candidates needed to surmount further obstacles, for they had to undergo a rigorous medical inspection. In the early years this was conducted by an army medical officer, but from 1839 it was the responsibility of the constabulary's own surgeon. In 1914 fully 30 per cent of candidates failed this examination. After at least two medical inspections in his county, Jeremiah Mee had his final medical at the Dublin depot in 1910. Mee noted that of the 39 recruits examined with him, only 16 were passed as fit by the force's surgeon. 'The medical examination for the RIC was one of the most exacting in the world', Mee concluded 'since the smallest defect such as a decayed tooth meant rejection.'[13] Mee speculated that the RIC was attracting too many recruits and that small physical 'defects' were being used as an excuse to reject men. However, at the time the RIC was in fact having increasing difficulty in finding suitable recruits.[14] The medical examination was rigorous simply because police duties could be very physically taxing. But the high failure rate

book of regulations compiled for chief constables and constables of the county constabulary established in 1822, but this was largely a list of duties drawn from various statutes. However, chief constables were instructed that 'the men should be respected by the people of the county and obtain the good opinion of the gentry. They will be extremely cautious in their demeanor, sober, regular, and orderly in their conduct, respectful to the gentlemen, and strictly obedient and zealous to execute the orders of the Magistrates …' *The standing orders and regulations, for the conduct and proceeding of the chief constables and other constables of the county of* … (Dublin, [1825]), p. 16. The need for the new national constabulary to win the approval of the gentry generally, and the magistrates in particular, is obvious in the wording of these regulations. 11 [Shaw Kennedy], *Standing rules and regulations*, 1837, p. 109. 12 *Report of Inquiry into the RIC and DMP*, 1914, pp 8, 182–3. 13 Jeremiah Mee, Memoirs (typescript in possession of the Mee Family, Belfast, n.d.), p. 1. 14 In December 1901 there were 721 first-class candidates on the RIC's recruitment lists, but by December 1912 this figure had plunged to ninety-one. Between December 1896 and March 1898 recruitment had been suspended altogether as candidates were so numerous. *Report of Inquiry into the RIC and DMP*, 1914, p. 182; Griffin, 'The Irish police', p. 136.

of candidates may also have been a reflection of the poor physical health of the Irish small-farming population.

Under the regulations of 1837 and later, candidates for appointment were also required to complete and sign a declaration setting out their name, place of birth, age, occupation and marital status – all of which information was entered into the force's Personnel Register. It is worth noting that religious denomination was not formally requested, although this fact did appear in the register. So at some stage recruits must have been questioned on the subject of religion, although the force was clearly reluctant to admit this. Men also had to state if they had previously served in the police or military; if they had ever been dismissed or resigned from such a position; if they were subject to 'fits, or any other bodily infirmity'; if they had engaged in a faction fight in the previous twelve months; and if they had ever been in jail. The reference to faction fighting is interesting, as is the surprisingly short twelve-month cut-off date, but it is perhaps puzzling that no mention was made of membership of secret societies. However, in the oath of allegiance to the crown that a recruit had to swear before he began his training there was the following final sentence: 'I will not, while I shall hold the said office, join, subscribe, or belong, to any political society whatsoever, or to any secret society whatsoever, unless to the society of freemasons.'[15] The exception made for the freemasons is striking and reflects the fact that freemasonry was strong among both Irish and English police forces during the nineteenth and twentieth centuries.

If a candidate was recommended by a head constable or sergeant, then by a district inspector and a county inspector and finally passed the medical examination, he was expected to go to Dublin to undergo six months' training at the constabulary depot in Phoenix Park.[16] Shaw Kennedy, who was always meticulous over details, specified that a recruit had to bring with him 'a suit of plain clothes and a hat', plus four linen shirts and two pounds 'for the purchase of necessaries and for his support until the next issue of pay'.[17] Two pounds was a considerable sum

15 [Shaw Kennedy], *Standing rules and regulations*, 1837, pp 110–11.   16 In 1839 it was decided to establish a central depot in Dublin to house the newly created reserve force and to supersede the existing four provincial training depots in Armagh, Ballinrobe, Philipstown (Daingean) and Ballincollig. The new buildings were not completed until 1842. Herlihy, *The Royal Irish Constabulary*, pp 49–50.   17 [Shaw Kennedy], *Standing rules and regulations*, 1837, p. 111.

as at the time it amounted to one month's pay for the most junior sub constables in the force. Only recruits with some personal or family resources could have put up this money, over and above the cost of clothes and journeys to the depot. So, while recruits were mainly the sons of small farmers and rural labourers, they were hardly from the very bottom of rural society.

TRAINING: CONSTABLES

When he was asked 'what it was that changed the country boy into a stern, suspicious policeman', Jeremiah Mee concluded that it was the 'atmosphere and discipline' prevailing at the Phoenix Park depot. In elaborating upon this, he wrote:

> For six months the recruit is entirely in the company of policemen in their dark, sombre uniforms. His one ambition is to imitate his seniors and in doing so he loses his own individuality and becomes part of a highly efficient machine. At the end of six months in such company he would not dream of standing at a street corner with his hands in his trousers' pocket or whistle while he walked along the street. He hears so much about crime and criminals during his course of training that he wonders whether there are any honest men left. Discipline has got a grip on him and he cannot shake it off even when he goes home on holidays . . .[18]

The discipline at the depot was severe and the atmosphere intimidating, as Mee indicates. For six months young farmers and rural labourers, who had seldom been absent from their own localities or away from their families before, were subjected to the full rigour of infantry training. That this experience transformed them is hardly to be wondered at.

An examination of the regulations governing the depot, its drill manuals, the memoirs of some of its recruits and cadets amply supports Mee's claim as to the depot's defining role in shaping Irish policemen.

18 Mee, Memoirs, p. 11.

Life at the depot was minutely regulated under standing orders. The depot was headed by a commandant, assisted by an adjutant, both of whom were long-serving inspectors. In addition there was a barrack master and a head constable major — the latter being the 'link' between the adjutant and the head constables and constables on the staff. A schoolmaster, a surgeon, a vet and various specialist teachers of drill, swordsmanship, musketry and riding were also attached to the staff.[19] As well as housing rank-and-file recruits and officer cadets, the depot was also the base for the constabulary reserve force, its mounted corps and its band. It had accommodation in all for around 800 men.[20]

As regards recruits, the depot was divided into two wings presided over by two district inspectors from the reserve. Each wing was further sub-divided into four divisions commanded by head constables and the divisions in turn were broken down into rooms run by constables. Standing orders set out the duties and responsibilities of each officer and man in some detail. Head constables had to 'insist upon the constables rigidly performing their respective duties', to 'check and report irregularities' and to 'pay the utmost attention to the behaviour and morals of every man' in their division.[21] Constables were responsible for the 'constant order and correct arrangement of every article' in the barrack room. A constable had to

> give all orders to the men in a firm and decided manner; and never permit a reply on point of duty, or suffer any man to conduct himself disrespectfully towards him ... He [was] at all times to treat the men with mildness and good humour; to instruct the awkward or ignorant; to encourage the young and diffident ... to teach them the duties and obligations of a constable; to show them the manner of packing their necessaries, arranging their boxes, bedding, knapsacks, etc., and fitting on their accoutrements.[22]

There were also wing and divisional orderly inspectors and constables, who made regular inspections. The constables, who were rotated

19 *Depot standing orders 1846* (Dublin, 1847), pp 17–21. At a later date the duties of the various staff of the depot were also set out briefly in *Standing rules and regulations for the government and guidance of the Royal Irish Constabulary* (6th ed., Dublin, 1911), pp 133–57. 20 Leatham, *Sketches and stories of the RIC*, p. 7. 21 *Depot standing orders 1846*, pp 7–8. 22 Ibid., p. 10.

weekly, had always to be in uniform with sidearms and were never to leave the depot except on duty. They had to ensure that the kitchen coppers and mess utensils were clean; they had 'to ascertain that the men wash their legs and feet, and put on clean linen, every Thursday and Sunday morning before breakfast'; and they had to see that the urine tubs were washed every morning. Each room also had an orderly who had to keep it clean, lay the tables and carry the food from the cookhouses to the room. He was dressed in fatigues and could only leave the room 'in case of necessity'.[23]

A visitor to the depot in 1852 described in some detail the rooms in which recruits lived during their training.

> In the infantry barracks, on the ground floor, I found the men's rooms, which are 33 feet by 20, newly whitewashed; and besides two lofty windows at each end, they were scientifically ventilated ... In every room were sixteen iron bedsteads, each containing a fresh bed and pillow of straw, a pair of sheets, two blankets, and a quilt. The tick beds are washed every six months, and the pillow-cases every four months. The men's accoutrements are arranged on shelves, and around each room were stands for their arms. For the lower panes of the windows I observed iron shutters, loopholed; in short, the Irish Constabulary in their barracks are, in fact, a select garrison of admirably drilled troops, occupying, very properly and very peacefully, a very snug little fortress of their own.[24]

The military character of the depot was reinforced by its emphasis on drill. The recruits were all assigned to drill squads and had to give their 'entire and undivided attention' to their drill instructors. In addition, they had to see to 'perfecting' themselves in reading, writing and accounting under the tutelage of the schoolmaster, and they were warned that no man could expect promotion who could not 'write with facility a good legible hand, and spell well'. Although recruits were supposed to be literate on appointment, the emphasis on teaching reading and writing at the depot suggests that abilities in these areas may sometimes have

23 Ibid., pp 23–9. 24 Head, *A fortnight in Ireland*, p. 62.

only been very basic. Recruits were also to memorise and transcribe into their copybooks 'crimes and punishments, barrack regulations and … sections of the standing regulations of the constabulary'.[25]

It is clear from standing orders and from accounts of depot life that a great deal of importance was placed upon drill, as was also true of the army.[26] In describing the depot buildings in 1886 the first point that Sergeant Michael Brophy made was that they formed three sides of a quadrangle and enclosed 'the finest and largest drill-exercise ground or square in the empire'.[27] In 1891 one former recruit recorded his experience of drill in verse form:

> I think I'm on the square again, and hearing Cody shout,
> Or Roger Kelly's fierce command, the order, 'Right about!'
>
> 'Left wheel! Front form! Mark time! or Yoult', then a volley of abuse:
> 'Hold up your head, you clout, you clod, you ignorant country
>   goose.'
> But hush! the Major's on the scene, his Kerry blood's on fire;
> Your gravity you'll scarce command when it you will require,
> For see he can no longer stand that masher on the right,
> And with his cane he thongs him, while we laugh with all our
>   might.[28]

It is clear from these lines that the ritual verbal and physical abuse of recruits, which was an essential part of drill in the British army, was also prevalent in the Irish constabulary.

In 1859 a special drill manual for the constabulary was issued under the name of Inspector General Henry Brownrigg and in 1906 another

---

25 *Depot standing orders 1846*, pp 15–16.   26 Even senior army officers had begun to question the value of mindless drill. In his memoirs published in 1909 one brigadier general observed that drill was 'brought to the condition of appearing to have for its object "precision and stiffness alone, in exercises not having any real object in war"'. It was imposed upon 'the rank and file until they responded to the word of command as the machine answers to the pressing of the button'. Quoted in Skelley, *The Victorian army at home*, p. 137.   27 Michael Brophy, *Sketches of the Royal Irish Constabulary* (London and New York, 1886), p. 25. For a description of the depot and its 'capacious … parade-ground' in the early 1850s, see Head, *A fortnight in Ireland*, p. 56. In his account, published in the late 1860s, Inspector Robert Curtis also drew attention to the 'extensive' nature of the 'parade-ground', enclosed by the hollow square of the buildings, and commented that 'admirers' often stood outside the 'handsome iron railing' on the fourth side to watch the 'evolutions of the force'. Robert Curtis, *History of the Royal Irish Constabulary* (2nd ed., Dublin, 1871), p. 57.   28 'Memories of the past' in the *Royal Irish Constabulary Magazine*, i, 7 (May 1912), p. 239. According to a footnote this poem was originally published in 1891 in a type-written RIC magazine entitled the *Constabulary Correspondent*, which only lasted for about three months. Copies do not appear to have survived.

was produced under the imprimatur of Neville Chamberlain.[29] The depot's 1846 standing orders instructed that recruits were 'frequently' to practise all elements of drill and especially 'light infantry drill'.[30] According to the 1859 manual recruits were to be taught marching, saluting, halting and firing on level or rough ground. They were to be trained individually, then in squads and finally in companies. They were to learn how to charge with bayonets and how to receive cavalry in squares.[31] A description of constabulary drill in 1852 noted that:

> For the purpose of clearing away a mob, the infantry advanced rapidly in the form of a solid wedge, which, as soon as it was supposed to have penetrated the mob, gradually extended itself into a line. They then quickly formed themselves into small defensive squares; and although they have happily never had occasion to carry it into effect, they went through a movement of street firing adapted for a small force, which it would be impossible for any undisciplined crowd to resist. Advancing in sections about the length of a narrow street, the leading men no sooner fired than a section from the rear in double quick time ran in front and fired again; and so on a rapid succession of volleys was administered. Besides this exercise, the men are taught first to fire blank cartridges, and then, with the help of a target, are (as it is professionally termed) 'finished off with ball', until, as I was informed, they can hit true and well at 100 yards.[32]

That the Irish constabulary had never used this mob-dispersal technique of firing into a crowd is hardly surprising. Like so much of depot drill, it was far more appropriate to wartime conditions than to routine policing.

Chamberlain's 1906 manual, which was nearly 230 pages long, continued the emphasis on military drill and was indeed based on the army's new 1905 infantry drill book. Men were drilled in squads, companies and battalions; they performed numerous firing exercises and were shown how to care for their weapons; they were instructed in skirmishing, in sentry and ceremonial duties and in saluting.

29 *A manual of drill for the constabulary force of Ireland* (Dublin, 1859); *Drill book compiled for the use of the Royal Irish Constabulary from the infantry drill book, 1905* (Dublin, 1906). 30 *Depot standing orders 1846*, p. 34. 31 *A manual of drill*, pp 39, 79, 103–5. 32 Head, *A fortnight in Ireland*, p. 60.

Officer cadets were expected to learn basic drill alongside rank-and-file recruits, although otherwise the two groups had little if any contact. One cadet has left a description of this experience.

> The morning after I joined I was roused by the orderly, who had my cold tub and uniform ready, and at 7.30 a.m., in answer to the bugles sounding the 'assembly', I turned out for my first drill. We cadets fell in with an awkward squad, who wore their often grotesque country garments until they commenced musketry. Learning how to stand as a soldier, to stand at ease and spring sharply to attention and the goose ... step, occupied some weeks, during which we were also gradually taught to march. There are not, even in the army, smarter drill-sergeants than ours, and the ability which they show in turning the country louts into smart infantrymen in a short time is surprising.[33]

Inspector George Garrow Green recognised that he and the 'country louts' were undergoing what was in effect infantry training. His obvious contempt for the rank-and-file recruits was fairly typical of the attitudes of many officers, who, as we saw in the previous chapter, regarded themselves as comparable to army officers and therefore as separated from constables by an unbridgeable social gulf.[34]

An examination of the RIC's drill books would seem to suggest that the force had as emphatic a military character in the early years of the twentieth century as it did in the middle years of the nineteenth century. Yet this would be a misleading impression. Despite the best efforts of the constabulary's commanders, not all the multitude of rules, regulations and orders appearing in constabulary publications were enforced to the letter. As we shall see in later chapters, military efficiency declined over the years, although the fiction of it was maintained in drill manuals and in the training given at the depot.

A number of officer cadets, like Garrow Green, have left memoirs of their training, but accounts by rank-and-file recruits are less common.

---

33 G. Garrow Green, *In the Royal Irish Constabulary* (London and Dublin, n.d.), pp 11–12. Although Green writes in a light-hearted fashion and, indeed, Comerford calls his book 'silly', I feel he makes a number of valuable points about depot training and thus I have quoted him at some length. Comerford typescript (NLI, MS 25530, p. 100).
34 It was often claimed that many army officers 'knew nothing of their men, rarely came in contact with them, and were indifferent towards their wants'. Spiers, *The army and society, 1815–1914*, p. 26.

One of the earliest is that of Robert Dunlop, a Protestant small farmer's son from Clough, Co. Antrim, who was born in 1825 and applied to join the constabulary in 1842. In April 1843 Dunlop and four other Ulster recruits travelled over-night by steamer from Belfast to Dublin. After a hearty breakfast at a public house in Smithfield market, they proceeded to the depot at 10.00 a.m. and reported themselves to the commandant. They were swiftly assigned to divisions and rooms. As the Phoenix Park buildings had only been completed in 1842, Dunlop was one of the first constables to train there.

He seems on the whole to have enjoyed his four months' training – at least his memoirs make few critical remarks. The head constable in charge of his division was also from Antrim and treated him as a friend, while the sub constable in charge of his room was 'kindly'. Obviously a natural athlete, Dunlop won respect by beating several of his room mates at boxing and running. He commented that the drill was 'severe' and complained that for firing practice recruits were issued with ancient flintlocks that could be dangerous. But he must have performed well for, on completion of his training, he was assigned to the reserve, which meant easier duties and higher pay. He had to attend parade at 11.00 a.m. every morning, but then, unless assigned to a particular task like guard- or escort-duty, his time was his own. Phoenix Park provided much recreation. He visited the Dublin Zoological Gardens regularly and watched military reviews on the Fifteen Acres. Most Saturdays he walked to the Pigeon House Fort and went swimming in Dublin Bay. There was also time for a lot of reading, although unfortunately Dunlop does not tell us what books he read. And there were even occasional duties. He was part of the police contingent sent to Clontarf in October 1843 to prevent Daniel O'Connell holding a monster meeting. When the constabulary was issued with new percussion cap carbines, Dunlop helped escort the carts distributing them to barracks in Cos Wicklow and Kildare.

By December 1843, however, Dunlop was tiring of this leisurely life and was eager for a posting. Through the influence of his friend the head constable he secured one in Co. Fermanagh, obviously preferring to return to the north. But the commandant, for unexplained reasons, switched him at the last minute to Co. Longford. A disappointed Dunlop commented: 'I certainly did not know where the County Longford was, or by what way I should get to it'. He was able, however, to join a group of constables being sent to Sligo and travel with them as far as Longford by fly-boat on the Royal Canal.[35] Men were not supposed to be sent to counties in which they had connections, nor was influence to be used to gain favoured postings. In Dunlop's case, an attempt to influence a posting failed, but it is hard to imagine such efforts did not succeed in other cases.

Another interesting account of depot training – this time during the late 1840s – occurs in the novel *Mervyn Grey; or, Life in the Royal Irish Constabulary*, which was published in Glasgow in the 1870s under the name of J.W. Montgomery. The novel is so detailed and precise that it clearly reflects personal knowledge, if not first-hand experience, of depot training.[36] Mervyn Grey joins the constabulary aged nineteen, with three others: a thirty-year-old who has lived for a number of years in the United States; the twenty-year-old son of a head constable; and the younger son of a 'respectable' farmer, who had failed to secure a clerkship in a mercantile office. This group offers an interesting and fairly accurate cross-section of recruits. Having taken an oath of loyalty before a magistrate, passed an examination by a doctor and satisfied the commandant as to their literacy, the new recruits were assigned to divisions and rooms. Each room housed twenty-four men and the new arrivals were immediately asked where they were from and what their religion was. They had missed supper and so went unfed. They were also liable to an initiation ceremony, which appears to have consisted of having a bucket of water thrown over them. But a man could avoid this ordeal if he paid half a crown.[37]

35 Eull Dunlop (ed.), *Robert Dunlop (RIC) of Clough, County Antrim: reminiscences (1825–75) of a northern boyhood, followed by service in County Longford and County Kildare, before retirement in Belfast* (Ballymena, 1995), pp 9–12. Dunlop's memoirs are in the Public Record Office of Northern Ireland, Belfast (PRONI, T2815), but they have also been published by the Mid-Antrim Historical Group. I would like to thank Dr Eull Dunlop for providing me with a copy of this pamphlet.   36 Stephen Brown, *Ireland in fiction: a guide to Irish novels, tales, romances and folk-lore* (new ed., Dublin and London, 1919), p. 213. Brown identifies the author as an antiquarian from Co. Cavan who died in 1911. In fact John Wilson Montgomery (c.1835–1911) was a poet and local historian, born in Cavan, who worked for many years as clerk to the poor law guardians in Downpatrick. But, being too young to train for the constabulary in the late 1840s, how did he come to acquire what appears to have been first-hand knowledge of the depot? A John W. Montgomery joined the constabulary as a sub constable in 1829, became a head constable in 1837, trained as an officer cadet in 1845–6 and served as a sub inspector from 1846 until his death on duty in 1870. Inspector Montgomery, as well as being at the depot in the late 1840s, had been posted in Co. Cavan between 1829 and 1845. See his personnel record in RIC General Register (PRO(L), HO 184/45). Circumstantial evidence would thus suggest that he may have been the father of his namesake, the Downpatrick poet and antiquarian, and that *Mervyn Grey* was based on his memoirs. It is striking that the book largely covers Grey's training and first posting in the late 1840s and early 1850s, but then jumps awkwardly to a final chapter set in 1871. Presumably this chapter was added after Inspector Montgomery's death in 1870 in order to complete the book. In light of the above information, I have chosen to regard the novel as based closely on the experiences of someone who trained in the depot in the late 1840s, and therefore as an accurate reflection of depot life at that time.   37 J.W. Montgomery, *Mervyn*

There were no servants for rank-and-file recruits, unlike the officer cadets, and so they had to see to their own beds and clothes. They slept, relaxed and ate all in the one room. These rooms 'only boast furniture of the plainest description'. There were deal tables, with iron-legged forms for chairs and bayonets stuck in the tables to serve as candle sticks. Meals were frugal: breakfast, for instance, consisted of unbuttered bread and coffee. But there was alcohol available.[38]

Dinner was at 3.00 p.m. and roll calls were at 7.00 p.m. and 10.00 p.m., although recruits could obtain permission to be absent from the first roll call. So it was possible for recruits to spend some of the afternoon in Phoenix Park or even to go into Dublin for extended periods. 'Rambling through the city has always been a favourite occupation of depot men – of the recruits in particular it forms the chief recreation.' The main duty of sentries – one 'much needed at the time' – was to ensure that 'none of the men returned from the city under the influence of drink'. But, even if men did not frequent the Dublin pubs, they could still drink in the depot, for the recruits smuggled in porter, ale and whisky. After the final roll call and the departure of the orderly constable on his rounds, the door to the barrack room was barred and the windows covered with quilts fixed to the woodwork by forks. The alcohol was brought out, plus bottles of cordial 'for the few inmates of the room who still adhere ... to the principles inculcated by Father Mathew'. A constable or sub constable presided at these drinking parties and tried especially to prevent political arguments among the recruits.[39]

But 'how was Grey's time employed in the depot?' He was taught reading and writing in the schoolroom and everyday the hours from 10.00 a.m. to 12.00 noon and 1.00 p.m. to 2.00 p.m. were spent in drill.

> Marching and counter marching, loading without ammunition, and firing without having even a report. These were the occupations of his drill hours. [After four months' training, he] was now in the first squad, wore regimental clothing, and was, in about a week, to pass the commandant; – that is, undergo with other first

Grey; or, Life in the Royal Irish Constabulary (Glasgow and London, [c.1875]), pp 9–10, 18–29. The only copy of this interesting book I have been able to locate exists in mint condition in the Belfast Central Library – or at least it did in 1990. It is inscribed by 'the author' to 'my friend, Thomas Beatty', but unfortunately this inscription is not dated. There is no publication date on the title page and the one given above is suggested by Stephen Brown. 38 Ibid., pp 32, 38. 39 Ibid., pp 41, 43, 52, 54.

squad men a strict inspection, where the commandant, the chief
officer of the depot, would be present picking out the effective
from the non-effective men; setting the former apart for active
duty, sending the latter back for further polish at the hands of
the drill sergeant.[40]

The fictional Grey, like Dunlop, impressed his superiors for he too was
assigned to the reserve.

In 1913 a former constable who had entered the depot as a recruit in
1870 recorded his reminiscences in the RIC's *Magazine*. He clearly found
the training far more irksome than did Dunlop or Grey. According to
him, the way recruits were treated at the time was very different from the
present situation. 'We were then "broken in" on much the same princi-
ple that country folk break in young horses, viz., give them very little
food, work them hard; and they won't kick over the traces.' The first item
of equipment that a recruit had to provide himself with was a patent
leather stock. This was about three and a half inches wide, very stiff and
hard and was fastened around the neck with a buckle and strap at the
back. It had to be worn during drill even if otherwise, at the beginning,
the recruit was dressed in plain clothes, for it forced the recruit to 'hold
his head up, as he could not look down'. The author of this article
remembered recruits trying to master the goosestep on the parade ground
during the snowy winter of 1870, wearing their stiff stocks and tall hats.
In retrospect, he felt that they must have looked 'ridiculous'.[41]

Jeremiah Mee summed up his training at the depot in 1910 as primarily consisting of 'foot drill, carbine and revolver exercises, physical
culture, swimming, rope climbing, ju-jitsu, first-aid, fire-fighting, criminal law and police duties'.[42] It is probably no coincidence that 'foot drill'
came first in Mee's list and 'police duties' came last. Even after 1900 depot
training remained stubbornly military in character.

The 'first thing that struck the new recruit', according to Mee, 'was
the absolute orderliness of everything both inside and outside the depot
buildings'. Even the parade ground was 'spotless'. This 'orderliness' was
rigorously enforced.

40 Ibid., p. 104.   41 'Yarns by the day-room fire' in the *Royal Irish Constabulary Magazine*, ii, 3 (Jan. 1913), pp 97–8.
42 Gaughan (ed.), *Memoirs of Constable Jeremiah Mee*, p. 12.

Each morning by nine o'clock all beds were neatly folded, boots polished and put carefully away, the floors cleaned and every room dusted. While the nine o'clock parade was on, the sergeants inspected the rooms and woe betide the man who had left even a handkerchief out of place. There was no parade on Saturday, that whole morning up to one o'clock being given over to scrubbing floors and cleaning the cookhouse. Once a week every room in the barracks was disinfected, and twice a week new sheets were supplied for each bed. Cleanliness and orderliness were a kind of religion. The change which the six-month course of training at the depot effected in a young, country boy was almost unbelievable.[43]

Maintaining such order and undergoing training were time-consuming activities. According to Mee: 'Every hour of the day was taken up with parades, drill, gymnastics, school and the everlasting cleaning and polishing of equipment'. Recruits were kept busy from 6.30 a.m. until 10.00 p.m., with barely time to write a letter. However, Saturday afternoons appear to have been free for Mee remembered recruits taking 'to the park or city in pairs walking straight as ramrods and shining like new pins'.[44]

Other reminiscences of rank-and-file training at the depot have survived for an even later date. All the fifteen elderly former RIC constables interviewed by John Brewer in the late 1980s had trained between 1917 and 1921. Most of them found the regime practised at the depot far less congenial than that described by Dunlop and Montgomery, and even by Mee. One commented succinctly:

Phoenix Park was tough, it was far worse than the army, the drill, oh, it was tough, although you were glad to have some kind of job. You didn't have the time or money to see much of Dublin ... The drill made you physically fit, do you see, built you up, straightened you and made you put out your chest a bit and all that. School was alright. It was all learning scraps of Acts of Parliament here and there. Food was plain and a bit rough. It was a bit stale; there was hardly any of the recruits that put on weight.[45]

43 Ibid., pp 13–14. 44 Mee, Memoirs, pp 10–11. 45 Brewer, *The Royal Irish Constabulary*, p. 49. The following quotations from constables' interviews are drawn from ibid., pp 44–55.

Others agreed that the depot was 'fairly rough' and 'very strict' and that training 'was a very hard six months'. There was reveille at 6.00 a.m. and tattoo at 10.00 p.m. Most of the day was taken up with drill on the parade ground, teaching in the school and physical training in the gymnasium, with about fifteen minutes between each activity. The beds were hard, with straw-filled palliasses and pillows. While some interviewees said the food was 'alright', others complained bitterly about it. They 'pinch on the food. You were very badly fed …' said one, and another described the recruits' mess as 'terrible'.[46] After 1918 most of the drill instructors were ex-army men – mainly policemen who had served in the Irish Guards – and the drills accordingly became even more military in character. Three weeks of intensive weaponry training was also required: 'nothing else only musketry, rifles, mill bombs, hand grenades and so forth'.

Most recruits enjoyed the schooling, although some found it easier than others. It mainly entailed the memorisation of large numbers of regulations and statutes. The RIC's *Manual*, which summarised the statute law enforced by the police, had to be learned by heart. Recruits passed this aspect of their training by being able to answer a series of questions on the material they had memorised. Information on the quality of teaching is not plentiful, but the poem 'Memories of the Past', published in 1891, offers some clues.

> I think I see the schoolroom, it appears as if of old;
> I see the desks and gallery, and my mentor's eye so cold.
> The culprit there is on the floor, the summons he obeyed—
> Come down, my lad, you on that seat, it's you, I mean, McQuaid.
> The front seat, with its occupants, possess some clever boys—
> There's Bennet, Quinn and Culleton, Paddy Stapleton and Boyce,
> Some chips from off the old block, and a youth called Jim
>   O'Shea—
> All have earned the title clever from the 'Pro's' immortal sway.[47]

The reference to 'chips from off the old block' suggests that the sons of RIC men may have had an advantage when it came to learning regula-

---

46 Again there are similarities here with the army, for soldiers also frequently complained that they were provided with food that was either badly prepared or insufficient. Skelley, *The Victorian army at home*, pp 63–8; Spiers, *The late Victorian army*, pp 140–1.   47 *Royal Irish Constabulary Magazine*, i, 7 (May 1912), p. 239. A footnote to the poem explains that the term 'pro' to refer to the depot's schoolmaster derived from his habit of telling recruits: 'You're only here, my lad, on probation.'

tions, and also an advantage in training generally. They were presumably more familiar with constabulary procedures and discipline than were recruits from non-constabulary backgrounds.

The post-1917 recruits had fewer opportunities than Dunlop and Grey, and even Mee, to explore Dublin. In order to obtain a pass one remembered that he 'had to grovel in front of the Adjutant'. In addition, as the political situation deteriorated from 1919, depot officers were reluctant to allow recruits into the city for fear that they would become targets for the IRA. But, even before 1917, it would appear that leave had become less generous. In the constabulary *Magazine* in 1912 'Sylvanus' claimed to have heard of a Kerry recruit who requested leave to meet his mother off the train at Kingsbridge (now Heuston) Station the following day. His application went to the room sergeant, then to the divisional head constable, next to the wing inspector and finally to the adjutant, who submitted it to the commandant. He returned it for a report on the recruit's progress in training. So it was passed around the recruit's various instructors, all of who submitted positive reports. But, by the time the request had been approved by the commandant and returned, via channels, to the recruit, the constable concerned had left the depot and been serving in Co. Tipperary for two months. Although probably apocryphal, this story reflects rank-and-file frustration after 1900 with the bureaucracy of the RIC in general, and of the depot in particular. In the final years of the force's existence contacts outside the depot were certainly restricted, so that the institution and those training there were even more isolated from the community than they had been during the nineteenth century.

There was a canteen at the depot from which men could buy 'various food stuffs and common personal necessaries', supposedly at prices lower than those prevailing in Dublin city. One section also sold beer and was to all intents and purposes a pub. Presumably it had been decided that it was preferable for the men to drink under controlled conditions than to have them smuggling in alcohol or spending time in Dublin pubs. The canteen was a profit-making enterprise. The editor of the *Constabulary Gazette* complained that, although the canteen was in theory managed by three officers and five rank-and-file men, it was the officers who made all the decisions. Its prices were not always cheaper than Dublin ones and its profits 'squeezed' from the 'poor man's pocket in the

R.I.C.' were 'not only [used] to provide luxuries for the better paid members of the Force, but to provide necessaries for which the State should be liable'. The depot gymnasium, for instance, had been paid for out of canteen profits. The editor wanted the canteen run by an elected committee of constables for the sole benefit of the rank-and-file.[48]

Discontent over the officers' management of the depot canteen is just one among many examples of tension between the rank-and-file and the officer corps. Such tensions were obviously evident even during training at the beginning of a constable's career.

TRAINING: OFFICERS

Officer cadets entered constabulary training by a different route from rank-and-file recruits and the two did not mix, although initially they were drilled together. Cadets were officers and therefore, as we have seen, by definition 'gentlemen'. They had to be between 18 and 24 years of age, unmarried, of 'sound' health and 'good moral character'; they had to be nominated by a senior government official, most commonly the chief secretary, and they had to pass an entrance examination. Chamberlain remarked in 1914 that during the previous decade the chief secretary had nominated 31 candidates of whom 19 presented themselves for the exam. Although more of them had university qualifications, he still considered that their 'quality' had deteriorated over the years. They were, he felt, not 'as fitted to command men'.[49] But Chamberlain came from a military background, while few cadets did in 1914. The depot with its military-style training was clearly intended to rectify this deficiency.

Entry to a cadetship was from the 1850s onwards regulated by an examination comparable to exams for entry to the civil service. David Harrel, who later rose to be under secretary in Dublin Castle (1893–1902), was forced by 'family circumstances' – presumably lack of money – in 1858 to give up his plans for a naval career and to apply to the chief secretary to have his name entered for a constabulary cadetship. After this nomination, Harrel had to sit a 'highly competitive examination', as normally four candidates were nominated for each vacancy.

48 [Harding], *The R.I.C.: a plea for reform*, pp 58–62. 49 Griffin, 'The Irish police', pp 269–70; *Report of Inquiry into the RIC and the DMP*, 1914, p. 237.

I had six months to prepare myself, and I spent the time by working with grinders in Dublin on an average of 12 hours a day. The subjects were, Tests of Spelling, Dictation, History, Geography, Arithmetic, Algebra, Euclid, English, Composition, Latin, Law. In April 1859, I was called up for the examination with three others and I had the good fortune to get first place and to secure the appointment.[50]

While cadets trained for five months in the 1850s, by the 1900s their training had been extended to eight months. The surviving memoirs of cadets paint a rather different picture of depot life from the memoirs of constables. Garrow Green, for example, tells us that he presented himself to the depot adjutant 'with no pensive thoughts'. 'My uniforms and sword', he goes on excitedly 'had come from the military tailor, and I was actually one of the officers whose smart get-up I had so fervently envied while being ground to powder in Dublin for the dreaded competitive examination'.[51] Like other cadets he was assigned a single room and given the services of a personal orderly. Nevertheless, he clearly considered the living conditions to be rather primitive. The barrack master informed him that:

I would have to pay 'damages' for any injury to the public property and for each nail driven into the wall. The 'public property' consisted of a plain wood table and two chairs, a small press, and a huge iron coal box, Her Majesty dispensing with such superfluities as bed, wash-hand stand, easy chair, &c., in officers' quarters. But a dealer on the quay aided in this direction for 12/– per month, and that afternoon I was fairly comfortable. I was to share an orderly, in plain clothes, with three others, and, as bells were wisely omitted, we had to yell for him when required to the orderlies' room below.[52]

Cadets, unlike trainee constables, did not eat in their rooms, but in the officers' mess. Garrow Green's first night in the mess was 'rather an ordeal' as he had to 'pass muster' before some twenty-three officers 'who

50 Recollections and Reflections by the Rt. Hon. Sir David Harrel, April 1926 (Typescript, Katherine Tynan Papers, John Rylands Library, University of Manchester, pp 30–1). 51 Garrow Green, *In the Royal Irish Constabulary*, p. 9. 52 Ibid., p. 10.

are no more prone than military men to accept a new comer on his intrinsic merits alone'. However, as was the custom, he stood his comrades 'half a dozen champagne' and this duly 'wetted' his commission, without even the necessity of a formal speech – a possible requirement he had been dreading. What followed he tells us was a 'fair sample' of the way depot officers passed the hours between dinner and bed. They played a game called 'fox-hunting', which involved competitors jumping over a large table while wearing spurs. There were songs with a piano accompaniment, although 'youngsters' could be required to sing solo 'under a penalty of a tumbler of strong salt and water'. Another 'diversion' was a game known as 'cock-fighting'. Two mess waiters – presumably sub constables – had their arms pinioned behind them and their legs tied just above their boots. They were then forced to fight with their toes until one was knocked over. There was a great deal of smoking, Garrow Green records, but no card playing or gambling. Other schoolboy pranks were conducted outside the mess. The game called 'hay-making' involved cadets, often assisted by officers, invading the room of a sleeping colleague late at night, hauling him out of bed, making a pile of his furniture and dousing it with water. Late returners from Dublin could find a bath of cold water inside their door into which they could be plunged by fellow cadets. Protest was futile, as complainers were ostracised while '[s]toical endurance ensured popularity'.[53]

These drunken, rather juvenile, games, particularly involving the humiliation of inferiors, were typical of officer messes of the British army throughout the century.[54] RIC cadets like Garrow Green clearly aspired to army-officer status and the depot catered to this aspiration in its mess etiquette, as much as in its training. Each week 'guest nights' were held at the mess to which officers from regiments stationed in Dublin were regularly invited. The hospitality offered was generous and the RIC band played throughout the evening outside the windows of the mess. Army officers reciprocated by inviting constabulary officers to their messes.[55]

53 Ibid., pp 16–17. 54 For the systematic bullying of young army recruits or those who were deemed to have offended against mess etiquette, which was referred to as 'hazing' or 'ragging', see Gwyn Harries-Jenkins, *The army in Victorian society* (London and Toronto, 1977), pp 96–7; Spiers, *The army and society, 1815–1914*, p. 25. 55 Comerford typescript, p. 101. John Regan, who joined the RIC in 1909 as an officer cadet and subsequently the RUC, left a memoir of his service that is now held by the RUC Museum in Belfast. For an extract dealing with his experience in the depot, see 'An RIC cadet officer in training', *Proceedings of the Royal Ulster Constabulary Historical Society* (summer 1997), pp 6–7; (autumn, 1997), pp 6–7.

In describing the depot in some detail in 1852 Sir Francis Head, him-self a former soldier, equated every constabulary rank with what he per-ceived as the equivalent army rank. The recruits he described as a 'well-organized body of regular troops', and he went on to note that they reminded him of the 'old 95th, now-a-days christened "the Rifle Brigade"'.[56] Indeed, the Rifle Brigade had influenced both the uniform and the drill of the Irish constabulary, as several of the first inspector generals had served in that regiment. The number of recruits and cadets who had previously been soldiers declined markedly after 1836 and yet the military character of the force, and particularly of its training, remained unmistakeable. Partly this reflected the fact that government considered Ireland required paramilitary-style policing. The vast major-ity of the RIC's inspectors general were long-serving British army offi-cers and so approached their Irish commands from a military point of view. And even the memoirs of civilian cadets, like Harrel and Garrow Green, reveal men who would have preferred a military career, but lacked the necessary money and connections. Thus the depot's officer mess appears to have differed little from an army mess.

Francis Head during his visit in 1852 also inspected the officers' quar-ters in the depot, with the commandant. They contained a 'good read-ing-room well supplied with newspapers, and an excellent mess-room, handsomely carpeted, with mahogany sideboard, plate, and other Constabulary comforts'.[57]

Among the officers, as among the rank-and-file, drinking was proba-bly the most popular recreation. In his memoirs Assistant Inspector General Samuel Waters concluded that the depot was not at all an 'admirable school for young men'. He noted that when he was training in 1866 '[h]ard drinking was the fashion and the permanent officers in charge of the staff and the recruits were all free livers and very thirsty souls'. Free living, however, was expensive and Waters remembered that he graduated

---

56 Head, *A fortnight in Ireland*, p. 57. 57 Ibid., p. 62. A former district inspector, Lionel Yates, who had joined the RIC in 1909, published a novel about the force in 1924, which included a final chapter describing the last mess dinner held at the depot in 1922. 'The band was playing softly in the great hall, whose walls were almost obscured by antlered heads, stands of arms captured in old, half-forgotten rebellions ... In the lofty mess-room, four long tables glittered with priceless silver and Waterford glass, and from the walls long-dead Inspectors-General of the Force gazed sadly down on the scene.' It was indeed a somber meal, for, according to Yates, 'now the restraining arm of the green-clad Force was about to be withdrawn, and Ireland ... stood on the brink of such anarchy and barbarism as her history had seldom known.' Lionel Yates and Honor Goodhart, *The eclipse of James Trent, D.I.* (London, 1924), pp 337–8.

from the depot considerably in debt, largely due to the cost of elaborate uniforms and of mess bills.[58] Brigadier General Frank Crozier, the commander of the RIC Auxiliary Division, recalled his last dinner at the 'beautiful Depot mess' early in 1921, and that there had been a great deal of drinking and laughter, as the mess guest night was always 'a long affair'.[59] Garrow Green recorded that, on promotion to the rank of sub inspector, cadets had to present four bottles of champagne to the mess cellar, as well as donating £4 to the mess fund. Any officer drawing his sword in the mess ante-room was obliged to pay for the evening's champagne.[60] That cadets left the depot in debt is hardly surprising; and, again, this was a circumstance in which their experience resembled that of young army officers.[61] Drinking, however, was not only restricted to the evenings. Another former cadet, in a novel set in the early 1920s, describes an orderly waking an officer at 9.25 a.m. after a long guest night in the mess with a jug of beer in one hand and a bottle of aspirin in the other. The officer – not surprisingly given the ethos of the depot – opts for the beer.[62]

After morning drill between 7.30 and 8.30 a.m., the cadets, according to Garrow Green, spent an hour in riding school where they were instructed by a riding master who had participated in the Light Brigade charge in the Crimea in 1854 – 'a fact which insured our deep respect'. Then at 9.30 a.m. they were allowed a brief breakfast of cold meats, bread, tea or coffee. A hot breakfast was available but had to be paid for. At 10.00 a.m. there was another hour of drills and parades before cadets reported to the school. There they were instructed by a head constable in 'writing reports, preparing returns, and the mode of keeping the cash accounts and pay-bills'. The last drill ended at 3.00 p.m., after which the cadets' time was their own, except that they were required to sleep in the depot.[63]

In terms of content, cadet training was thus fairly similar to rank-and-file training, except for the emphasis on horse riding. Cadets were

---

58 Stephen Ball (ed.), *A policeman's Ireland: recollections of Samuel Waters, RIC* (Cork, 1999), p. 26. 59 Crozier's long night ended unhappily. As his car left the front gate of the depot he heard a shot and saw a body on the side of the road; a passing squad of Black-and-Tans denied responsibility for the shooting, but Crozier did not believe them. Inside the iron rails of the depot, he mused, 'the King's writ ran', but not 'ten yards outside'. He resigned his command shortly afterwards. F.P. Crozier, *Ireland for ever* (London, 1932), pp 192–3. 60 Garrow Green, *In the Royal Irish Constabulary*, p. 17. 61 For the chronic indebtedness of many army officers, mainly due to uniform, equipment and mess bills, see Spiers, *The army and society*, p. 23. The editor of the *Constabulary Gazette* claimed in 1907 that 90 per cent of rank-and-file recruits also left the depot in debt due to their inadequate pay, combined with the expense of outfits and equipment. [Harding], *The R.I.C.: a plea for reform*, p. 32. 62 Yates and Goodhart, *The eclipse of James Trent, D.L.*, p. 65. 63 Garrow Green, *In the Royal Irish Constabulary*, pp 12–13.

examined on their riding skills by the commandant before being passed out of the depot. Cadets also had to learn to give commands during drill and to compile statistical returns for their districts. Some seemed satisfied with their training, but others clearly were not. In his recollections, written in 1911, the former inspector general, Sir Andrew Reed, said that he had had a 'very good time' at the depot in 1859. But initially he had his doubts. One of his depot instructors had warned him off a constabulary career, complaining that promotion was too slow. However, he had invested so much money in uniforms and equipment that he felt he must persevere. Reed noted that he left 'not owing a shilling'. But this was clearly unusual, and Reed went on to explain that he had arrived at the depot with £100. This was a large sum and, although he did not get into debt, one wonders how much of Reed's money remained after his four or five months of training.[64] Sir David Harrel, who trained in the same year as Reed, described his period at the depot as 'a very happy one' and remembered the morning and afternoon drills, riding and 'police school' and instructions in official duties. When he took up his first posting in Co. Tyrone he found his duties 'not exacting' and clearly considered that he had been trained adequately to perform them.[65] Garrow Green's assessment was rather different – typically flippant, but more insightful nevertheless.

> When I left the Royal Irish Constabulary Depot – having blossomed from the chrysalis state of cadetship into a full-blown district inspector – to take charge of a country district, I was not disposed to agree with Mr W.S. Gilbert regarding the woes incidental to a policeman's career. I had gained distinction, as a ringleader in the pastime of 'haymaking', had mastered the intricacies of the goose-step, had fired twenty rounds of balled cartridge at Sandymount – chiefly to the disturbance of the local mud – and was unrivalled in my sublime ignorance of both statute and common law, and the detection of criminals. I could draw a map of Chinese Tartary, but had a profound contempt for Taylor on Evidence. I could form a hollow square, but of the necessary

64 Andrew Reed, *Recollections of My Life*, 1911 (typescript, Reed Papers, Private Collection, pp 13–14). I would like to thank A.D. Powell of Tonbridge, Kent, Andrew Reed's grandson, for allowing me to microfilm these papers.
65 Harrel, *Recollections and Reflections*, pp 31–2.

steps to be taken in a murder case my head was about equally empty. With these advantages I started to assume command of a lawless station in the wilds of Kerry, and to instruct the 50 peelers therein in all that pertained to crime and outrage.[66]

Andrew Reed also remarked that during his first posting in Co. Tipperary in the early 1860s, his head constable 'did all the office work'.[67] Many head constables appear to have agreed that cadet training was inadequate for they frequently complained that they had to do the jobs of newly-qualified cadets until these young inspectors learned their duties through experience and instruction by their subordinates.

THE DEPOT AS 'TOTAL INSTITUTION'

The depot had many of the qualities that later sociologists have ascribed to 'total institutions'. The classic definition of a total institution was provided in the 1950s by the Canadian-born sociologist Erving Goffman. According to him, it was 'a place of residence and work where a large number of like-situated individuals, cut off from the wider society for an appreciable period of time, together lead an enclosed, formally administered round of life'.[68] Goffman identified five types of total institution, highlighting the mental hospital and the prison in particular. But one of his types was

> ... institutions purportedly established the better to pursue some worklike task and justifying themselves only on these instrumental grounds: army barracks, ships, boarding schools, work camps, colonial compounds, and large mansions from the point of view of those who live in the servants' quarters.[69]

The RIC depot was certainly like an army barracks; indeed, it was modelled on an army barracks. It took the recruit abruptly out of his previous milieu, isolated him from society and sought to control every aspect of his waking day: not only what he did, but even what he thought. And

66 Garrow Green, *In the Royal Irish Constabulary*, p. 24.   67 Reed, *Recollections*, p. 16.   68 Erving Goffman, *Asylums: essays on the social situation of mental patients and other inmates* (New York, 1961), p. xiii.   69 Ibid., p. 5.

memoirs of recruits suggest that the degree of isolation and control increased rather than diminished over time. This regime was deliberately intended, not just to *teach* specialised skills, but to *create* a particular type of individual with certain well-defined attitudes and values. Jeremiah Mee obviously recognised the crucial role of the depot when he wrote that training there destroyed the recruit's sense of 'individuality' and made him feel part of a 'machine'. The much-hated drills were an essential aspect of this process. Like soldiers, Irish policemen were required to function as a group and to obey orders unquestioningly.

Yet the newly trained constables and inspectors were not assigned to large regiments and huge barracks, as regular soldiers would have been, where collective discipline could be maintained. Policemen were scattered throughout Ireland in small groups of half a dozen men or less, living mostly in ordinary houses fitted out as barracks in small towns or rural areas. They were certainly trained like soldiers in the depot, but thereafter they did not live or generally work like soldiers. The depot imparted discipline, but most policing skills had to be learnt on the job.

CHAPTER FIVE

Constabulary duties:
'arithmetic and fear'[1] in a 'policeman state'

He [Thomas Drummond, under secretary for Ireland (1835–40)] found the constabulary in a very inefficient state. By his power of organization, and administrative skill, he converted it into the most efficient police in Europe. It became under his hands an almost perfect machine, which, like a delicate musical instrument, responded at once from the remotest part of Ireland, to his touch in Dublin Castle.[2]

Everything in Ireland, from the muzzling of a dog to the suppression of a rebellion, is done by the Irish constabulary.[3]

It [RIC service] was a constant grind, studying Acts of Parliament, circular orders, *Hue and Cry*, burnishing and polishing arms and equipment, keeping barracks and premises in apple-pie order, and moving within the rigid limits of discipline. He read the daily newspapers, but little else in the shape of literature. He was part of a machine ...[4]

A career in the Irish constabulary between the 1820s and the 1920s could have afforded a secure and fairly undemanding life, or it could have entailed considerable toil and danger. The nature of a policeman's career very much depended upon when and where he served. The constabulary was under considerable strain during the Famine (1845–9); under even greater strain during the Land War (1879–82); and, during the Anglo-Irish War (1919–21), it was literally stretched to breaking point.[5]

1 Heaney, 'A constable calls', *North*, p. 66. 2 Sir Thomas Larcom, under-secretary for Ireland (1853–68), quoted in Curtis, *History of the Royal Irish Constabulary*, p. 22. 3 H.A. Blake, 'The Irish police', *The Nineteenth Century*, ix, 48 (Feb. 1881), p. 390. 4 Thomas Fennell, *The Royal Irish Constabulary: a history and personal memoir*, ed. Rosemary Fennell (Dublin, 2003), p. 19. 5 W.J. Lowe, 'Policing the Famine', *Eire-Ireland*, xxix, 4 (Winter 1994), pp 47–67; Richard Hawkins, 'An army on police work, 1881–2: Ross of Blandensburg's Memorandum', *Irish Sword*, xi, 43 (winter, 1973), pp 75–117; Townshend, *Political violence in Ireland*, pp 105–80; Fitzpatrick, *Politics and Irish Life, 1913–21*, pp 1–45; Peter Hart, *The I.R.A. and its enemies: violence and community in Cork, 1916–23* (Oxford, 1998), pp 53–6, 60–2, 75–7.

Policing parts of the country, like Belfast or counties such as Tipperary and Roscommon, also sometimes posed severe problems. It is no coincidence that the three most serious outbreaks of police disaffection to occur in Ireland between 1822 and 1922 happened at the end of the Land War in 1882, in Belfast in 1907 and during the Anglo-Irish War in 1920.[6] But, outside particular periods and particular places, police service could be a rather mundane and tedious occupation, dominated by routine patrolling and a great deal of paperwork.[7]

It is difficult therefore to present a picture of 'typical' policing. In addition, police duties expanded very considerably over time. Thus, whereas the first edition of the constabulary's rulebook, the *Code*, produced in 1837, consisted of 730 sections, the sixth and final edition in 1911 had 1,978 sections, plus ninety pages of appendices. Yet there were certain duties that most constables and officers would have undertaken and certain regulations that all had to abide by.

This chapter offers a general portrait of the working life of an Irish policeman, taking account of both day-to-day and extraordinary duties. It examines the peeler in a number of different roles: as information collector or clerk, as patrolman, as soldier, as gauger, as detective or intelligence agent and as officer of the courts. Not all policemen played all these roles. The first two, information collector and patrolmen, were most common and few constables would have escaped them. Appearing as a witness in a trial, or assisting the courts in other ways, was also a role that most policemen would have been familiar with. Especially before the Famine, and in Ulster after the Famine, many constables were also called upon to put down large-scale public disorder and in doing so to exercise military skills. From the late 1850s, mainly in the west of Ireland, suppressing illicit distillation formed a significant part of police duties. Related to this, after the 1830s, the constabulary was increasingly called upon to enforce the liquor licensing laws. The constabulary from the late 1840s also sought to develop specialised detective forces and detective

6 Lowe, 'The Constabulary agitation of 1882', pp 37–59; John Gray, *City in revolt: James Larkin and the Belfast Dock Strike of 1907* (Belfast, 1985), pp 111–36.   7 Ian Bridgeman argues the point persuasively and at some length in his thesis that after the Famine most policemen were engaged in carrying out fairly routine duties in relatively peaceful rural communities. Much attention has been paid by politicians and historians to the RIC in terms of its role in combating political and social unrest, but Bridgeman is right to stress that such activities were not typical of Irish policing in the latter part of the nineteenth century. See Ian Bridgeman, 'Policing rural Ireland', pp 1–4.

skills. And last, but far from least, some policemen recruited spies and informers or acted as spies themselves.

An examination of each of these diverse roles in turn provides a collective picture of the extremely wide-ranging and varied duties that policemen were called upon to undertake in nineteenth- and early twentieth-century Ireland. At the same time it illustrates how pervasive and powerful the constabulary became during the post-Famine period.

PAPER WORK: THE PEELER AS ENUMERATOR AND CLERK

Irish policemen had a great many tasks and much of what they did had little connection with apprehending those who had broken the law. The RIC was used by Dublin Castle as an all-purpose government agency. The constabulary was composed of some 8,000 to 10,000 men scattered in nearly 1,400 barracks throughout Ireland, from the most populous cities to the most isolated rural areas. Their job necessitated policemen becoming familiar with the districts in which they served: getting to know personally as many of the local inhabitants as possible and watching out for trouble and for troublemakers. Probably no other arm of the state was quite so ubiquitous, so intrusive or so rigidly centrally controlled. But exploiting the full potential of the constabulary for wide-ranging state purposes involved the construction of a complex bureaucracy and the use of a vast amount of paper and ink. If Irish policemen were trained at the Phoenix Park Depot as soldiers, many of them later spent a great deal of their time employed essentially as clerks.

The RIC acted as an information-gathering service for Dublin Castle. Under the force's 1911 *Standing Rules and Regulations*, or *Code*, county inspectors had to keep 22 books, from registers of public houses to postage books to a personal journal – the latter in the officer's own hand. In addition, county inspectors were required to make 65 returns each year to the inspector general, including monthly financial statements, quarterly returns of farms from which the tenants had been evicted and annual returns of the numbers of sheep killed by dogs and of hotel accommodation in the county. District inspectors had to maintain 18 books, including registers of police pensioners and of forges in their areas. They had to keep a personal journal, a cashbook and registers of crime and crime special – all in their own handwriting. They made 51 returns, mainly to their county inspector. These ranged from monthly summaries of cases of boycotting, to quarterly accounts of fees collected for pedlars' and chimney sweeps' certificates, to annual reports on police revolver practice. Head constables had to keep a daily diary of all duties performed by them. In addition head constables and sergeants in charge of stations had to maintain 13 books, from a patrol diary to a register of householders.[8] Most books and returns compiled by the constabulary had little to do with crime.

Except for patrol diaries, no official book was to be removed from the barracks. All barracks were liable to inspection and, indeed, were inspected regularly. County inspectors were instructed to inspect every barracks in their county quarterly. District inspectors had to make monthly inspections during the day of all barracks and, in addition, inspections at night of barracks within the vicinity of their residence. All such visits were to be made 'unexpectedly' and during them the station's books were to be examined. Not maintaining books properly or wasting official forms was a serious offence. The *Code* warned officers and head constables that such lapses would attract 'severe censure'.[9]

County inspectors appointed promising constables as clerks to assist them with their paperwork, thus guaranteeing such men accelerated promotion. But district inspectors had to rely on the head constables under their command in a more informal manner. The *Code* allowed district inspectors to seek the aid of head constables in preparing estimates, accounts, returns and reports, but instructed them 'not to abuse this privilege by requiring the Head Constable to perform an undue share of such work'.[10] However, it was widely recognised that new district inspectors, straight out of the depot, usually relied heavily on their head constables to keep their paperwork in order.[11] Samuel Waters, although he later rose to be an assistant inspector general, remembered during his first posting at Grange, Co. Sligo, in 1866–9 spending a great deal of time hunting, shooting, fishing and playing cricket, while his head constable 'took all official care off my hands'. Unfortunately for Waters, while he was confined to bed with a broken collarbone, the result of a hunting accident, his district was inspected by Colonel George Hillier, the deputy

8 *Standing rules and regulations*, 1911, pp 11, 15, 17–18, 458–63. 9 Ibid., pp 72–3, 214–15. 10 Ibid., p. 16. 11 *Report of the Commissioners*, 1873, p. 40.

inspector general and a noted martinet. Waters' head constable, in his absence, paraded the men improperly armed and demonstrated total ignorance of a recent important circular on detective duties. Hillier signed the inspection book, remarking that this was the 'worst district' he had ever inspected, and Waters was immediately transferred with a reprimand in the form of an unfavourable record entered upon his personnel file.[12] But, this was probably an exceptional case, as in the main long-serving head constables were far more knowledgeable regarding RIC procedures than were newly appointed junior inspectors. Inspector Garrow Green captured something of the head constable's key role when he termed him, an officer's 'grand vizier'.[13]

The 1911 *Code* included nearly twenty pages of instructions on 'correspondence'. Forms, letters and reports had to be submitted to the inspector general in a prescribed fashion. Reports were to consist of sheets of foolscap, no more than 13 by 8 inches in size. Pages were to be folded lengthwise and the communication written on the left-hand half of the sheet. The right-hand half was reserved for comments by the inspector general or other government officials to whom the document had been circulated. At the beginning of the first page, precisely two inches from the top, was to be written the name of the county concerned. Handwriting had to be 'distinct and legible', and men were warned that sending reports or returns to headquarters written 'in a cramped or slovenly manner' would 'expose themselves to censure'. The *Code* then went on to give detailed instructions on all manner of correspondence, including telegrams and letters to the public.[14] The collection of precise and accurate information on numerous topics and its transmission to Dublin Castle in a precisely standardised manner were clearly vital constabulary duties.

Yet some felt that this obsession with the minutiae of administration detracted from the real function of the force. Clifford Lloyd, an Englishman who had served in the Burma police and was posted to Ireland as an RM during the Land War, complained in his memoirs that 'wrongly heading an official report, giving a margin of foolscap unauthorised by regulation, or other breach of [the *Code*'s] contents, would give rise to much more correspondence and to a greater reproof than any

12 Ball (ed.), *A policeman's Ireland*, pp 29–30. 13 Garrow Green, *In the Royal Irish Constabulary*, p. 26. 14 *Standing rules and regulations*, 1911, pp 97–115.

shortcoming in [a young officer's] efforts to unravel the threads of some criminal mystery'.[15] While Lloyd's comments were certainly justified, nevertheless, the RIC did serve a vital function in providing government with a great deal of valuable data. The topics it reported upon were wide ranging and serve to give a flavour of the varied character of police service at the beginning of the twentieth century.

The constabulary's *Manual* or *Guide*, a catechism of duties that men were required to learn by heart,[16] made clear that a 'good local knowledge' was essential. Constables had to acquire 'an accurate knowledge' of all persons and places in their sub-district and a 'fair acquaintance' with those in the neighbouring districts. With regard to people, they needed to become familiar with 'appearance, character, habits, dress, employments, resorts, family circumstances, connections and relationships'. This information was to be gained by 'entering into friendly conversation' with the locals, winning their confidence and 'impressing on them that the police are their friends and protectors'. Any strangers were to be watched and inquired about, but 'without exciting suspicion'. Constables or sergeants were expected to study the twice-weekly *Police Gazette: Hue-and-Cry*, which contained descriptions of wanted men and women, to keep a record of those wanted in their areas in a notebook and to instruct their men on who they should be looking out for.[17] The men were also to know the natural features of their sub-district, its topographical divisions, its communication routes and public transport timetables, its places of public resort like churches, pubs, hotels, dispensaries and workhouses, its tradesmen's workshops especially forges and its fair, market, court and saints' days. All this information was to be gained by an 'intelligent policeman' within six months of his arrival.[18]

While officers and men were expected to have a thorough general knowledge of their areas, their duties also included the collection of specific information. Every ten years from 1841 to 1911 the constabulary acted as enumerators for the Irish census. This entailed selected men entering

---

15 Lloyd, *Ireland under the Land League*, p. 37.   16 Many men complained about having to 'learn off such dry stuff'. *Report of the Commissioners*, 1873, p. 40.   17 Such a notebook belonging to Constable Denis Shields of Co. Galway survives from 1869. Interestingly, inside the front cover there is a note written by Shields, reminding himself 'not to drink with Hanratty or Connell' during Lent in 1869 and 1870. Mary F., Salthill, Co. Galway, to ELM, 10 Sept. 1990 (RIC Letters, V/178), enclosing a photocopy of her great grandfather's police notebook.   18 *The Royal Irish Constabulary manual; or Guide to the discharge of police duties* (6th ed., Dublin, 1909), pp 30–1.

every house, establishment and institution in their district and recording information on all the inhabitants, whether permanent dwellers or visitors. In addition, the constabulary enumerated crops and animals on an annual basis; they supplied annual returns of the number of horses and vehicles and quarterly returns of the number of licensed and stray dogs in their areas; they sampled food for sale, checked weights and measures, inspected common lodging houses, supervised fairs and markets, licensed pedlars, transported vagrants to the workhouse and lunatics to the asylum, made notes at meetings where subversive speeches were likely to be delivered; and, at ports, they checked the safety of boats and watched the comings and goings of passengers. All these activities involved the collection of statistical information and the writing of reports which were despatched up the chain of command to district and county inspectors and usually finally to the inspector general in Dublin Castle. When any local newspaper contained a report about the police which was 'either incorrect or highly exaggerated', the district inspector or head constable was to forward an accurate account to the Castle as soon as possible.[19] Virtually all these activities fall into the categories of supervision and information-gathering rather than crime detection.

The constabulary, however, did collect crime and judicial statistics, relating to offences, prosecutions and convictions. These were compiled from crime registers kept at each station; details of private prosecutions supplied by court clerks were also included.[20] For how long these registers of crime, or outrage books as they were commonly known, were preserved in barracks is not altogether clear. Under the 1908 Old Age Pension Act no person could receive a pension who was in prison or who had been released from prison less than ten years earlier. In assisting pension officers, the constabulary were instructed to check their crime registers in the case of 'suspicious or known bad characters'.[21] This suggests that records of district crime were retained by the local police for at least a decade, and probably far longer.

Not surprisingly the constabulary took an especial interest in firearms and explosives and, by the turn of the century, these were heavily supervised. This had not always been the case, however. Up until 1870

19 *Standing rules and regulations*, 1911, p. 102.   20 Ibid., pp 127, 282.   21 Ibid., pp 280–1. Under section 3 of the 1908 act, no pension was to be paid to a person who had been sentenced to penal servitude or to imprisonment without the option of a fine during their imprisonment and for ten years after their release.

control of firearms had been sporadic and mainly restricted to pro-claimed areas, but under the 1870 Gun Licence Act all firearms required a licence. Although such licences were issued by the customs and excise authorities, the police were supplied with lists of holders and expected to enforce compliance. A policeman could challenge anyone seen carry-ing a gun whom he suspected of not having a licence.[22] Under the 1875 Explosives Act RIC sergeants acted as inspectors in rural Ireland. They inspected all premises holding explosives twice a year, collected samples for analysis, arranged police escorts for explosives in transit and pro-vided annual reports on the explosives held in their districts to the inspector general.[23]

Dublin Castle's use of the constabulary to collect all manner of infor-mation and statistics meant that few, if any, people escaped the prying eyes of the police. One did not have to break the law to come under police surveillance. It was the job of the constabulary to know every-one in their district: where they lived; what employment they had, if any; what land and animals they owned; where they drank and if to excess; and especially whether they happened to be mad or bad.

PATROLLING AND INSPECTING: THE PEELER ON THE BEAT

Aside from formally collecting statistical information, policemen got to know their districts well by simply walking through them *every day*. The one duty that all constables, including sergeants and head constables, had to perform was patrolling.[24] Many policemen did not like patrolling, and especially complained that being out for long periods in all weather con-ditions undermined their health. It may well have as we shall see in a later chapter, but patrolling was essential if policemen were to know their dis-tricts thoroughly and to fulfil their many responsibilities.[25]

The constabulary *Code* stated that the objects of patrolling were 'the prevention and detection of crime, the protection of life and property,

22 Ibid., pp 201–3. 23 Ibid., pp 173–4. The outbreak of the Anglo-Irish War or Irish War of Independence is tra-ditionally dated to an incident in January 1919 when two RIC constables, guarding explosives in transit to a quarry, were killed by Irish Volunteers at Soloheadbeg in Co. Tipperary. 24 In the 1890s a guidebook was produced by District Inspector Dagg to give policemen advice on the nature and state of the roads they patrolled. George Dagg, *The road and route guide for Ireland of the Royal Irish Constabulary* (Dublin, 1893). 25 For a lengthy correspondence on the nature and value of patrolling, see the letters and memoranda exchanged by Inspector General Duncan McGregor and Lieutenant General Lord de Ros, 1847/8 (NLI, Larcom Papers, MS 7617).

and the preservation of the public peace'. Patrols were to follow no set pattern in terms of time or location, and if a head constable or sergeant was in charge of a patrol, he was not even to inform his men where they were going. This was the theory, but in fact patrols normally occurred at regular times and followed regular routes. Day patrols between 6.00 a.m. and 6.00 p.m. usually consisted of one man, but night patrols had to have at least two. Men carried batons, but half of night patrols also carried unloaded firearms.

There were four major types of patrol: ordinary, ambush, special and conference. On ordinary patrol men proceeded along the sides of roads at a pace of two and a half miles per hour. Ambush patrols had to avoid roads and instead cross fields, concealing themselves in places where they were likely to detect offenders. Special patrols were to protect individuals or property liable to attack, while conference patrols were held at least every three months so that the officers and men of adjoining districts could meet and exchange information. However, patrols were not to take place during church services on a Sunday morning, as policemen were expected to attend their respective churches. Only if a district was 'in a state of disturbance' were men to patrol on Sunday mornings, and then arrangements were to be such that men missing one service would be able to attend another the following week.[26]

George Crawford, the son of an RIC man, who joined the force in 1920 and subsequently the RUC, described routine patrolling in Navan, Co. Meath.

> You did two patrols in a day, two three-hour patrols ... You got instructions going out, your sergeant paraded you going out to see that you had your equipment proper, and that you were clean and regular. Then he gave you instructions as to what you were to keep a look out for on different dates, different things ... You were paraded as you came in off patrol to see that you were regular, as they called it. We looked for various things, according to the locality, you see ... Cattle wandering on the road at that time was very common, they'd break out of the fields. You were supposed to caution the people first and afterwards if they persisted

26 *Standing rules and regulations*, 1911, pp 284–91.

in allowing their cattle to wander, you had to issue a summons against them; and there were other things. You got complaints from people, something was stolen from them ... you had to look into that, and check that in the town there was no disorderly conduct, that footpaths were kept clear, and traders didn't obstruct the footpath with boxes. General police work.[27]

Crawford's description suggests that ordinary patrolling was a fairly tedious affair. Certainly removing boxes from footpaths and recovering stray cattle hardly sound like stimulating activities. However, ambush and special patrols were rather different matters. As we shall see in the next section, patrolling towns constantly in order to prevent public disorder could also be a very demanding and dangerous duty.

Officers too undertook patrol duties, which they often combined with regular inspections of barracks in their districts. But, while men walked, officers rode or drove; and while men patrolled every day, officers generally spent a great deal of time handling paper work. Some, however, clearly relished getting out of their offices. Andrew Reed, serving in Co. Donegal in the late 1870s, later wrote: 'No man ever enjoyed any kind of sport more than I enjoyed driving by myself in a light car through the wild County, calling at the Police barracks for my inspections'.[28] A rare, handwritten, officer's personal journal survives from 1874 to 1884, which provides a detailed record of the day-to-day duties of a rural sub inspector[29] and, at the same time, illustrates how much more onerous police work became during the Land War.[30]

Before the outbreak of the Land War, Sub Inspector E.J. Kerin,[31] who joined the RIC in 1871 and was stationed in Co. Fermanagh until 1878,

27 Brewer, *The Royal Irish Constabulary*, p. 64.   28 Reed, Recollections, 1911, p. 46.   29 Another officer's diary has recently been acquired by the NLI. It belonged to County Inspector William R. Burke, who later rose to be assistant inspector general. The diary covers the period March 1865 to April 1872, when Burke was serving in Cos Wexford and Dublin. The vast majority of Burke's time was taken up with 'office duties'. He rarely investigated crime, but inspected barracks about twice a month, attended assizes, supervised drill and issued licences for firearms. His diary highlights the largely administrative role played by county inspectors. Official Diary of County Inspector William R. Burke, 1865–72 (NLI, Accession Number 5706). I would like to thank Dr Mark Radford for drawing my attention to this book and arranging to have parts of it copied.   30 The discussion below draws upon Sub Inspector E.J. Kerin's Day Book, 1874–84. I would like to thank Charles Byrne, Kerin's grandson, for allowing me to read and take notes from this book, and also for providing me with information on Kerin's subsequent career as 'more or less a professional entertainer'. Charles Byrne, Harlow, Essex, to ELM, 30 May and 20 Nov. 1991 (RIC Letters, III, 99).   31 Kerin's father, a Catholic from Co. Clare, had joined the constabulary in 1837, aged twenty-five, and retired as a first-class county inspector in 1881. It was unusual at the time for a Catholic to

when he was transferred to Co. Cork, spent the greater part of his time on what he termed 'office work'. But, at least five or six times every month he mounted his horse and set off on patrol, to inspect barracks or attend a fair, an election poll or an inquest, to be present at a petty sessions court or, even occasionally, to investigate a crime. Sometimes he inspected barracks as late as midnight; during day inspections he often put the men through drill and firing exercises. Some days he rode ten or fifteen miles; occasionally he also walked, recording in February 1875 that he had walked that day eight miles, while investigating a case of suspected infanticide. When inspections were late in the evening, he slept overnight at the barracks. Sometimes he also stayed overnight if he was leading a party searching for illicit stills.

But his duties in Fermanagh in 1874–8 seem relatively undemanding compared to his life in Cork from 1879. During 1880, for instance, there were months when he was on patrol, investigating 'outrages', attending Land League meetings and leading police parties at evictions virtually every day.[32] One day in July 1881 he patrolled, inspected barracks and pursued tinkers suspected of coining from 2.00 p.m. until nearly 3.00 a.m., covering he calculated nineteen miles. The same month he severely reprimanded a sub constable whom he found in bed at a protection hut at 11.30 a.m. and again at 2.20 p.m. the same day. The man complained that 'he was fatigued'. Given his own heavy schedule at the time, it is clear that Kerin was not impressed by this excuse.

But after the Land War patrol duties for officers seem to have resumed their more leisurely character. A newly appointed district inspector, Osborne G. de C. Baldwin, wrote from Ballinamore, Co. Leitrim, in November 1912 to a former army colleague describing his life. According to Baldwin, he was 'in charge of 800–900 sq. miles of bog & mountain, with a force of 30–40 police, in 6 stations' and was leading 'quite a jolly life'. His duties were 'not too hard as a rule', with only six day and some

reach this rank. Kerin (1851–c.1938) joined in 1871 and retired in 1899, but he never advanced beyond the rank of district inspector. He was suspended and reduced in rank on more than one occasion for getting into debt, borrowing money from a publican and signing worthless cheques. He married young and had nine children, and his career was clearly blighted by debt – an experience not uncommon among RIC officers. RIC General Register (PRO (L), HO 184/45). 32 Andrew Reed's memoirs also illustrate graphically the pressures of the Land War. In June 1881 he was transferred to Dublin to head the Crime Division. From the day of his arrival until early November 1882, that is for nearly eighteen months, he says he worked seven days a week, being absent from his office for only one day. The word Reed chose to characterize his work at this time was 'slavish'. Reed, Recollections, pp 51–2.

night inspections each month. But there was a 'good deal of patrol duty, & a certain amount of Petty Sessions and office work'. He complained about the likelihood of Home Rule, which 'if it comes … will ruin our job'. But, like so many officers, D.I. Baldwin reserved his bitterest comments for his economic circumstances. 'Money is the damndest nuisance. I am drawing in pay & [allowances] £280, which should be £300 shortly – but I have to keep a horse & man out of that – as well as paying my own board & lodging etc. – so that I don't get much good from it'. When writing this letter, Baldwin was 'laid up with a game leg, having fallen off my bicycle one dark night'.[33] The advent of the bicycle increased the mobility of the RIC, although it did not mean the end of patrolling either on foot for constables or on horseback for officers.

MAINTAINING PUBLIC ORDER: THE PEELER AS SOLDIER

Little has been said so far about the role of the police in maintaining public order, although initially the Irish constabulary was created in the 1820s and 1830s as a paramilitary force largely to take over from the army the task of suppressing widespread popular unrest. Before the Famine public order duties were especially time consuming, and even after 1850, in parts of Ulster and at times of political tension, these duties could still prove exceedingly demanding. Parties of police routinely attended markets and fairs, large sports gatherings, controversial political meetings, election polls, evictions, auctions of goods distrained in lieu of rent, sectarian marches and popular religious festivals. All had the potential to produce rioting and large-scale disorder.

When Thomas Drummond, under secretary in Dublin Castle, circulated stipendiary magistrates in March 1837 regarding the duties of the newly consolidated constabulary, he highlighted their role, not just in investigating crime, but specifically in preserving public order. The Whig administration wanted to use the police to suppress faction fighting at fairs, to prevent Orange marches, to stamp out secret societies and to end drunken popular gatherings.[34] However, as Theodore Hoppen has

33 Baldwin re-joined the army at the outbreak of war and was killed in action in January 1916, aged thirty. His letter is reproduced in Peter McGoldrick, 'My life as a 3rd class district inspector', *Proceedings of the Royal Ulster Constabulary Historical Society* (spring 2002), p. 3. 34 M.A.G. Ó Tuathaigh, *Thomas Drummond and the government of*

pointed out, in pre-Famine Ireland, for large sections of the population, 'violence occupied a recognized place within the wider world of celebration, enjoyment, and festivals'.[35] The Whigs were well aware that insisting upon the police controlling violence at mass gatherings could make the force very unpopular and provoke major clashes between police and people.[36] Nevertheless, they were committed to the creation of a more controlled and regulated society in Ireland.

Beginning in December 1835 a series of circulars was issued by Dublin Castle instructing chief constables to 'make it their business to acquire early information respecting the leaders of factions, whose movements should be narrowly watched'. In June 1836 this was followed up by a general order on the same subject from Inspector General James Shaw Kennedy. Declaring that fights were 'calculated to keep up habits of ferocity and ill-will; [and to train the population in] habits that are in total violation of law, of humanity, and good order', Shaw Kennedy announced the 'fixed determination' of the government 'to call upon the constabulary force for a persevering and uniform system of exertion to put down fights arising from whatever cause'. Chief constables were to be held responsible for anticipating fights and sub inspectors were to decide if the army was to be called upon to aid magistrates and police.[37] If there was insufficient time to organise military assistance, chief constables were to attend fairs with sufficient men to prevent a disturbance.[38] Drummond himself monitored the policing of fairs. One luckless chief constable who was unable to stop a faction fight in May 1836 received the following angry rebuke.

> This occurrence is discreditable to the police. Chief Constable
> Armstrong will state:— Why he was not on the alert several days

Ireland, 1835–41 (O'Donnell Lecture, Galway, 1977), pp 20–1; R.B. O'Brien, *Thomas Drummond, under secretary in Ireland, 1835–40: life and letters* (London, 1889), pp 245–6.   35 Hoppen, *Elections, politics, and society in Ireland*, p. 408.   36 For an example of the constabulary refusing to intervene at a fair, specifically to enforce a writ for non-payment of tithes, see Major Miller to Thomas Drummond, 27 May 1836 (NAI, CSORP 1836/1606). Sir John Harvey, inspector general of constabulary for Leinster, also voiced fears about the use of police at mass gatherings. However, they appear to have proved groundless. Between 1824 and 1844 thirty-nine people died in fights at fairs, but only five of these deaths occurred after 1835. During the same period two policemen died in clashes with faction fighters, but both deaths occurred before 1835. Palmer, *Police and protest*, pp 332, 334.   37 The military were reluctant to assist the police in curbing public disorder and, although troops were sometimes called upon, they were not used as extensively as Drummond wished. Crossman, 'Preserving the peace in Ireland: the role of military forces, 1815–45', p. 268.   38 *Minutes of Evidence taken before the Select Committee of the House of Lords, appointed to enquire into the State of Ireland, since the Year 1835, in Respect of Crime and Outrage*, iii, H.L. 1839 (486–III), xii, 107 (hereafter *Report on Crime*, iii).

previously? What force he assembled at the fair? What force he might without difficulty have assembled? How near is the nearest military station to the village? And he will further state whether forty men armed with guns, blunderbusses, and pistols could have entered the village unknown to the police if the police had been doing their duty? ... and let him well and fully understand that he is expected to use more diligence and show more intelligence in bringing these offenders to justice than he has done to prevent the exhibition, so disgraceful to the police, of a village being in the possession of a band of armed ruffians.[39]

Despite occasional failures, many observers noted a decline in faction fighting in the late 1830s, with Samuel and Anna Marie Hall proclaiming confidently 'we are mainly indebted to [the constabulary] for the extinction of [faction fights] as a national reproach'.[40] In March 1840 a questionnaire was sent by Inspector General Duncan McGregor to sub inspectors and resident magistrates in twelve counties in the south and west of Ireland seeking information on the impact of Fr Theobald Mathew's temperance crusade. Out of 46 replies received from the constabulary, 42 agreed that fighting and drunkenness at public gatherings had diminished and, in most cases, diminished markedly. However, a number of respondents made the point that faction fighting had been in decline for some time before the advent of Mathew, 'restrained by the vigilance and interposition of the constabulary'.[41]

In addition to faction fighting, Drummond also took a close interest in the policing of Orange marches. The Orange Order had been banned during 1825–8 and was banned again in 1835, while the Party Processions Act of 1832 made it an offence for anyone to attend a meeting or parade carrying a weapon or a banner or emblem calculated to provoke animosity. Circulars condemning Orange marches were issued each July by Dublin Castle to police and magistrates and were displayed in public places.[42] But the constabulary found policing Orange celebra-

39 Ibid., p. 104. 40 Mr and Mrs S.C. Hall, *Ireland: its scenery, character, &c.* (London, n.d.), i, 426. 41 Sub Inspector Leavis, Newport, Co. Tipperary, to Inspector General, March 1840 (NAI, OPMA 131/10). Whether or not there was a real decline in such disorder is difficult to determine. The method of collecting crime statistics was changed in 1832, again in 1837 and for a third time in 1844. It is not possible therefore to compare crime figures accurately during the 1830s and early 1840s. Hoppen, *Elections, politics, and society*, pp 362–3; Palmer, *Police and protest*, p. 369. 42 For examples of such circulars, see *Third Report from the Select Committee on Orange Lodges, Associations or Societies in Ireland,*

tions no easy task. Frequently there were not enough policemen available to prevent marches; the army was reluctant to become involved in clashes with Orangemen; sometimes magistrates, many of whom were members of the order themselves, would not act; and, even if the police were able to identify and summons marchers, sympathetic magistrates and juries usually threw out the charges. Orangemen were also ready to retaliate against the constabulary. Sir Frederick Stovin, inspector general for Ulster from 1834 to 1836, told the 1835 select committee on Orange lodges that if the 'police do their duty in the county of Down', where he was based, they were 'hooted and called papists'. His secretary, Chief Constable David Duff, although a Protestant, was widely known as 'Papist Duff' because of his support for the curbing of Orange parades. Both Stovin and Duff had been burned in effigy by Orangemen in Dungannon in August 1834 and Stovin himself had been shot at in front of his house during an Orange gathering in the following December. Around the same time Duff's wife had found a letter hidden in her prayer book in church, threatening both Stovin and Duff with death if they continued to obstruct Orange marches.[43]

But Drummond was determined to enforce the banning of the order. In July 1835 there were over 40 processions in the 9 counties of Ulster, with serious disturbances at 11 of them – a woman was killed in Belfast during clashes between marchers, police and soldiers. In July 1836 Drummond wrote to his mother in Scotland: 'I am very busy with arrangements for the 12th of July – the day on which the Orange demons walk. It is very difficult to allay their fiendish spirit; but we are improving.' That year Dublin Castle despatched 33 stipendiary magistrates, 34 companies of infantry and 12 cavalry units to assist the constabulary in parts of Ulster where trouble was anticipated. However, by 1839 only 5 infantry companies and 9 cavalry units were required; 28 processions occurred, but there were no serious disturbances.[44]

The use of government-appointed magistrates bypassed local pro-Orange magistrates, while the use of the army reinforced the constabulary. Stovin in his evidence in 1835 noted that 'a great many' Orangemen

H.C. 1835 (476), xvi, pp 418–22. 43 Ibid., pp 323, 325, 328–9, 339. **44** *Report from the Select Committee on Orange Lodges in Ireland*, H.C. 1835 (377), xv, pp 134–41; Return of Places Where Orange Emblems were Displayed and Processions Took Place, 12 July 1839 (NAI, CSORP 1839/103/6538); O'Brien, *Thomas Drummond*, p. 232; Ó Tuathaigh, *Thomas Drummond*, p. 21.

had been appointed to the constabulary by Orange magistrates during the 1820s. There had been instances of policemen wearing Orange lilies and refusing to assist in the identification of Orange marchers, but on the whole Stovin had confidence in his men, because, as he said, 'I know they would obey me to the letter'. Of his officers' loyalty he seemed less sure however, admitting that there were a number 'I would not trust'.[45] Chief Constable Duff was in the process of having three of his men dismissed for pro-Orange behaviour. He acknowledged that 'a great part of the Ulster constabulary' were the sons of Orangemen or had been Orangemen themselves and confessed he had been told that several men in his own district were actually lodge masters.[46] Clearly the Irish constabulary was not immune to the sectarian divisions of the period. There were certainly Orangemen in the constabulary during its early years and, indeed, there is some evidence suggesting that there were Ribbonmen as well.[47]

Some indication of what public order duties before the Famine were like for ordinary constables can be gleaned from the few surviving patrol diaries and from the evidence given by the rank-and-file before parliamentary committees investigating the police. Ulster patrol diaries of the 1830s and 1840s make it clear that the celebrations connected with 12 July were the busiest time of year for the police, even if in fact no trouble occurred.

The five men stationed at Moy barracks in Co. Tyrone were despatched to Dungannon on 11 July 1836 to be inspected at 7.00 a.m. on the 12th by the new inspector general, James Shaw Kennedy, then on a fact-finding tour. Immediately after inspection they had to walk back to Moy and spend all day and all night patrolling as there was 'a great concourse of people' in the town. But there was no Orange march and '[all] passed away quietly'. The following year, 1837, the police patrolled the town all night on the 11th and all day on the 12th. They removed an Orange arch put up across the main street, but otherwise there were no incidents. However, the diary regularly reported arrests made at fairs for fighting or drunkenness, while on 28 July 1837 a 'riot took place between parties of carters at the quay of this town … it being our duty to enterfair [*sic*] we separated the parties and got peace restored and the parties set to work'. On 19 August 1837 the Moy force patrolled all day until midnight, there 'being a great

45 *Report on Orange Lodges*, pp 341–2. 46 *Third Report on Orange Lodges*, pp 417,145–6. 47 For a suspected case of Ribbonism among the constabulary in Co. Kilkenny in 1839, see *Report on Crime*, iii, 48–9.

quantity of labourers paid in this town'.[48] With violent disorder anticipated, patrolling was obviously vital, for having policemen constantly visible on the streets was a way of forestalling outbreaks.

This, however, did not always work. At 7.00 a.m. on 23 May 1838 the
head constable and five sub constables stationed in Coleraine marched
to Garvagh to help police a fair. There was a riot at a public house called
Perry's and the police arrested a man named Hill. But, while they were
taking him to the barracks, 'the mob endeavoured to rescue him and
pelted the police with stones'. One sub constable 'received a severe blow
on the back with a stone'. The Coleraine party did not leave Garvagh till
midnight and it was 3.00 a.m. before they had covered the twenty miles
back to their own barracks, 'having formed a patrol on the way'. Later
that morning the head constable recorded in his journal: 'No parade, the
party being fatigued were allowed to rest in bed and afterwards employed
cleaning up their appointments.'[49] So it would seem that allowance was
made for lengthy and tiring duties.

Obviously small parties of constables could not deal with large-scale
disorder. An entry in the Stewartstown patrol diary dated 1 July 1844 indicates the tactics that the police employed in these circumstances.

> ... at 10 pm there came into town between 7 and 8 hundred men
> and boys with fife and drum. They had 10 drums and 8 fifes. They
> played party tunes and went through the different streets and fired
> shots from pistols. A great many were armed with blugens [*sic*] of
> which number the police identified 4 persons ... they passed away
> about 1 a.m. ... at 2 a.m. on Tuesday morning all was quiet.[50]

At large gatherings, where they were vastly outnumbered, the constabulary simply sought to identify the ringleaders or the most disorderly
elements of the crowd. Then they laid their evidence before a magistrate
who would issue a summons. Patrol diaries show that a great deal of
police time was spent serving summonses. Those breaking the law were
thus made liable to punishment without it being necessary for the police
to provoke a violent confrontation with a large crowd.

48 Patrol Diary, Moy, 1 Dec. 1833 – 30 Sept. 1839 (PRONI, D804/3). 49 Barrack Journal, Coleraine, 20 Feb.
1838–26 Apr. 1839 (TCD Library, Goulden Papers, MS 7367). 50 Patrol Diary, Stewartstown, 16 Jun. 1844–16
Mar. 1847 (PRONI, DOD548/7).

Unfortunately for the police, however, even the use of summonses did not always guarantee punishment. In Coleraine on 9 July 1838 between 9.00 and 10.00 p.m. 'a large number of persons men and boys had assembled at Killowen Street near the church with fifes and drums playing party tunes'. When Chief Constable Thomas Thornley proceeded to the spot with five men 'the mob ... dispersed on hearing of the approach of the police'. Concluding that there would be no further trouble, Thornley set off with four sub constables on 11 July to attend a fair fifteen miles away in Newtownlimavady, where disorder was anticipated, and did not return to Coleraine until 10.00 p.m. on 13 July. The town of Coleraine, with a population of around 6,000, was thus left with but one policeman, Sub Constable Gilmore, on duty during the potentially explosive day of 12 July.

Gilmore's day began early. He was awakened at 3.00 a.m. by a watchman to assist in arresting two boys who had locked themselves in an outhouse after being detected robbing a garden. At 5.00 a.m. Gilmore was informed that about 200 men and boys, 'chiefly of the lower order of society', were marching through the town with two drums and two fifes, playing party tunes like 'The Boyne Water'. This march continued for two hours until the mayor came to the barracks and then went with Gilmore to the Shambles Gate where he 'desired them to stop the music'. The Orangemen responded by dispersing quietly. But three Orange arches had been erected in the town and three public houses were displaying Orange flags. During the course of the day shots were fired from the windows of one of the pubs. Aside from noting the names of those involved in these illegal activities, there was little that Gilmore could do on his own, although he patrolled the town until 2.00 a.m., assisted after 10.00 p.m. by a night watchman. On the 16th, however, he got summonses against twenty-five people for marching and against three publicans for displaying illegal flags. But at the petty sessions court held on the 20th the charges against all the Orangemen were dismissed by four magistrates, who included the mayor, and only one of the publicans was fined a small sum.[51]

Although the under secretary in Dublin Castle and the inspector general of the constabulary issued repeated orders for the suppression of faction fights and illegal marches, barrack records show that the police in many cases were simply too thinly spread to be able to take effective

---

51 Barrack Journal, Coleraine, 20 Feb. 1838–26 Apr. 1839 (TCD Library, Goulden Papers, MS 7367).

action. This was especially so in Ulster, which was the most lightly policed of the provinces during the 1830s.[52] The fact that many local magistrates disliked the new police and failed to convict those arrested or summonsed by them made the constabulary's task even more difficult.

It wasn't only magistrates who objected to the deployment of an expensive, centrally controlled police force; the Irish constabulary was widely unpopular both before and during the Famine. Catholics regarded it as a Protestant force and resented its attempts to curb popular recreation, while during the Famine its role in policing public works' projects and escorting food convoys to ports outraged a starving population.[53] Ratepayers complained at its expense; clergymen objected when it was withdrawn by the Whigs in the late 1830s from the protection of tithe proctors; while farmers and landlords were aggrieved when during the 1840s it was used to protect the collectors of poor law rates.[54]

Unlike English borough and county police forces, the Irish constabulary was armed and thus during violent confrontations the force's last resort in order to maintain its authority was the bullet. But 'firing', as it was termed in constabulary manuals, was strictly controlled – in theory at least. The regulations governing the use of firearms were set out in Shaw Kennedy's 1837 *Rules and Regulations* and they were substantially repeated in all editions down to the last in 1911. Shaw Kennedy began with the stern warning that the policemen must 'observe the utmost forebearance that humanity combined with prudence can dictate, before incurring the awful as well as legal responsibility of firing upon the people; a measure which should never be resorted to until the very last extremity'. If firing was necessary however, 'it ought to be at the leaders of a riot, or the assailants of the police – and, if possible, with effect. Firing over the heads of mobs engaged in an illegal pursuit must not be allowed, as a harmless fire, instead of intimidating, would give confidence to the daring and the guilty'. Shaw Kennedy, as an ex-solider, indeed a Waterloo veteran, had been trained to fire in order to kill and destroy the enemy, not just to frighten them. The regulations also made clear that men were to fire only on the command of an officer, head constable or

---

52 In 1831–2 there was only one policeman for every 1,890 persons in Ulster and by 1841–2 this ratio had improved to 1:1,586. In comparison, the same figures for Leinster, the most heavily policed province, were 1:723 and 1:628. Palmer, *Police and protest*, p. 555; W.E. Vaughan and A.J. Fitzpatrick (eds), *Irish historical statistics: population, 1821–1971* (Dublin, 1978), pp 15–16. 53 Lowe, 'Policing Famine Ireland', passim. 54 Brian Griffin, 'The Irish police', pp 350–4.

sergeant; they were not to obey an order to fire given by a sheriff or magistrate. The senior policeman ordering firing was not to fire himself and firing was to cease immediately the order to stop was given, even if given by a sheriff or magistrate. Aside from defending themselves against mob violence, the police could also fire if their barracks were attacked and if there was an attempt to rescue their prisoners or to steal their arms.[55]

However, with regard to firing, the constabulary did not always follow its own strict regulations. There were two particularly notorious incidents in the 1880s, when parties of police retreating into their barracks from attacking crowds opened fire indiscriminately and without orders.

One occurred at Mitchelstown, Co. Cork, in September 1887 when two people were killed. Although publicly the chief secretary, Arthur Balfour, staunchly defended the RIC's actions, thus winning for himself the sobriquet, 'Bloody Balfour', in private he expressed an altogether different view. He seems to have had a low opinion of many constabulary officers and especially of the then inspector general, Andrew Reed. After the Mitchelstown 'Massacre', Balfour wrote to his uncle, the prime minister, Lord Salisbury, castigating the police and magistrates involved. According to Balfour, the magistrates should have prevented the meeting taking place; the police officers present did not behave 'with judgment or presence of mind'; while their men panicked and began trying to use their rifle butts as batons. Balfour ordered that a memorandum be prepared giving the police new instructions on how to repel a violent mob.[56]

The incident at Mitchelstown occurred in the wake of a royal commission that had conducted a lengthy investigation into the riots that broke out in Belfast in the summer of 1886. In terms of their death toll of thirty-two, these were the worst sectarian riots of the century. Much evidence was heard that did not reflect well upon the constabulary.[57] Their crowd control methods had simply not worked on a number of occasions; local officers did not give decisive leadership; reinforcements rushed in from

55 [Shaw Kennedy,], 1837, pp 82–5; *Standing rules and regulations*, 1911, pp 191–3. 56 Balfour to Salisbury, 21 Sept. 1887 in R.H. Williams (ed.), *The Salisbury–Balfour correspondence, 1869–92* (Cambridge, 1988), pp 207–8; L.P. Curtis, *Coercion and conciliation in Ireland, 1880–92: a study in conservative unionism* (Princeton, NJ, 1963), pp 196–200, 436–7; Virginia Crossman, *Politics, law and order in 19th-century Ireland*, pp 168–70. 57 In his memoirs, Inspector General Andrew Reed, who served in the constabulary for forty years and had had experience of Belfast riots during 1866, described duty during the 1886 riots as the 'most arduous and responsible in my whole service'. Interestingly, he did not mention the Mitchelstown incident the following year and presented a positive picture of his relations with Balfour. Reed's memoirs, though informative, tend to gloss over significant problems. Reed, Recollections, pp 81–92, 105–6.

country areas did not know the town or what they were expected to do; and, after days of facing rioters, accompanied by little sleep and irregular meals, constables were too exhausted and bewildered to follow orders.

The experience of one officer and his party highlights many of the problems of public-order duty in Belfast. Edward Mulliner was a young English-born district inspector who had served only four years in the RIC – and those in rural Co. Westmeath. He had never been to Belfast before. After a long railway journey, Mulliner and his men arrived in Belfast late in the afternoon of 8 June and were immediately despatched to Boyne Bridge to face a stone-throwing crowd. They stood around for several hours, with Mulliner apparently being reluctant to take any action against the crowd without an order from a superior officer. Finally they were sent to the Shankhill Road, but the rioting there had subsided and so they were allowed to go to their 'temporary barracks'.

We know from other evidence that country policemen hurriedly posted to Belfast in 1886 were forced to sleep in what were known as 'straw lodges' or 'straw barracks'. These were empty houses in Royal Avenue. Large numbers of police came and went at all hours and slept – if they could get any sleep – on straw laid across the floor. Their so-called 'barracks' had no chairs or tables and nor was any food provided. Men had to get food from Belfast cafés and restaurants, whenever an opportunity arose. But meals were usually rushed and sometimes men went for long periods without eating at all. Also they had to pay all their own expenses. Meal allowances were provided, but they were not paid in advance and had to be claimed later. If, after several weeks serving in Belfast, a man ran out of money, then he was forced to borrow from his colleagues or his officer in order to eat.

On the afternoon of the 9th Mulliner was ordered to Bower's Hill barracks on the Shankhill Road, but, not knowing where it was, he had to get directions from the local police. On arrival he could not find an officer to tell him what to do and, while standing outside the barracks, he and his men were heavily stoned by an angry crowd. A Catholic public house in the road was being attacked and Mulliner led his men in a number of baton charges, but failed to drive off the attackers. Finally he entered the barracks and telegraphed for reinforcements. After some delay both the resident magistrate and the inspector in charge of the district arrived and ordered all the police into the barracks. Consultations occurred between the RM, the inspector and local magistrates, but Mulliner was not privy to these and no orders resulted from them.

By now, however, the crowd had set the pub on fire. Mulliner and his men were sent out to disperse them, but again they failed. At this juncture, the Reverend Hugh Hanna appeared from among the crowd and asked the police to withdraw. The local inspector ordered them back again into the barracks. But, large numbers of policemen, rushing into the narrow hallway of the building, under showers of stones, blocked the entrance. Those caught outside panicked, turned and began firing. Constables upstairs, believing that an order to fire had been given, commenced firing out the windows. Seven people were killed, five of whom were not involved in the riot, which suggests that the police fired wildly. Mulliner admitted before the royal commission that after five hours of battling stone-throwing mobs, his men were exhausted and confused. He appears to have been confused as well, for he was jammed in the melee in the barrack hallway and did not know himself if an order to fire had been given or not. Eventually reinforcements arrived from the depot in Dublin, accompanied by three companies of soldiers. Mulliner and his weary men finally got back to their straw beds at 3.00 a.m.[58]

Yet when confronted by a large, angry, stone-throwing crowd, armed policemen were at an advantage, even if they panicked, as they clearly did at Mitchelstown in 1887 and on the Shankhill Road in 1886. Stanley Palmer calculated that between 1824 and 1844 forty-four policemen were killed in 'affrays', which occurred when the constabulary were either breaking up faction fights at fairs, supervising elections, protecting tithe collectors or trying to thwart prisoner rescues. However, the ratio of police to civilian deaths in these clashes was 1:4, which clearly demonstrates that the police wielded the more lethal power.[59]

THE PUB AND POTEEN: THE PEELER AS GAUGER

While on patrol, as well as ensuring that the roads and footpaths were kept clear, constables also devoted a good deal of their attention to the

---

58 This account is largely drawn from District Inspector Mulliner's evidence in *Belfast Riots Commission 1886, Report of the Belfast Riots Commissioners. Minutes of Evidence and Appendix* [C 4925 I], H.C. 1887, xviii, pp 245–9, 696–7. For a more comprehensive account of the riots, see also Radford, 'A trial of strength', pp 169–209.   59 Palmer, *Police and protest*, pp 332–3, 336–7. See Chapter 8 for further discussion of police death rates.

enforcement of the licensing laws. In the 1830s when the constabulary was reorganised and instructed to improve public order, it is no coincidence that new, stricter, licensing laws were introduced at the same time. Dublin Castle was convinced that Irish violence and disorder were fuelled by whiskey – some of it legally-produced, but much of it distilled illicitly. The police were a vital part of a general assault on Irish drinking practices launched by the state from the 1830s onwards.

In 1836, the year that the constabulary was reformed, the Whig government passed a major licensing act (6 & 7 Wm. IV, c.38). This act substantially increased the role of the constabulary in the policing of licensed premises. It specified that publicans required a good character certificate from their local chief constable before their licences could be renewed. In addition constables were empowered to enter licensed premises during closing hours and to eject anyone found drinking or gambling within.[60] Publicans were also prohibited from allowing illegal meetings in their houses and the display of the flags and emblems of illegal societies. These latter provisions were aimed specifically against Orange lodges. But the act's provisions were wide-ranging, taking in outdoor as well as indoor drinking. Section 5 specified that booths and tents erected by licensed retailers at fairs, races or other gatherings were to close between 6.00 p.m. and 9.00 a.m. in summer and between 3.00 p.m. and 9.00 a.m. in winter; and they were not to open at all on Sundays or public holidays. In other words, drink could not be sold out of doors during the hours of darkness or during holidays. This was a clear attempt to curb drunkenness at fairs, markets, sports meetings and popular festivals. Section 12 of the act gave the police the power to arrest any person they considered drunk in a public place. Public drunkenness, or more accurately police perception of public drunkenness, was thus criminalised. From the 1830s onwards for most Irish policemen taking home drunks, whom they knew, or arresting those they did not know or were suspicious of, formed a significant part of their duties.

But the constabulary was not only used to limit drinking on licensed premises, it was also used from the late 1850s in an attempt to stamp out

---

60 The police also took an interest in the songs being sung in pubs and at outdoor gatherings, such as fairs and markets. For an Irish-language song that occasioned much correspondence between the Cork constabulary and Dublin Castle in December 1836, see Niall Brunicardi, 'The police and the language', *Avondhu*, 3 Jan. 1991. I would like to thank Lieutenant Commander Brunicardi for sending me a copy of his article, plus copies of the ballad and related correspondence. Niall Brunicardi, Fermoy, Co. Cork, to ELM, 5 Jan. 1991 (RIC Letters, II, 58).

the illegal production and sale of whiskey. Illicit distillation had developed into a major cottage industry in Ireland during the late eighteenth century. Landlords and magistrates often turned a blind eye to this law breaking as, particularly in parts of the west and north, it enabled tenants to find the money for their rents.[61] A special police force, the Revenue Police, devoted to enforcing laws against illicit production and sale was established in 1818. However, this force became noted for its inefficiency and its corruptness.[62] In 1854 a parliamentary inquiry came out against the constabulary taking over the policing of illicit distillation.[63] Nevertheless, in 1857 this substantial task was added to the growing list of police duties.

According to constabulary regulations, still-hunting parties had to consist of at least three men, all armed with revolvers or carbines, except for one man who was to carry extra handcuffs, plus an imperial gallon measure. Parties could enter suspected premises without a warrant. If poteen was found each man in the party had to taste it and confirm that it was indeed illicit whiskey. It was to be measured and then the spirit had to be spilt on the ground.[64] Malt or grain was to be burned or thrown into the sea. If an officer was leading the party, the distilling equipment could be destroyed on the spot, but without an officer in attendance constables had to remove the still and worm to their barracks, along with one stave and two hoops from the vessels containing the wash. Illicit malt or still houses were to be 'completely destroyed'.

Seizures of stills generated a good deal of paper work. Full particulars of the seizure were to be entered into a Revenue Seizure Book, 'without erasures or interlineations', and signed by every member of the party. District inspectors were to examine the seized equipment, check that it matched the description in the seizure book and then have it destroyed in front of all the men at the barracks. Reports in duplicate and triplicate were to be written and submitted to the county inspector, the inspector general and the petty sessions court. Those convicted of illicit distillation were liable to fines ranging from £6 to £100. The RIC *Code* included a standard table of the value of poteen, its constituents

61 Elizabeth Malcolm, '*Ireland sober, Ireland free': drink and temperance in nineteenth-century Ireland* (Dublin, 1986), pp 33–7. 62 Dawson, 'Illicit distillation and the revenue police'. 63 See *Report of the Select Committee of the House of Lords ... appointed to consider ... extending the Functions of the Constabulary in Ireland to the Suppression or Prevention of Illicit Distillation*, H.L. 1854 (53), x. 64 For an ingenious scheme used by some constables to preserve spilt poteen for their own consumption, see Vere Gregory, *The House of Gregory* (Dublin, 1943), pp 187–8.

and the equipment used to produce it. On the basis of this, policemen were rewarded for successful prosecutions.[65] Some policemen appear to have enjoyed revenue duty; others clearly did not.[66]

In his memoirs Andrew Reed mentioned John Croker, who was a sub inspector in Glenties, Co. Donegal, in the early 1860s. According to Reed, he 'devoted his whole time to rearing young horses and preparing them for the turf'. One of the few of his duties that Croker actually undertook was revenue duty, but only because this allowed him to race around the countryside exercising his horses.[67]

The constable's experience of revenue duty was not always so pleasant. Writing under the pen name 'Gauger' in the *RIC Magazine* in 1912, one constable noted that the public often thought revenue duty was 'a mild sort of walking exercise indulged in on a nice bright day' by police who were in collusion with illicit distillers. Yet, while the 'tourist may gloat over the beauties of "wild Connemara", . . . the average policeman soon tires of its charms' for he needs more than 'a tuft of heather' to protect him from the often bitter weather. A typical day's revenue duty could involve a six- or seven-mile walk across bogs to a bleak mountainside. Bog holes and ponds had to be searched for hidden distilling equipment and it was not unknown for policemen to sink up to their armpits in water-logged turf. Scouts would often see the party's approach and warn the distiller who would then make off with his equipment. A lot of distilling was done at night and night searches were even more arduous than day-time ones. If the police came across an abandoned fire or an empty still house, they might have to hide and watch all night or until the distiller reappeared. If the equipment was captured in most cases it then had to be carried back to the barracks.[68] Another constable writing in the *Magazine* in 1913 described how he and his sergeant captured a still consisting of a

65 *Standing rules and regulations*, 1911, pp 372–9. 66 When serving in Dungloe and Gweedore, Co. Donegal, during the 1870s, the future inspector general of the RIC, Andrew Reed, spent a good deal of time trying to suppress illicit distillation. He found such work 'heavy' and 'severe', but still concluded: 'I enjoyed it'. Reed, Recollections, pp 19–23, 26–8. 67 Ibid., pp 23–4. Croker, who joined the constabulary in 1837, accumulated an extraordinary twenty-five 'unfavourable records' over a period of thirty years. He was transferred sixteen times, in a number of cases as punishment for offences, and reduced in rank five times. In 1865 he was reduced in rank and transferred for keeping a racehorse and getting into debt. He was finally dismissed for insubordination in 1869, aged fifty-six. Yet it is remarkable that he survived for so long with such a record of persistent offences. Nevertheless, some years after his dismissal he published a pamphlet attacking the RIC. [John Croker], *The Croker inquiry: miscarriages of justice exposed: brief pamphlet* (Dublin, 1877). For his personnel record, see RIC General Register (PRO(L), HO 184/45, pp 93 and 211). 68 *RIC Magazine*, i, 8 (June, 1912), pp 245–7.

twenty-gallon iron pot and then had to carry it, with the arm and worm, between them the four miles to their barracks. Although the constable eventually received a reward of thirty shillings, he concluded that he would never want to carry a still again even for double the amount.[69]

However, 'Gauger' acknowledged that, while there was '[h]ardship and fatigue' in still hunting, there was also a 'certain amount of excitement and absence of monotony about it – craft and cunning [had] constantly to be employed to be on equal terms with the smugglers'. 'Gauger' preferred revenue duty to the 'hum-drum work of patrolling the roads ... year in and year out'.[70] Section 1667 of the *Code*, which specified that all policemen had to taste captured poteen, seems at times to have been interpreted loosely for, writing in 1914, 'Connemara Dan' described policemen who had been out all night in cold weather taking far more than a sip for tasting purposes.[71] Articles written by policemen about still-hunting duties are usually couched in a lighthearted tone, which suggests that the men did not take it too seriously.[72] One ex-policeman suggested that, although £100 was the maximum fine for having an unlicensed still or poteen, many magistrates levied the minimum fine of £6, which distillers came to regard 'as the legal penalty for the bad luck of being caught by the police' or as 'a tax paid to the government' that made few inroads upon their profits.[73] For all concerned still-hunting and the prosecution of illicit distillers had become something of a ritualised activity.

THE PEELER AS DETECTIVE AND INTELLIGENCE AGENT

Today it is taken for granted that the intensive investigation of serious crimes, especially politically inspired crimes, and the apprehension of their perpetrators are fundamental aspects of police duties. Yet, in both Ireland and England during the nineteenth century, the role of police detectives was highly problematic.[74] The Irish constabulary initially only

69 Ibid., ii, 8 (June, 1913), p. 286. 70 Ibid., i, 8 (June, 1912), p. 247. 71 Ibid., iii, 7 (May, 1914), p. 197. 72 Samuel Waters offers an amusing account of still hunting on Inishmurray Island, off the Sligo coast, during the late 1860s, while Jeremiah Mee also found his duties on the island humorous in 1918/19. Both suggested collusion between the police, the inhabitants and the distillers – partly perhaps why, despite fifty years of policing, illicit distillation survived. Ball (ed.), *A policeman's Ireland*, pp 34–5. Gaughan, however, has edited out some of Mee's references to collusion. See Mee, *Memoirs*. 73 *Tales of the R.I.C.* (Edinburgh and London, 1922), p. 71. 74 For a more detailed account of early Irish detectives, see Elizabeth Malcolm, 'Investigating the "machinery of murder":

established a small, part-time force, that even avoided the name 'detective'. Later, detectives were used more extensively, especially in cities[75] and to investigate politically motivated crime. But full-time detective work was always confined to a very limited number of policemen.

Detective forces were first introduced in Dublin,[76] and also in London, during 1842/3, and largely devoted their energies to the pursuit of thieves and the recovery of stolen property. There was a reluctance to allow detective constables, almost all of whom were of working-class origin, to investigate serious crimes that might necessitate them questioning middle-class witnesses or suspects, especially women,[77] and working side-by-side with officers and magistrates.

Rural areas and small towns were even slower to introduce detectives. In rural Ireland investigations into serious offences were led by justices of the peace, resident magistrates and constabulary sub inspectors, assisted by crown solicitors in the lead-up to trials. These groups, who were often at odds with each other over the conduct of enquiries, were at least agreed on one thing: that is, they did not want to surrender any of their investigative powers to lowly constables employed as detectives.

Therefore the Irish constabulary did not employ detectives until 1847, when it was faced with a huge upsurge in famine-related crime, and then they were used in a very circumscribed fashion. Indeed, these men were not even called detectives initially. They were known by the euphemism, 'disposable men', reflecting the fact that they operated on a part-time basis, being 'disposed' or assigned to detective duties temporarily. The reluctance even to use the term 'detective' is indicative of Dublin Castle's anxiety that such an innovation could well encounter considerable resistance, as many equated plain-clothes detectives with spies, informers and *agent provocateurs*.

Inspector General Duncan McGregor, who established the first constabulary detective force in 1847, indicated that he had been in favour of

Irish detectives and agrarian outrage, 1847–70', *New Hibernia Review*, 6, 3 (fall, 2002), pp 73–91.   75 The activities of Belfast's detective force are described, and also criticised, at some length in *Belfast Police Commission, 1906. Appendix to Report of the Commissioners: Minutes of Evidence, Appendices and Index* (Dublin, 1907), pp 3–4, 10–15, 23–4.   76 The Dublin detective force, attached to the Dublin Metropolitan Police (DMP), was the renowned G Division. Herlihy, *The Dublin Metropolitan Police: a short history and genealogical guide*, pp 122–53; Cochrane, 'The policing of Dublin, 1830–46, pp 82–6.   77 For an examination of gender and class anxieties in England associated with detectives, and police forces in general, see Anthea Todd, 'The policeman and the lady: significant encounters in mid-Victorian fiction', *Victorian Studies*, xxvii, 4 (summer, 1984), pp 435–60.

such an initiative since his appointment in 1838, but was well aware that 'monstrous evils … are supposed, by some, to be inherent in such as body'.[78] Under his scheme, which operated until the late 1860s, four or five experienced men in each county, who were noted for their 'respectability and ingenuity in tracing crime', were to be selected and made available for detective duties should 'any heinous outrage' occur. In such a case, they would proceed 'in disguise to the scene of the crime, and endeavour by every legitimate means to discover the perpetrators'.[79] McGregor's stress on the 'respectability' of the men concerned and their use of only 'legitimate' means to investigate only a 'heinous outrage' reflects unease about the acceptability of detectives in Ireland. And, due to this unease, disposable men were not employed extensively by the constabulary during the mid nineteenth century.

Aside from the fact that police officers and magistrates resented what they perceived as the interference of detectives and that country people regarded constables in plain clothes as spies, there were serious practical limitations on detective work in rural Ireland.

An analysis of a sample of the early detectives shows that most of them were long-serving constables or head constables. Nearly half were Protestants and they had received an above average number of good service awards. Clearly the detectives selected during the 1850s and 1860s were highly reliable and loyal policemen, and thus answered the essential requirement of 'respectability'.[80] But their very success as policemen proved to be a liability when many of them were called upon to investigate rural crime in disguise. It is – somewhat ironically – a tribute to the rigorous military training that policemen underwent in the Phoenix Park Depot, and subsequently, that when these sons of small farmers were required to shed their uniforms and resume the appearance and manners of a rural labourer or small tenant farmer, or perhaps an itinerant artisan or pedlar, they proved extremely unconvincing in these roles. Critics of the constabulary complained that they made poor detectives; and even the force itself eventually conceded their shortcomings.

According to the second edition of the constabulary's *Rules and Regulations*, published in 1860, while on detective duties, disposable men

78 Notes by Colonel Duncan McGregor, 1 Jan. 1848 (NLI, Larcom Papers, MS 7617/3). 79 Ibid.; Lord de Ros to Colonel Duncan McGregor, 23 Jan. 1848 (NLI, Larcom Papers, MS 7617/4). 80 Malcolm, 'Investigating the "machinery of murder"', pp 80–3.

were to wear plain clothes; they were not to have their hair cut short in the usual police fashion; and they were not to wear moustaches as many policemen then did. Despite these attempts at disguise, however, critics claimed that detectives were easily recognisable. For instance, they walked in a distinctive way due to the influence of the army drill they had undergone when training at the depot. Before a select committee investigating Ribbonism in Co. Westmeath in 1871, one witness asserted: 'A man comes down with his hair cut short behind, and his very walk is recognised at the end of a mile upon the road.' Before the same committee, the RIC inspector general, Colonel John Stewart Wood, conceded that detectives were more effective in towns than in rural areas, for 'whenever a stranger goes into the country, the children of eight or ten years will say: "Bedad, that's a paler [peeler]"'.[81]

The failure of policemen in plain clothes to successfully investigate crime in rural Ireland[82] is certainly indicative of close-knit communities that were suspicious of strangers, but it is also a measure of just how far police service had removed men from their roots. Many detectives had been born and grew up in small farming communities, yet after their intensive training in the depot and perhaps twenty years of service in the constabulary, they could not hide the fact that they were policemen — even from children.

Irish detectives were more successful in investigating urban crime, such as burglaries, and also political crime committed in towns and cities. The RIC maintained, for instance, a body of plainclothes detectives in Belfast who appear to have proved fairly effective against the city's many petty criminals. Detectives were able to go 'undercover', convincingly, in cities in a way that was impossible in the countryside. Indeed, some of the constabulary's disposable men, who had singularly failed in investigations of rural homicides in the early 1860s, were strikingly successful when investigating Fenianism in cities like Dublin during the mid and

81 *Report of the Select Committee on Westmeath, etc. (Unlawful Combinations)*, H.C. 1871 (147), xiii, pp 625, 699.   82 For a study of a number of cases of murder during the late 1850s and early 1860s in which detectives were employed unsuccessfully, see Malcolm, 'Investigating the "machinery of murder"', pp 84–9. For other recent studies of particular homicides, which throw light on the problems of investigating such crimes in rural Ireland, see Angela Bourke *The burning of Bridget Cleary* (London, 1999); Jarlath Waldron, *Maamtrasna: the murders and the mystery* (Dublin, 1992); W.E. Vaughan, *Sin, sheep and Scotsmen: John George Adair and the Derryveagh evictions, 1861* (Belfast, 1983); Ann Murtagh, *Portrait of a Westmeath tenant community, 1879–85: the Barbaville Murder* (Maynooth Studies in Local History 25, Dublin, 1999); Frank Sweeney, *The murder of Conell Boyle, County Donegal, 1898* (Maynooth Studies in Local History 46, Dublin, 2002).

late 1860s. While they were unable to convince rural communities that they were merely farmers or labourers, they were able to persuade urban Fenian tradesmen and shopkeepers that they were supporters or sympathisers. Thus Head Constable Thomas Talbot, a Protestant from Co. Westmeath, who had failed to solve several notable murder cases in that county in the early 1860s, nevertheless was very successful in infiltrating and betraying Dublin Fenian cells during the mid 1860s.[83]

Attempts to combat Fenianism in the 1860s and again in the 1880s led to the development of various agencies within the RIC, the DMP, Dublin Castle and the Home Office in London aimed at gathering and evaluating political intelligence. This development was rather haphazard, however, being a reaction to specific threats rather than a considered, long-term strategy, and thus coordination and consistency were often lacking.[84] The RIC established a Crime Branch Special in 1882 to investigate and, if possible, prevent politically inspired crime. The DMP's long-standing G Division handled political as well as ordinary crime. But not until World War One did the RIC and the DMP set up formal mechanisms for cooperation between them as regards intelligence.

Crime Branch Special essentially consisted of a small number of men spread throughout the country in six divisions, plus Belfast. In 1890, for instance, there were forty-two men, mainly sergeants, collecting information. In theory their work was to be kept secret from even their fellow policemen, although it is hard to imagine that this was possible in barracks where men lived and worked so closely together. Special Branch men reported directly to their county inspector, who sent a confidential monthly report to Dublin Castle, which in turn synthesised county reports, in combination with relevant newspaper articles, into what were

83 Talbot took early retirement after his exploits among the Fenians, rewarded with a generous annuity, but he was murdered in 1871, probably in revenge. Malcolm, 'Investigating the "machinery of murder"', p. 90. For the failure of attempts to prosecute those responsible, see V.T.H. Delany, *Christopher Palles* (Dublin, 1960), p. 57. Isaac Butt defended the man accused of Talbot's shooting and managed to convince a jury that Talbot had died, not because of his wounds, but due to the incompetence of the surgeon attending him.   84 The long and complex story of political intelligence gathering in Ireland, and also among Irish communities abroad, will not been examined here in any detail as it has been discussed by a variety of other writers. For first-hand, if somewhat unreliable, accounts of the years before 1900, see Robert Anderson, *Sidelights on the Home Rule movement* (London, 1906); Henri Le Caron [Thomas Beach], *Twenty-five years in the secret service: the recollections of a spy* (10th ed., London, 1893; Wakefield, Yorks., 1974). For secondary accounts of the same period, see Leon Ó Brion, *Fenian fever: an Anglo-American dilemma* (New York, 1971); idem, *The prime informer: a suppressed scandal* (London, 1971); K.R.M. Short, *The dynamite war: Irish-American bombers in Victorian Britain* (Dublin, 1979); Christy Campbell, *Fenian fire: the British government plot to assassinate Queen Victoria* (London, 2002).

known as the 'Intelligence Notes', which were regularly forwarded to the chief secretary.[85]

A great deal of information was thus accumulated. But how useful much of this was is very much open to question. Experienced sergeants may well have become very knowledgeable regarding political activities in their areas and the police clerks processing data in Dublin Castle doubtless also developed a degree of expertise. But whether the busy county inspectors who filtered the local information before forwarding it to the Castle were quite so skilled is questionable.[86]

Special Branch men concentrated on 'shadowing' suspects.[87] That is they identified leading Nationalist activists in their areas and kept them under constant surveillance, in particular observing those they met with, where they travelled to and what speeches they made.[88] Typically, the whole system was rigidly structured, with suspects divided into categories, according to their perceived importance within the Nationalist movement, and with reporting procedures strictly standardised. At the same time Special Branch men also recruited and controlled spies and informers within organisations considered suspect. In 1890 Crime Branch Special employed 105 spies, who were paid anything from £3 for a specific piece of information to a regular stipend of £100 per annum. Large numbers of informers operated on a less regular basis, providing occasional intelligence for which they too were usually rewarded.[89]

From the government's point of view Crime Branch Special was expensive and its surveillance and spying activities were sensitive and controversial matters, which could easily cause embarrassment. After 1900, as the country remained relatively peaceful and the probability of Home Rule being granted increased, the branch had its funding cut by successive Tory and Liberal governments.[90] While Republicans would later revile

85 For a published selection of these notes during the lead-up to the 1916 Rising, see Brendan MacGiolla Chiolle (ed.), *Intelligence notes, 1913–16: Chief Secretary's Office, Dublin Castle* (Dublin, 1966). 86 A British army report of 1922, reflecting on the Anglo-Irish War, specifically identified the county inspectors as the weak link in the RIC's intelligence-gathering chain, largely because they received little if any guidance on how to sift information. O'Halpin, *The decline of the Union*, p. 103. 87 For the account of a parliamentary debate on 'shadowing', see *Irish Times*, 20 June 1890. 88 For a typical Special Branch report of speeches made and a riot during an election campaign in Co. Meath in January and February 1893, see Chief Secretary's Office, Crime Branch (Special), 1893 (NAI, Police and Crime Records, 1887–1917, Crime Branch Special, 6338/S). 89 RIC Crime Department, Special Branch, Divisional Lists of 'Special Men', 28 Apr. 1890 (NAI, Police and Crime Records, 1887–1917, Crime Branch Special, 501/239/S). Bridgeman, 'Policing rural Ireland', pp 229–32. See also Ian Bridgeman, 'The constabulary and the criminal justice system in nineteenth-century Ireland'. 90 W.F. Mandle, 'Sir Antony MacDonnell and Crime Branch Special' in Oliver MacDonagh and W.F. Mandle (eds), *Ireland and Irish-Australia: studies in cultural and*

the RIC as spies, the truth is that this aspect of the Irish police work was in serious decline in the years before 1916.[91]

THE PEELER AS WITNESS AND PROSECUTOR

In discussing the many duties that policemen were called upon to perform, there is a tendency to isolate the constabulary and not to portray it as merely one aspect of a far larger and more complex criminal justice system.[92] As already demonstrated in this chapter, RIC men played many roles, some of which had little to do with crime, but at the same time they were an essential element in a structure charged with arresting, prosecuting, convicting and punishing those who had breached the laws of the land. So the police worked closely with magistrates, coroners, witnesses, prosecutors, judges, juries and prison authorities. Like collecting information and patrolling, working both for and in courts was a duty most policemen would have experienced during their careers.

Policemen arrested suspects, with or without a warrant, and issued summonses; they often held prisoners awaiting trial in cells in their barracks and transported them to and from court; they arranged for bail if it had been granted by the court, and conveyed those convicted at the end of trials to prison; they were on occasion required to protect witnesses and jurors; they briefed crown solicitors or sometimes acted as prosecutors themselves; and, most importantly, they gave evidence in court. The giving of precise and detailed evidence, calculated to convince a jury, was naturally considered by the RIC authorities as crucial to the success of the force. The *Code* set out exactly what was expected of police witnesses.

> ... they should give their testimony in a manly straightforward manner, without caring or appearing to care, about the effects of it, either as to the conviction or acquittal of the accused ... They should briefly answer the questions put to them without remark

political history (London and Sydney, 1986), pp 175–94; Eunan O'Halpin, 'British Intelligence in Ireland, 1914–21' in C. Andrew and D. Dilks (eds), *The missing dimension: governments and intelligence communities* (Basingstoke, Hants., 1984), pp 55–77. 91 For contemporary official critiques of intelligence gathering, see Peter Hart (ed.), *British intelligence in Ireland, 1920–1: the final reports* (Irish Narratives, Cork, 2002). 92 For an attempt to counteract this tendency, see J.F. McEldowney, 'Policing and the administration of justice in nineteenth-century Ireland' in Clive Emsley and Barbara Weinberger (eds), *Policing Western Europe* (London, 1991), pp 18–35.

or commentary, and if cross-examined, they should carefully avoid making a disrespectful or an intemperate reply ... Any member of the Force who prevaricates, or gives partial or vindictive evidence before any court ... renders himself liable to punishment.[93]

In this extract there is an obvious emphasis upon appearance and presentation. Policemen were acting a role in the drama of a court case and their role was to appear 'manly', 'straightforward', respectful, temperate and apparently uncommitted as regards the guilt or innocence of the defendant. The *Manual* went further, instructing policemen to 'give their evidence with *perfect* [my italics] impartiality, not showing any desire to convict the prisoner' as this was the best way in which to 'make a favourable impression on the court and jury'.[94] But of course policemen were committed – as much as the prosecutor – being like him part of a system bent upon securing a conviction. Before petty sessions courts, policemen themselves often acted as prosecutors.[95] But the *Code* and the *Manual* expected that in superior courts they should play a double – even a hypocritical – role: offering evidence calculated to convict, while not 'appearing to care' one way or the other – and moreover, doing this *perfectly*.

An experienced barrister, J.A. Curran, in his memoirs expressed admiration for the RIC as witnesses.

> I have almost invariably found that the police, considering the difficulty of their position, especially in Ireland, in obtaining evidence in the various cases in which they represent the public, and the temptation to supplement testimony by imagination, discharge their duty with commendable fairness.[96]

Yet even Curran conceded that the police were 'often honestly mistaken'. Others would have agreed with the words 'often ... mistaken', but chal-

93 *Standing rules and regulations*, 1911, pp 171–2. 94 *The RIC Manual*, 1909, p. 314. In his popular police manual, Inspector General Andrew Reed warned men not to feel 'disappointed, and regard it as a slur cast upon their official reputation by the acquittal of an accused'. That such a warning was necessary suggested that policemen were by no means impartial witnesses. Andrew Reed, *The policeman's manual, intended for the use of the constables of the Royal Irish Constabulary* (2nd ed., Dublin, 1883), p. 11. For an account of the 'Parnellism and Crime' controversy of 1887–9, questioning Reed's own integrity in terms of the evidence of witnesses, see Ó Broin, *The prime informer*, pp 34, 36, 47, 60, 160–1. 95 For the regulations governing constabulary prosecutions, see *Standing rules and regulations*, 1911, pp 339–40. For Andrew Reed's account of his own experiences as a prosecutor, see Reed, *Recollections*, pp 34–5. 96 J.A. Curran, *Reminiscences of John Adye Curran, K.C.* (London, 1915), p. 75.

lenged the notion that such frequent mistakes were necessarily always honest.[97]

Fortunately for the police, however, much of their court work took place at the petty sessions level, before local magistrates and RMs, where the crimes being tried were relatively minor ones. One RM stationed in Co. Donegal before 1914 listed in his memoirs the most common cases to come before his court as: drunkenness, with or without disorderly conduct; failure to maintain a light on a donkey cart at night; allowing cattle to wander on to a public road; using obscene or threatening language to a neighbour; 'family squabbles'; illicit distillation; and breaches of the liquor licensing laws by publicans.[98] In such cases the RIC usually acted as both prosecutors and witnesses, and so a pretense of impartiality was hardly necessary. But, at this level, the police could also exercise a degree of discretion in what breaches of the laws they chose to prosecute. Head Constable Thomas Fennell, while noting that some men, 'in order to establish their efficiency were familiar figures in the witness chair in Petty Session courts', claimed that most RIC men 'were not out to harass the people by dragging them into court and causing them trouble and expense for matters which they, themselves, could as effectively settle'. In rural areas where policemen 'had practically a free hand in ordinary violations of the law', according to Fennell, they 'gave no trouble that could be avoided'.[99]

This survey of police duties, which is by no means exhaustive, highlights the fact that the constabulary was far from being a body of men intended solely to prevent or investigate breaches of the law. Policemen certainly did work closely with crown solicitors, stipendiary magistrates and judges in order to arrest, prosecute and convict those they believed responsible for crimes. Irish criminal statistics are problematical, but recent studies do strongly suggest that there was a marked decline in inter-personal violence in Ireland during the late nineteenth and early twentieth centuries and that heavy policing of the country played a role in this trend – although exactly how great a role is difficult to determine.[100]

---

97 Accusations of policemen intimidating witnesses, giving false evidence themselves or assisting in jury packing were common in the Nationalist press. For one notorious case, see Murtagh, *Portrait of a Westmeath tenant community*, pp 38–51. 98 Christopher Lynch-Robinson, *The last of the Irish R.M.s* (London, 1951), pp 103–5. 99 Fennell, however, was very critical of the operation of the criminal justice system at the level of the assize courts. Fennell, *The Royal Irish Constabulary*, pp 33, 78–88. 100 The most important recent study of the role of the police in terms of

Apprehending and successfully prosecuting those who broke the law was, however, only one aspect of police duties. The leading English historian of crime, V.A.C. Gatrell, in an outspoken 1990 article on the 'policeman-state' advised: 'Historians might profitably remind themselves that the history of crime is a grim subject, not because it is about crime, but because it is about power.'[101] When one surveys the many duties of the RIC, it is clear that the force was more about power than about crime. It was a ubiquitous, all-purpose arm of government, rigidly disciplined and strictly controlled, and intended to observe and regulate most major aspects of Irish political, economic and social life. It is thus perhaps not entirely inappropriate to borrow Gatrell's term and characterise Ireland 1822–1922 as a 'policeman-state'.

crime is Mark Finnane, 'A decline in violence in Ireland? Crime, policing and social relations, 1860–1914', *Crime, Histoire and Sociétés/Crime, History and Societies*, i, 1 (1997), pp 51–70. I would like to thank Professor Finnane for providing me with a copy of this article. For the levels and nature of post-Famine violence, see also Carolyn Conley, *Melancholy accidents: the meaning of violence in post-Famine Ireland* (Lanham, MD, 1999) and Ian O'Donnell, 'Lethal violence in Ireland', *British Journal of Criminology*, 45 (2005), pp 671–95. 101 V.A.C. Gatrell, 'Crime, authority and the policeman-state' in F.M.L. Thompson (ed.), *The Cambridge social history of Britain, 1750–1950* (Cambridge, 1990), iii, p. 246.

1 and 2 Sub Inspector Henry Denny (1837–72), IC/RIC, 1854–72

These photographs, taken in the early 1850s and early 1870s, illustrate typical officers' uniforms of the period. Despite obvious changes, uniforms continued to adhere to military models. Denny, from a Kerry Anglo-Irish family, served mainly in west Cork and resigned from the RIC shortly before his untimely death. (Photographs provided by Canon A.E. Stokes, Co. Wicklow, SI Denny's great grandson.)

3 County Inspector R.C. Rainsford (b. 1858), RIC, 1882–1920

This photograph shows Rainsford, who was from Co. Louth, as a young district inspector during the 1880s. In a career spanning nearly forty years, beginning in the Land War and ending during the Anglo-Irish War, he served in eight different counties and was county inspector of Mayo (1907–12) and Leitrim (1912–20). He is fairly typical of the career officer of this period. (Photograph provided by Air Commodore F.F. Rainsford, Hereford, C.I. Rainsford's son.)

4 Tralee RIC, c.1890

Tralee was the headquarters of the RIC in Co. Kerry and was therefore the home station of the county inspector. The county inspector at the time this picture was taken was S.A.W. Waters (1846–1936), RIC 1866–1906, Kerry 1890–6, and he is probably the officer, with sword, seated in the centre of the front row. In his memoirs Waters described Kerry as a 'very cheery place'; the people were 'hospitable'; he did a good deal of shooting and took up golf; while six of his daughters met their future husbands during his time there. But he also admitted he was 'going a bit too fast', that is, getting into debt. (Photograph provided by Patrick H. Waldron, Dublin, whose grandfather, Thomas, 1855–1917, was serving in Tralee RIC at this time.)

O HOLY CROSS UNDER THY SHADOW I WILL REST.

COMPASSIONATE
LORD JESUS,
GIVE HIM
ETERNAL
REST.

SWEET. HEART
OF
MARY,
BE HIS
SALVATION.

SWEET JESUS
have mercy on the soul of

Philip St. J. Howlett Kelleher
D.I. R.I.C. M.C.

LATE LIEUT. 4TH. LEINSTER REGT.
SHOT AT GRANARD, CO. LONGFORD.
OCTOBER 31ST. 1920. AGED 23 YEARS,

MAY God the Father refresh thee, God the Son
redeem thee, God the Holy Ghost comfort thee
May the loving Mother of Mercy and all the Saints pray
for thee May the Incarnation and Bitter Passion of
Jesus succour thee. May my fervent prayers for thy
souls speedy rest relieve thee, and may the Holy
Trinity grant my request and give thee eternal bliss.
Do thou, in return praise, bless and adore God in my
name, of my weal for time and eternity have the care,
and at the hour of my death come to my aid.   Amen

5 District Inspector Philip Kelleher (1897–1920), RIC, 1920

Kelleher, from Macroom, Co. Cork, was shot dead in October 1920 at Granard, Co.
Longford, in the hotel belonging to the Kiernan family, friends of Michael Collins.
Local rumour suggested he had been involved in the murder of Tomas MacCurtain, lord
mayor of Cork, in March. But Kelleher only joined the RIC in July. (Mass Card,
Author's collection.)

6 Sergeant Terence Donaghy (b. 1838), IC/RIC, 1858–88

Donaghy, a Catholic labourer from Co. Monaghan, joined the force in 1857, resigned and re-joined in 1858. Perhaps he had second thoughts about the job, although his only alternative seems to have been emigration. In a notebook he jotted down addresses of relatives in America and recorded the departure of his parents from Derry in 1869. (Photograph provided by F.M. Donaghy, Belfast, Sergeant Donaghy's grandson.)

7 Constable James Ferry (1858–95), RIC, 1881–95, and family, 1891

Ferry, from Co. Tyrone, joined the RIC in 1881 and served in Co. Limerick until 1888 and then in Belfast. He married Susan Duncan in 1889 and they had three children, William, pictured (b. 1891), Elizabeth (b. 1893) and James (b. 1895). Ferry died of peritonitis after being kicked in the stomach by a prisoner he was escorting – his youngest son was a month old. His widow was awarded an RIC pension of £10 per annum, plus £8 for the maintenance and education of her two sons until they reached the age of fourteen. (Photograph provided by Richard Albury, Belfast.)

8 Sergeant and three constables with carbines, c.1900

The man second from left in this photograph is probably Constable Thomas Gillan (1877–1950), RIC 1899–1922, who served mainly in Co. Sligo and Belfast. Although this group looks formidable with their carbines, plus bayonets and handcuff cases fixed to their belts, by 1900 the RIC had ceased to be an effective paramilitary force. (Photograph provided by Thomas Gillan, Co. Leitrim, Constable Gillan's son.)

9 Head Constable Patrick O'Brien (1865–1935), RIC, 1885–1917

O'Brien, then a sergeant, is on the left in the photograph taken around 1900. Cycling not only allowed men greater mobility, it helped keep them fit. O'Brien, who was an avid reader and writer, noted in his diary in 1899 that he was eating and drinking too much. He served mainly in Co. Cork and in 1907 married a woman twenty-two years his junior. They went on to have eleven children. (Photograph provided by Finbarr O'Brien, Co. Cork, HC O'Brien's son.)

10 Skibbereen RIC, 1921

This photograph, taken in September 1921, shows a mixed group of RIC men, some of whom had served in the British army. After the truce in July 1921, the RIC in west Cork could afford to relax somewhat. Perhaps that is why the photograph was taken, and includes the sergeant's son, as well as the station's pets or mascots. The constable, third from the right in the back row, is Joe Canty. (Photograph provided by May Mulqueen, Co. Limerick, Joe Canty's niece.)

11 RIC barracks, Rathmullan, Co. Donegal, *c.*1909

The barracks is the grim three-storey building on the right, with its lower windows barred, but with a seat outside on which local men often sat to chat in good weather – encapsulating the varied and contradictory roles of the police in small communities. (Postcard provided by J.V. Ballantine, Belfast.)

12 and 13 Former RIC barracks, Kinnitty and Killoughy, Co. Offaly, 1991

Some RIC barracks, such as Kinnitty, were taken over by the Garda Síochána and used throughout the twentieth century. Others, such as Killoughy were turned into private homes. The former Killoughy barracks had bars on its windows into the 1980s and the words 'Day Room' were still visible painted over the doorway of one room. (Photographs taken by Pat McKeon and provided by Jim Madden, Banagher, Co. Offaly.)

14

THE BLACK PIG TURNED SUDDENLY, AND BROUGHT ACTING-CONSTABLE FINUCAN DOWN WITH A TERRIFIC CRASH.

15

THE RENT WAR IN IRELAND: AGENT AND EVICTION PARTY CONSULTING OPERATIONS AT GLENBEIGH, COUNTY KERRY.

14 The Peeler and the Pig

This illustration, satirising the ineffectiveness of heavily armed policemen in rural Ireland, plays upon the fact that RIC men themselves were sometimes referred to in Irish as 'black pigs'. (Charles J. Kickham, *For the Old Land: a Tale of Twenty Years Ago*, Dublin, 1886, p. 45.)

15 'The Rent War in Ireland: Agent and Eviction Party Consulting Operations at Glenbeigh, Co. Kerry'

Although drawings or photographs of armed police parties helping to carry out evictions during the 1880s, like the one above, are frequently reproduced as though reflecting regular police duties, in fact most constables would not have had this experience. (*Illustrated London News*, 5 Feb. 1887, p. 150.)

16 '"Your bright smoile haunts me still", as Barney said to the Peeler when discovered making a dhrop of Poteen', 1906

This postcard, sent from Ireland to London in August 1906, demonstrates that the RIC's attempts to suppress illicit distilling had become a source of popular humour — which to some extent reflected the attitude of many policemen to this particular duty. (Postcard, Author's collection)

HOMAGE FROM THE BRAVE.

"Old Contemptible" (*to Member of the Royal Irish Constabulary*). "WELL, MATE, I HAD TO STICK IT AGAINST A PRETTY DIRTY FIGHTER, BUT THANK GOD I NEVER HAD A JOB QUITE LIKE YOURS."

17 'Homage from the Brave'

A British army officer, a veteran from 1914, greets an RIC officer in 1920. Despite its obvious uplifting message, this cartoon is far from optimistic. The veteran is uninjured after four years of war; his Irish police counterpart, on the other hand, is already wounded and apparently facing a far more dangerous enemy than the German army.

(*Punch*, 19 May 1920)

18 Motorised RIC patrol, near Kilrush, Co. Clare, Dec. 1920

Men travelling in these noisy, open vehicles were exposed to all weathers and were very
vulnerable to attack by snipers. (Photograph provided by Commander
C.E. Eckersley-Maslin (b. 1900), RIC 1920–2, Tasmania, driver of the tender.)

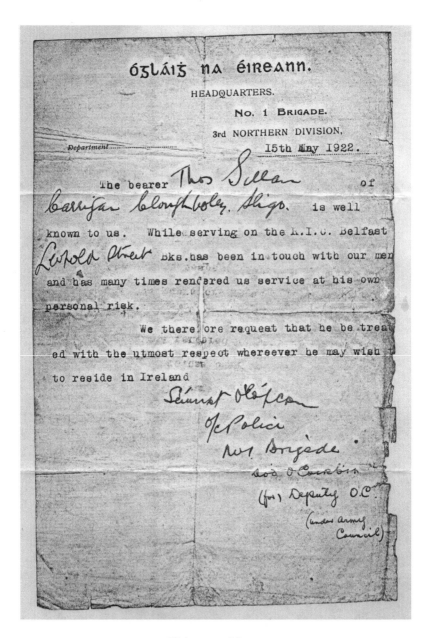

ógláiġ na éireann.

HEADQUARTERS.

No. 1 BRIGADE.

3rd NORTHERN DIVISION,

Department... 15th May 1922.

The bearer *Thos Gillan* of *Carrigan Cloughboley. Sligo.* is well known to us. While serving on the R.I.C. Belfast *Leopold Street* bks.has been in touch with our men and has many times rendered us service at his own personal risk.

We therefore request that he be treated with the utmost respect whereever he may wish to reside in Ireland

19 IRA pass, 15 May 1922

Even after the truce in July 1921 and the passage of the Treaty in January 1922, the IRA continued to attack RIC men. Some were shot, while some received letters ordering them to leave Ireland. But others, like Constable Gillan, who had provided information to republicans, were given letters guaranteeing their safety. (Letter provided by Thomas Gillan, Co. Leitrim, Constable Gillan's son.)

CHAPTER SIX

Police service and its discontents

There is no Department in His Majesty's Service so urgently in need of radical reform and re-organisation as the Royal Irish Constabulary. Founded some seventy years ago, when British ships of war were made of wood and dependent on the winds of Heaven for speed, the R.I.C. has undergone little change, and is at present in its constitution and management as antiquated and out of date as these wooden walls would be in a modern naval engagement. Any changes effected have been mere patchwork, and although various valuable suggestions have from time to time been made by Commissioners appointed by Government, yet the Headquarters' influences have always been able to resist them. The result has been doubly prejudicial to the Taxpayer, adding substantially to the expense of maintaining the Force, and at the same time insidiously sapping its efficiency ... The claims and prospects of the Constable have been consistently disregarded ...[1]

Service in the constabulary offered various benefits, which have been highlighted in earlier chapters. Most rank-and-file recruits came from small farming families in the south, west and midlands of Ireland. Work on the land was hard and unrelenting. Younger sons were essentially unskilled labourers subject to the authority of their fathers or, in some cases, their widowed mothers. Their prospects of independence, material betterment and marriage, especially after the Famine, were decidedly limited. Many emigrated, often with the encouragement of their families. Jobs in Ireland for such men outside of farming were few. The church took small numbers, as did the army; some moved to towns or cities to work as labourers or in shops; bright boys might get into teaching or the civil service. But for a century around 10,000 farmers' sons each year enjoyed secure and steady employment as policemen. As discussed already, service in the constabulary offered regular pay, allowances and a pension; food and accommodation were subsidised; policemen exercised a degree

1 [Harding], *The R.I.C.: a plea for reform*, p. 1.

of power in rural Ireland and generally commanded respect; they enjoyed
the *camaraderie* of a group, as opposed to the isolation of small farming;
and most long-serving policemen married and were able to ensure the
education of their children.

Obviously, police service held out a number of material and social
benefits for the sons of small farmers who had aspirations to better
themselves and their children. This is not to suggest, however, that policemen were happy with their lot. On the contrary, as we shall see in this
chapter, there was a great deal of discontent in the force at various times
– discontent that not only resulted in a significant number of resignations, but that even spilled over into widespread organised agitation.
Policemen were ambitious and the conditions of service often frustrated
their ambitions. So what made policemen discontented? Pay, pensions
and promotion were all major sources of grievance, and in this chapter
we shall look at each, before examining three major outbreaks of police
unrest. But, as we shall see, discontent never seriously compromised the
functioning of the RIC, at least before 1920. The rigorous discipline
imposed on policemen helped maintain loyalty, while emigration was
always available as an alternative for those who were irretrievably disaffected.

PAY AND ALLOWANCES

For both constables and inspectors police pay was regular and reliable.
This was certainly not true of the wages of labourers, whether rural or
urban, since much of their employment was seasonal. Nor was it always
true of the pay of army officers, who could be reduced to half pay when
their services were not in demand. But pay and allowances were far from
generous, and both officers and men frequently found it difficult to make
ends meet.

As we have seen, cadets regularly graduated from the depot seriously
in debt. Their aspirations to live like infantry officers entailed heavy clothing and mess bills. Once posted, they sought to maintain the life style of
a country gentlemen, but this too was expensive – and sometimes beyond
their means. In his memoirs Samuel Waters described in some detail his
life as a young sub inspector posted to Grange, Co. Sligo, during the late

1860s. He was paid the 'princely' sum of £125 a year. He lodged cheaply with the local postmistress and his father sent him a horse as a present. His mounted police orderly helped him break in the animal. Waters tells us little about his duties, which appear to have mainly involved watching suspected Fenians, putting down election riots and pursuing illicit distillers; instead he devotes far more space to accounts of his hunting, fishing, sailing and cricket matches with members of the Gore Booth family of Lissadell House, who were the leading landlords in the area. Waters attended country house parties and balls, as well as hunts, not only among the gentry of Sligo, but of Roscommon as well. He took holidays in London, where he belonged to various clubs, and on occasion he indulged heavily in gambling. Not until he was posted in 1870 to Ballyvaughan, Co. Clare, married and came under the influence of the 'sternest and most severe officer in the force', did he begin, he informs us, to 'take seriously to the work of a police officer'[2].

The life style that Waters describes during his bachelor days in Sligo would have been an expensive one. He had gotten into debt at the depot and it is probable that he spent – if not over spent – his 'princely' salary in order to maintain his comfortable life style. Marriage, while encouraging him to take his career more seriously, did not ease his financial problems, however – rather the reverse. He and his wife produced ten daughters and three sons. Providing for this large family was a hard struggle on an inspector's salary; and during the early 1890s, in desperation, Waters travelled all the way to Australia in search of what turned out to be a phantom inheritance. After his retirement in 1906, aged sixty, Waters was forced to take on further work in order to pay off his debts.[3] This he successfully did. Yet it is an interesting reflection on the lives of RIC officers that Waters was only able to finally clear himself of debt *after* he had retired from the constabulary. His case illustrates the fact that officers aspired to, and often lived, life styles that were frequently beyond their incomes.

Financial indebtedness among officers was therefore a serious problem. The RIC even found it necessary to introduce a regulation prohibiting officers from borrowing money from their men;[4] and, as we have

2 Ball (ed.), *A policeman's Ireland*, pp 26–37. 3 Ibid., pp 66, 71–3, 86–7. 4 Among the papers of Inspector General Andrew Reed is a damaged sheet containing a handwritten list of sub inspectors dismissed in 1869. Of the seven listed, two were dismissed for borrowing money from their men and one for embezzlement. Sub Inspectors

seen, in 1878 Sub Inspector Kerin was demoted for borrowing money from a publican. Over the years various officers were accused of mismanaging police funds or of outright embezzlement. In one notorious incident in Co. Tyrone in 1871, an officer, heavily in debt due to speculation in shares, resorted to bank robbery and murder in order to solve his financial problems.[5] At the time a sub inspector's pay ranged from £125 to £200 per annum, while a county inspector, who normally would have served around twenty-five years as a sub inspector, received from £270 to £300.[6]

Levels of pay were also one of the major grievances felt by constables. Pay rises were infrequent and usually took place only after much complaint and a government enquiry – and sometimes not even then. In the post-Famine period there were pay rises in 1866, 1873, 1883, 1908 and 1919. The increases in 1866 and 1873 were partly attempts to overcome high levels of resignation and difficulties in attracting suitable recruits. The 1850s and 1860s witnessed increasing prosperity in Ireland and corresponding price inflation and wage increases. Also the constabulary's duties expanded: it took over the policing of illicit distilling in the late 1850s and during the 1860s it was heavily involved in suppressing Fenianism. Understandably, all ranks became deeply discontented with pay levels that had been fixed during the Famine.

The committee that investigated the constabulary in 1866 acknowledged that the 'inadequacy of pay' was 'almost universally alleged to be the reason equally of resignations, of the falling off in the supply of recruits from a better class, and of the difficulty of obtaining recruits even from an inferior class'. The committee baulked, however, at recommending a substantial pay rise as it was not wholly convinced that this would have much of an effect in the face of growing prosperity and a 'very general' desire to emigrate. Moreover, it was concerned that the expense of the force had grown from £486,000 per annum in 1847 to over £700,000 by 1865. It therefore fixed the minimum annual salary for sub constables at £31 4s. 0d. and the maximum, after twenty years' service, at

Dismissed, 1869 (Reed Papers, Private Collection). 5 This was Sub Inspector Thomas Montgomery (1842–73), a former accountant and the son of a police officer, who joined the constabulary in 1866 and was convicted of robbing the Northern Bank in Newtownstewart, Co. Tyrone, and killing the cashier in 1871. Montgomery was hanged in Omagh in 1873. For an account of his trial, see M.M. Bodkin, *Famous Irish trials* (1918; new ed., Dublin, 1997), pp 95–103; and for his police career, see RIC General Register (PRO(L), HO 184/43, p. 236.) 6 *Report of the Commissioners appointed ... to enquire into the condition of the Civil Service in Ireland on the Royal Irish Constabulary*, [C 831], H.C. 1873, xxii, p. 5.

£42 18s. od. Constables were to receive £49 8s. od. and head constables up to £70 4s. od. But this meant that senior head constables were only receiving around half the salary of junior sub inspectors. Discontent over pay therefore continued.[7]

The 1872 inquiry, which reported in 1873, was concerned that the force was about 950 men below its establishment strength and that, despite the modest pay increases in 1866, resignations had jumped from 332 in 1867 to 704 in 1872. Men often joined the police as an alternative to emigration, but, in their first few years of service, young, unmarried constables became very aware of the rigours of policing life and of the poor pay on offer. Having chosen policing over emigration, many then changed their minds and opted for emigration over policing. As the inspector general, Sir John Stewart Wood, told the 1872 inquiry: after three or four years in the force young men tended to become restless, looking for better pay elsewhere, and after four or five years many transferred to English forces, or emigrated to America or the colonies.[8]

The committee noted that the classes from which constables mainly came, such as 'minor artisans, porters and superior farm servants', were earning from 15s. to £2 per week, while the pay of sub constables started at a mere 12s. a week and had only reached 16s. 6d. after twenty years' service. First-class head constables received only £1 9s. 6d. per week. The committee therefore revised the pay scales to match those being paid to rural labourers and artisans, so that the most junior sub constables would receive 15s. per week and the most senior head constables £2. Sub inspectors received no increase, but county inspectors were granted from £30 to £50 per annum more. These were significant rises and did much to restore police service as an attractive job option for young labourers. As we shall see, they also helped cut the rate of resignations and desertions.[9]

The 1882 inquiry, which reported in 1883, took place in response to RIC discontent in the wake of the stresses of the Land War, which will be discussed in more detail below. But the committee was sceptical of some of the claims made in regard to pay, concluding that 'the single men can, with due care and prudence, live comfortably on their pay, and in stations which are not exceptionally expensive, save some money'. Prices

---

7 *Report of the Commissioners*, 1866, pp 11,14,16. 8 *Report of the Commissioners*, 1873, p. 133; Griffin, 'The Irish police', p. 121. 9 *Report of the Commissioners*, 1873, pp 4–5; Griffin, 'The Irish police', p. 133.

had increased since 1873, but not as dramatically as during the 1860s. Moreover, the committee was concerned that a practice had arisen of over charging the RIC, especially when men were on special duty and serving outside their own districts, as many had done during the Land War. But men were paid allowances to cover expenses incurred in such cases, and so the committee rejected the suggestion that price increases justified a pay rise. At the same time it noted that single men lived free in barracks, while men with families living outside barracks had to pay rent. In most cases houses used for barracks were rented from private owners and paid for by the Treasury. The committee decided that constables should contribute towards the cost of barrack accommodation and therefore it instituted a charge of one shilling a week per man to cover the cost of the rent of barracks.[10] In general the committee took the view that the men's discontents arose from temporary problems involved in policing the Land War. It offered a smug lecture of dubious historical accuracy, assuring them that:

> History – at lease modern history – does not furnish an example of any country in which the strained relations of classes existing in Ireland during the last two or three years have been kept up for any lengthened period. When they have passed away the policeman survives, and is recognised by every man in the restored community who has anything to lose as a valuable support of peace and prosperity. The anarchy of the French Revolution – the greatest social upheaval in history – did not last more than five years, and from the hour that it terminated the French people became … excellent friends with their police. The same process has already commenced in Ireland.[11]

The committee was more impressed, however, by the claims of married men. More men were marrying after around ten years' service and 'evidence tends to show that married men with families must exercise some denial in order to live on their pay and avoid indebtedness'. While rejecting a separate pay scale for married men, the committee neverthe-

10 *Report of the Committee of Inquiry into the Royal Irish Constabulary*, [C 3577], H.C., 1883, xxxii, pp 259–60, 265. Later, some discontented constables would characterise the 1882 enquiry as having given with one hand, while taking away with another. Men were awarded a pay rise, but then much of the money was clawed back by the introduction of rent for their accommodation in barracks. *Irish News*, 2 Aug. 1907. 11 *Report of the Committee*, 1883, p. 268.

less decided to raise the wages of sub constables and constables, who had served for more than seven years and were thus qualified to marry. These men were awarded two shillings extra per week, while head constables received four shillings extra. The committee also recommended that the ban on policemen's wives working should be eased, so that they might supplement the family income.[12]

The pay rises granted by the 1866 enquiry and especially by the 1872 and 1882 enquiries appear to have dampened down discontent in the force and made police service more attractive, as rates of recruitment and retention improved markedly.[13] But by 1900 discontent was on the rise again. This led to another enquiry in 1901.[14] This enquiry, however, firmly rejected any substantial pay increases announcing that the present rates were 'sufficient to attract an excellent class of recruit ... and to maintain them ... in the condition of comfort and independence ...'[15] Policemen were naturally angered by the rejection of their pay claims, but even more galling was the tone often adopted by government enquiries. Reports frequently called into question the veracity of evidence given by constables before committees and lectured the men in a condescending manner on the advantages of their position. The 1901 report, wrote the editor of the *Constabulary Gazette* in 1907, 'produced a feeling of extreme soreness in the R.I.C.' Claiming that the force was characterised, on the one hand, by 'extravagance' in the provisions made for its officers and, on the other, by 'parsimony' in the treatment of its constables, the editor complained that:

> Time and again they [constables] had been lauded to the skies by various and sundry persons of eminence, including the Sovereign, his Viceroys, Cabinet Ministers, Judges and Magistrates: they have been told that they were the Model Police Force of the Empire, and the Saviours of Ireland – but when it came to a revision of their pay after twenty years without a change, then the door was shut with a bang ... as the years went by the Constable gradually came to realise that already isolated, his master, whom he had served long and faithfully was giving him the cold shoulder.[16]

12 Ibid., pp 261, 264. 13 In his memoirs, however, Head Constable Fennell described the 1883 reforms and other similar changes as, 'cheese-paring improvements that merely aggravated rather than allayed discontent'. Fennell, *The Royal Irish Constabulary*, p. 29. 14 *Royal Irish Constabulary. Evidence taken before the Committee of Inquiry, 1901*, [Cd 1094], H.C. 1902, xiii. 15 Quoted in [Harding], *The R.I.C.: a plea for reform*, p. 5. 16 Ibid., pp 5–6.

The 1908 rise was relatively modest, but in 1919 pay was raised substantially to reflect the massive inflation of prices that had occurred during World War One.

Related to pay was the issue of allowances. Policemen were required to wear uniforms, to have various pieces of equipment and to live in or near their barracks. Such clothing, equipment and accommodation, taken together, were costly. On occasion, as well, men were sent out of their districts on special duties and so faced additional travel and lodging expenses. Allowances were paid to offset these work-related costs. Yet policemen were expected to bear some of the financial burden themselves. What police should pay for and how much they should pay were perennial sources of controversy and discontent.

As early as 1820, even before the establishment of a national constabulary, a group of sub constables in Limerick were writing anonymously to the chief secretary, Charles Grant, complaining about the prices they were being charged for clothing and equipment. For a set of brushes three shillings was being stopped out of their pay, even though some men had brushes already. Moreover, they had been 'informed that Brushes of the same quality can be purchased in Limerick for one shilling per set'. Their memorial pointed the finger at the chief clerk in charge of procurement, accusing him of profiteering. In addition five shillings was to be stopped for ten weeks to pay for new clothing. In 1828 the new inspector general of Munster, while admitting he was ignorant of the cost of his men's uniforms, complained to Dublin Castle that they often did not fit properly and that the cloth was 'too coarse in texture'.[17] Clearly cost was not the only problem connected with uniforms. In 1820 these and other charges were to come out of wages that were only 16s. 10½d. per week. For married men, who had had to pay to move their families to Limerick, such additional expenses were especially onerous. The anonymous constables pleaded with Grant 'not to suffer them to be drove [sic] to destruction'.[18]

Among the Goulden Papers in the library of Trinity College, Dublin, are detailed accounts, covering the years 1862 to 1877, relating to the Moate police district in Co. Westmeath and to the barracks at Boyanna, which was situated within this district.[19] These provide an insight into

17 W. Miller, Clonmel, to Dublin Castle, Oct. 1828 (NAI, Outrage Papers 1828 II 584).   18 Sub Constables, Limerick, to Charles Grant, 5 Aug. 1820 (NAI, Outrage Papers 1820 II 489).   19 The following discussion is based

the pay, allowances and expenses of constables living in rural Ireland during years when there was considerable discontent over conditions of service. They also throw light on the question of whether officers 'fiddled' allowances – a claim sometimes made by the force's critics.

Boyanna was manned by one constable and from three to five sub constables. The barracks consisted of a dayroom; a 'strongroom', that is a cell; a kitchen; a dormitory for the sub constables; plus a sitting room, bedroom and office for the constable. The building had a slate roof and a chimney that 'draws well'. The site included an enclosed yard, a privy, 'convenient' water and fifteen perches of land. For all this the RIC paid £14 a year in rent to the owner. Furnishing and bedding were basic, even by late nineteenth-century standards. There were five rugs, three iron candlesticks, a tin lantern, three noticeboards and two buckets. Each man was supplied with two sheets, two blankets and one 'bolster tick'. Presumably there were also beds, tables and chairs, but these were not listed. In addition, in terms of weaponry, the barracks boasted five carbines, five batons, 100 ball cartridges and 250 percussion caps.

The barrack accounts that survive relate to the early 1870s, when, in addition to the constable in charge, Nicholas Neilan, there were four sub constables living in the building. Below is a list of their names, years of service and pay for the month of November 1873.

Constable
Nicholas Neilan (22 years)   £5 19s. 6d.

Sub constables
Michael Brady (15 years)   £4 18s. 2d.
William Daughton (7 years)   £4   9s. 8d.
Owen Reilly (4 years)   £4   9s. 8d.
James Byers (3 years)   £4   5s. 4d.

As we saw above, pay rises recommended by the 1872 enquiry had meant that the minimum monthly pay of a new sub constable was £3 and the maximum pay of a senior head constable was £8. So the men stationed at Boyanna late in 1873 fell roughly into the mid range of the constabulary pay scale.

upon Moate District Returns and Accounts, 1862–77 (Goulden Papers, TCD Library, MS 7376/5, 163, 215, 246–8, 288)

The barracks received several allowances, which in November 1873 included: for fuel and light, 11s. 4d.; for arms, 1s. 3d.; for straw, 0s. 10d.; for stationary 1s. 0d.; and for postage, nil. So the lighting and heating of the barracks were paid for, as were the men's weapons, straw – probably for their ticks or quilts – and the constable's stationary.[20] It would seem though that no letters needed to be dispatched during this month. Out of their wages each man had paid the following expenses:

Turf	1s. 3d.
Cooking	3s. 6d.
Groceries	8s. 11d.
Milk and butter	5s. 8d.
Bread	4s. 0d.
Beef	5s. 10d.
Laundry	2s. 0d.
Total	£1 11s. 2d.

So sub constables earning between 21s. and 24s. a week paid nearly 8s. in living expenses – that is about one-third of their wages. This included having their cooking and laundry done by the barrack servant, Harriet Eagney, who was illiterate and signed her account with a cross. Unfortunately, the accounts do not mention families. Sub constables Byers, Reilly and Daughton would not have been married, while Sub Constable Brady may well have been and Constable Neilan very probably was. These accounts would appear to confirm the findings of the later 1882 enquiry, which suggested that unmarried, young sub constables could live reasonably well on their wages in rural barracks, but that married men with dependent wives and children had a serious struggle to make ends meet.

In charge of the Moate district, which included the Boyanna barracks, in August 1876 was Sub Inspector William Jacques. He had under him: 61 men, including one head constable, 10 constables, 3 acting constables and 47 sub constables. Jacques was responsible for ensuring that they all received their monthly pay and allowances, which amounted to nearly £365. Jacques himself was paid some £15 per month, that is £180 per

20 For a discussion of these allowances, see *Report of Commissioners*, 1873, pp 5–7.

annum. The pay scale for sub inspectors at the time was £125 to £200 per annum, so Jacques was a fairly senior inspector.[21] In addition to his salary, he was also paid the following allowances in August 1876:

Stationary	3s. 4d.
Postage	10s. 0d.
Servant allowance	£3 15s. 0d.
Pension payment allowance	0s. 11d.
Travelling expenses	£1 0s. 3d.
Forage	£4 3s. 4d.
Extra pay	5s. 0d.
Total	£9 17s. 10d.

Thus allowances increased Jacques' income substantially: in this particular month by nearly two-thirds.

Jacques' pension payment allowance reflected the fact that, as well as being responsible for the payment of his men, he was also responsible for the payment of pensions. In his district there were ten police pensioners, who had been discharged between 1848 and 1875 and were drawing pensions amounting to £28 4s. per month. Sub inspectors, like Jacques, thus handled significant sums of money on a regular basis; in his case during the mid 1870s, around £400 every month. While pay and pensions were fixed, allowances were both variable and potentially substantial. For officers in financial difficulties there was an obvious temptation to 'fiddle' their own or their men's allowances.

More than half of Jacques' allowances went on travel and forage expenses. Policemen had to be highly mobile. Constables patrolled their rural districts or city beats on foot, and from 1883 they received boot allowances, which recognised the fact that they wore boots out relatively quickly. Officers were obliged to keep a horse, as one of their principal duties was to regularly inspect all the barracks in their districts. They were expected to provide their own horse, but were entitled to a forage

---

21 Jacques, a Protestant from Co. Kilkenny, had joined the constabulary as a sub constable in 1846, aged nineteen, rising to head constable in 1865, and had acted as a detective investigating Fenianism in 1867. He was rewarded in 1870 by being promoted into the officer corps as a sub inspector. He was assigned to detective duties again during the Land War, being 'highly commended' for his role in the 1882 Barbavilla murder case in Co. Westmeath. He retired in 1889, after a career spanning forty-three years. For his personnel record, see RIC General Register (PRO(L), HO 184/45, p. 259).

allowance. Up until 1882 they were also assigned a mounted orderly, one of whose jobs was to care for the officer's horse. In addition, they could claim for costs entailed when they were obliged to spend nights away from their homes on official duties. It was up to them, however, to report these sometimes substantial travel expenses honestly. Some probably did so, but there is evidence that many did not.

In his indiscreet memoirs Samuel Waters, who from 1892 to 1906 served successively in the senior positions of county inspector of Kerry, head of Crime Branch Special and assistant inspector general, made no attempt to hide the fact that he had at times 'fiddled' his travel allowance – and 'fiddled' it substantially. Indeed, he seemed rather proud of his ingenuity in doing so. In 1874 he was transferred to Castletown Berehaven in Co. Kerry and found himself 'particularly hard up, a condition, I regret to say, not altogether unknown to me at other times!' He was reduced to making the furniture for the small house that he and his wife rented. There was little crime in his district, except for the occasional drunken brawl at a fair or market. His closest local friend was a young doctor, George Armstrong. After a fight at one fair, Armstrong agreed to exaggerate the extent of the victim's injuries so that Waters could class the incident as a case of aggravated assault causing actual bodily harm. Armstrong's father, another doctor and also a magistrate, obligingly returned the case for trial at the assizes held in Cork. According to Waters:

> This meant a delightful trip at the public expense to Cork for George and me. How profitable it was may be guessed from the fact that we had 112 miles to drive to and from Dunmanway to catch the train to Cork, and this meant 112 ninepences to me, and the same to George, in addition to what we could save out of liberal nightly allowances in Cork ... George ... had pleasant friends in Cork who put us up free of expense, so that, after a high old time in the city, we came back with our pockets full [of] money.[22]

Waters does not tell us what the outcome of this concocted case was, nor does he show any sympathy for the defendant, who presumably did not find his trip to Cork either profitable or enjoyable.

22 Ball (ed.), *A policeman's Ireland*, pp 41–3.

But Waters' 'biggest haul', as he described it, at this time came in connection with a shipwreck. A sailing ship carrying timber from Central America was wrecked ten miles from Castletown and all the crew save two were drowned. Waters and Armstrong rushed to the scene to secure the wreck. Knowing that there was an enquiry sitting at the time in London into ship safety, Waters submitted a lengthy report on the incident as he considered the ship to have been unseaworthy. In consequence, he and Armstrong were called to London twice to give evidence. As they stayed with one of Waters' uncles, while being paid lodging and living allowances, they 'made quite a little fortune' out of their trips. In addition, policemen who protected wrecks were entitled to payment by the owners. So, as well as profiteering from his London trips, Waters was 'liberally paid by Lloyds Insurance people'.[23] Waters' memoirs demonstrate that throughout his career he sought opportunities to maximise his pay and allowances. He worked hard to support his large family and eventually rose to be an assistant inspector general of the RIC, but it is clear that he regarded it as perfectly acceptable to 'fiddle' his allowances. In this attitude presumably he reflected the culture of the constabulary officer corps generally.

Constables were aware of how officers exploited their allowances, which doubtless only added to their discontent with their own meagre provision. In his 1907 'plea for reform', the editor of the *Constabulary Gazette* railed in particular against what he termed, disparagingly, the 'ornamental department' of the RIC. Under this heading he included the officers' horses and, indeed, the whole mounted corps of the force. He noted that while an officer had to provide his own horse, he was allowed up to £50 per annum for its maintenance, plus another £45 to pay for a groom. This latter allowance had been instituted in 1883 when the system of assigning each officer a mounted orderly had been ended. In addition, officers travelling outside their districts could claim a travel allowance of nine pence per mile. Officers' horses alone cost the force £23,000 a year. Yet this was 'only one item in the enormous and altogether absurd cost of command'.[24]

That officers were at pains to look after themselves and to maintain a comfortable and undemanding life style, while they had little if any interest in the welfare of their men was a common – and justified – com-

23 Ibid., pp 43–4. 24 [Harding], *The R.I.C.: a plea for reform*, p. 8.

plaint among the rank-and-file. In his memoirs, Head Constable Thomas Fennell, who served from 1875 to 1905, recognised that officers 'differed widely': some being 'haughtily domineering', some 'exacting' and others 'petty and mean'. Nevertheless, the majority he characterised as 'reasonable'. Yet, he noted that at the various parliamentary enquiries held into the RIC the officers never backed up the men's complaints. Fennell thought that this was not only a matter of disinterest on the officers' part. Rather, the officers knew well that governments did not want to recognise discontent in the constabulary and thus it was politic for them to dismiss and disregard it.[25]

PENSIONS

A major attraction of police service was the fact that the job was pensionable. During the nineteenth century, before state old-age pensions and when few jobs carried an automatic retirement pension, this was doubtless an important consideration in the minds of those opting for a police career. One Belfast sub constable, who had joined the force in 1857, told the 1872 enquiry that he had become a policeman although the pay was poor and he could have found higher paid work elsewhere. What determined his decision was the fact that the job was pensionable, while the alternatives were not.[26] Therefore, pensions were of great concern to the rank-and-file, and attempts to reduce or restrict pensions were a source of serious discontent.

The regulations governing pensions were complex and changed substantially over time. Rather than attempting to describe them in any great detail here, this section will highlight aspects that proved especially controversial.[27]

Essentially, pensions varied according to length of service, age and rank. When the Irish constabulary was consolidated in 1836 it was decided

---

25 Fennell, *The Royal Irish Constabulary*, pp 22, 28. Others also complained that the RIC was so restricted by regulation and so cowed by government, that the police did not dare say anything that might be construed as critical by their political masters. The Nationalist MP, R. Barry O'Brien, joked that: 'It has been wisely said when in doubt "ask a policeman". The policeman in Ireland when in doubt asks the Castle.' R. Barry O'Brien, *Dublin Castle and the Irish people* (Dublin and Waterford, 1909), p. 124.   26 *Report of the Commissioners*, 1873, p. 30.   27 For a more detailed account of RIC pensions, see Griffin, 'The Irish police', pp 189–204.

that only men who had reached the age of sixty, with at least fifteen years' service, could retire voluntarily on a pension. This was fixed at two-thirds of their salary. All others less than sixty years of age wishing to retire had to be certified by a police surgeon as incapable of performing their duties due to physical or mental infirmity. In addition, they required letters from their superiors testifying to their diligent service. If they were able to satisfy the surgeon and their inspectors, then they could be permitted to retire on a pension graduated according to their length of service. For men with more than twenty years' service, their pension would equal their full salary. Similarly, any man found unfit due to injuries suffered in the course of duty was also entitled to a pension of his full salary.

These were fairly generous provisions, but they were enacted at a time when few in the force were expected to serve more than twenty years. Pension regulations were amended in 1847, 1866, 1874, 1882 and 1908, usually following the recommendations of committees of enquiry. In most cases the amendments to the original provisions involved reducing or restricting pension entitlements. For instance, in 1847 it was decided that only men serving thirty years or more should be entitled to a pension of their full salary. In 1866 further qualifications and cut backs were introduced when a committee of enquiry recommended that men joining the force after that date should still be able to retire voluntarily at sixty after at least thirty years' service, but their pension should only amount to 60 per cent of their salary, not, as previously, to their full salary.[28] In 1874, however, voluntary retirement was extended to all those who had served thirty years, regardless of age, while in 1882 it was extended further to include all those who had joined the force after 1866 and served at least twenty-five years. Men retiring after twenty years service would receive 40 per cent of their salary; after twenty-five years 60 per cent; and after thirty years 66 per cent.[29] This slight easing of the restrictions imposed in 1847 and 1866 reflected a desire – as already mentioned above in relation to pay – to attract and retain more recruits. In 1908, however, with retirements on the rise, the regulations were amended once again by another committee, which recommended that men should serve at least thirty years and be at least fifty years of age before they could retire voluntarily.

28 *Report of the Commissioners*, 1866, pp 9–11. 29 *Report of the Commissioners*, 1873, p. 7; *Report of the Committee*, 1883, p. 268.

Not surprisingly, this rather haphazard pattern of tightening, easing and then again tightening pension regulations created a good deal of discontent and anger. Men could see no real logic in the pensions policy beyond short-term financial and administrative concerns. While there was a general unhappiness about pensions, certain aspects attracted particular hostility. One was the fact that, whereas the pensions of the rank-and-file were calculated on the basis of their pay, those of the officers were based on their pay, plus allowances. This was an innovation introduced by a pensions act passed in 1874. Given, as we have seen, that officers' allowances were substantial, this change in the regulations made a significant difference to their pension rates. Understandably, the rank-and-file wanted to know why their pensions were not also calculated on the basis of pay and allowances. To this question they received no satisfactory answer.[30]

Another especial source of grievance was the requirement that men, who had served for less than thirty years, had to satisfy the RIC surgeon, based at the Phoenix Park Depot, before being permitted to retire on a pension. Eugene Le Clerc, who was appointed surgeon in 1857, told the 1872 enquiry that any man who appeared before him, suffering from a curable disease, was sent to hospital, usually Dr Steevens' Hospital in Dublin, which contained a ward reserved for policemen. If the seriousness of the disability was unclear, as in the case of rheumatism, then the man was assigned light duties for a time and had to reappear later for another examination.[31] Only in a 'very bad' case did Le Clerc recommend that a man should be pensioned immediately. The surgeon informed the enquiry that 'malingering' was a problem and that '[m]any men pretend to be seriously ill', and therefore he had a 'great deal of responsibility' in having to decide such cases. Le Clerc, who was essentially arguing for his own pay rise, not having received one since his appointment, informed the committee that he examined from 300 to 400 men applying for retirement each year, plus thirty to forty civilians applying for officer cadetships.[32]

---

30 For a letter to the *Constabulary Gazette* setting out this grievance at length, see [Harding], *The R.I.C.: a plea for reform*, pp 68–71. 31 This policy of giving unfit men light duties appears to have applied to officers as well. In his memoirs, one RM recalled working in a 'very isolated district' of Co. Donegal with 'an old D.I., who had been promoted from the ranks. He had been sent to this quiet spot, where there was very little for him to do, because he had been badly shaken in a nasty railway accident in the South and he had only a couple of years to serve before retirement on pension'. Lynch-Robinson, *The last of the Irish RMs*, pp 100–1. 32 *Report of the Commissioners*, 1873, pp 55–6.

Many of the men, on the other hand, were convinced that the surgeon was not neutral – that is judging solely on the basis of medical criteria – but rather that his decisions reflected the priorities of the force's commanders, and ultimately of government. If, for whatever reason, the government wanted to retain more experienced men in the force or boost numbers, then the surgeon rejected many applications for retirement; conversely, if government wanted to reduce the size of the force, the surgeon was more prone to approve retirements on medical grounds. The health and welfare of individual constables were not the prime considerations, as the men thought they should be.

Moreover, appearing before the surgeon was a stressful, and potentially humiliating, experience for a long-serving and conscientious constable or head constable. He could be quizzed closely about his health, lifestyle and family, and about the way he did his work. If it was felt that his disability had been self-inflicted, in particular caused by excessive alcohol consumption, then, while permitted to retire, his pension could be reduced substantially.[33] If, however, the surgeon rejected his application, there was inevitably the suggestion that he had not told the truth; that he was in fact exaggerating the extent of his disability. Head Constable Anthony Ransome of Cork City, with twenty-eight years of service, complained to the 1872 enquiry that long-serving men were being kept in the force when they were simply unfit for duty.

> Men having thirty years' service are brought up before the surgeon for medical inspection, and though broken down in constitution, they are sent into hospital for months, sent on then to the station, kept in the force and paid their salary for two years. I know men two years without doing anything for the public service.

In similar vein, a Galway sub constable complained of men remaining in the force who were 'wearing spectacles and going on sticks'.[34] But it wasn't only the men refused retirement who suffered, the significant numbers assigned to light duties had the effect of increasing the demands placed upon their comrades.

33 Griffin, 'The Irish police', pp 195–6. 34 *Report of the Commissioners*, 1873, pp 19, 41.

PROMOTION

Aside from pay and pensions, the other major source of discontent among the Irish constabulary was promotion. Men complained that it took too long for them to be promoted; that the grounds on which they were promoted were inappropriate or unfair; and many argued that the officer corps should be more open to head constables. We touched upon some of these issues in an earlier chapter, when discussing the composition of the force.

Much evidence was presented before the 1872 enquiry, by both officers and men, on the issue of promotion. This highlighted considerable tensions between the two groups. Head Constable Robert Shore, representing men from Galway, told the commissioners that, 'the officers have not the feeling towards the men that they ought to have'. By this he meant that the officers showed little interest in the welfare of their men. When asked why, Shore said he did not know.[35] Several men, however, made reference to religious differences between officers and men, implying that this created a significant barrier between the two. A Catholic head constable from Derry, James O'Connell, who had served for twenty-four years and had volunteered to fight in the Crimea, told the enquiry that as 'three quarters of the constabulary are Roman Catholics ... it would give them greater confidence if they had more Roman Catholics [in the Castle headquarters] or [as] superior officers'. A sub constable from Galway said his comrades felt that not enough Catholics were even being promoted to the rank of constable.[36] In both cases, the witnesses had volunteered these comments and the commissioners chose not to follow them up with questions. Nor in their detailed report did they make any mention of dissatisfaction about the religious composition of the force. That religious discrimination operated in the constabulary was not a problem that either Dublin Castle or the British government wanted to hear about.

On the question of promotion, many constables gave evidence suggesting that officers had too much influence over who was promoted and who was not. Promotion was supposed to be based on seniority and good service, plus an examination. But Sub Constable John Doosey from Cork city claimed that it was the officers who determined eligibility for the

35 Ibid., p. 35. 36 Ibid., pp 44, 39–40.

exam according to their own prejudices. He said that despite fourteen years' exemplary service he had not been promoted and this was because he had 'never been fortunate enough to secure the influence of an officer'. He also strongly recommended that all officers should be promoted from the ranks, as was the situation in the DMP.[37]

There were also complaints about the favouritism shown towards men who served as clerks in county inspector's offices. County inspectors chose their clerks from among constables, but this put the selected men on a fast track to promotion. After six years they could be promoted to head constable, and most of the small numbers achieving the rank of sub inspector during the early 1870s came from the ranks of these men. In effect therefore, county inspectors had considerable power to bypass the system of promotion based on seniority and merit and ensure that their own protégés rose rapidly to the top of the rank-and-file and even into the officer corps. Sub inspectors could also facilitate the promotion of favoured men. Each was entitled to appoint a mounted and a private orderly from among the sub constables. Again, it was claimed that such men, with the support of their sub inspector, tended to rise much more rapidly than men who did not work so closely with officers. Men like Doosey were clearly aggrieved by a system, supposedly fair and based on ability and length of service, that they saw was actually open to manipulation by officers who were more interested in their power and status than in the welfare of the men under their command.

Another aspect of the promotion system that many men complained of concerned rewards and punishments. These were very much at the discretion of officers and determined whether men were promoted or not. Officers regularly inspected barracks and men on parade. If, for whatever reason, a county inspector was dissatisfied with a man, he could fine him up to 10s. The sub constable or constable concerned had no appeal against this penalty, nor did the county inspector have to justify his decision in writing.[38] If a man was fined twice, an 'unfavourable record' was entered in his personnel file, which remained there no matter how long and faithfully he served thereafter. This record not only impeded promotion, but also leave. A man applying for leave had to indicate on the

---

37 Ibid., p. 24. 38 Andrew Reed abolished this practice when he was inspector general (1885–1900), saying in his memoirs that he thought it 'calculated to dishearten the men'. Reed, Recollections, 1911, pp 78–9.

form if he had any unfavourable records.[39] Equally, the men complained that 'favourable records' were also too much at the whim of officers. In 1872 one fairly junior sub inspector from Co. Clare conceded that the award of favourable records was not regulated adequately and largely reflected the personal opinions, and prejudices, of officers.[40]

Most officers vehemently opposed promotion from the ranks. It is true that officers tended to be Protestant in religion and Unionist in their politics, while the rank-and-file were strongly Catholic and generally Nationalist. It is therefore easy to see religious and political prejudices operating in this context – and they undoubtedly did. But we should not overlook the very important matter of class. This has been remarked upon before. RIC officers regarded themselves as 'gentlemen' and saw themselves as coming from a different class to their men. Promoting the sons of small farmers into the officer corps in large numbers was perceived by officers as a direct threat to their social standing. They were not prepared to treat such men as either professional or social equals and they argued that magistrates and landlords too could not possibly be expected to deal with former constables on the same footing as they dealt with 'gentlemen' officers.

One officer informed the 1872 enquiry that the men did not respect promoted officers in the way they did appointed officers. When asked to explain, he said that they were too 'familiar' with the promoted sub inspectors, sometimes continuing to call them by their first names or even by nicknames. He claimed further that most promoted men themselves 'greatly regretted' their elevation into the officer corps. They could no longer associate with their former friends among the rank-and-file, yet they were not accepted by their new colleagues among the appointed officers. When asked by the commissioners, officers who had been appointed as cadets readily admitted that they never mixed with promoted officers except when obliged to do so by their duties. In addition, suggested appointed officers, the lifestyle of an officer was much more expensive than that of a constable and the promoted men had difficulty handling the increased financial demands placed upon them. Another officer told the committee that many of the men themselves did not like to serve under sub inspectors who were promoted head constables. This was

39 *Report of the Commissioners*, 1873, p. 35. 40 Ibid., p. 68.

because such experienced men knew far better than appointed sub inspectors how the force operated, and thus they were better able to detect lapses among the rank-and-file. They tended to be more strict and harsher in terms of discipline.[41]

Despite these ingenious arguments suggesting that the men themselves opposed promotion of officers from the ranks and that such officers were unhappy with their lot, the evidence given by the rank-and-file, and also by promoted officers, was overwhelmingly in favour of the creation of an officer corps largely, if not wholly, by promotion rather than appointment. Indeed, most of the official enquiries that investigated the constabulary from the 1860s onwards tended in their reports to favour more promotion from the ranks. The 1873 report was typical, with the commissioners concluding that 'the prospect of promotion to the higher ranks would undoubtedly stimulate the men to greater efficiency, and probably attract to the service a higher class of recruits'. Yet, the officers, from the inspector general down, almost to a man, opposed a promoted officer corps. Thus, after putting forward the arguments in favour, the 1873 report abruptly backtracked in a sentence replete with social anxiety:

> The Inspector-General has, however, pointed out that, on account of age and other reasons, Head Constables are but rarely well fitted to fill the post of Sub-Inspector; and undoubtedly the change in his *social position*, and the additional expense it involves, render promotion to a different *class* less desirable to a Head Constable than increased rank and pay in his own. [my italics]

The commissioners, while leaving the door open to more promotions from the ranks, nevertheless concluded that, in the main, constables lacked both the 'social position and education' essential to fit them for command.[42] It is surely no accident that the commissioners placed 'social position' ahead of 'education'.

As we have seen, during the 1890s, it was decided that in future half of all sub, or – as they had been re-named in the early 1880s – district, inspectors would be promoted from the ranks. But, even then, such men languished as junior inspectors, with the senior positions of county

41 Ibid., pp 68, 66, 78. 42 Ibid., p. 9.

inspector and assistant or deputy inspector general being still dominated by Protestant appointed officers.[43] There was a clear gulf fixed between officers and constables, which officers fought hard to maintain and constables repeatedly challenged. In the main the gulf remained until the final years of turmoil in 1919–21, when, due to necessity, large numbers of Catholic constables and junior officers were swiftly promoted to fill the gaps left by numerous retirements, resignations and deaths among senior officers.

THE LIMERICK AGITATION, 1882

It is obvious from the above review of discontents about conditions of police service that the job had significant drawbacks. Constables were undoubtedly glad of an occupation that gave them a reliable wage and a degree of status. Their training and the force's own ethos also engrained in them a powerful sense of solidarity and loyalty. But, on the other hand, as we shall see when we come to discuss constabulary family life, many policemen were ambitious – if not for themselves personally, then certainly for their children. They were what is often popularly termed, 'an upwardly mobile class'. From the late 1860s more and more of them were marrying. They needed to provide for wives and families. Pay and allowances initially introduced in the 1830s, and revised during the Famine, which were geared towards single men were no longer adequate.

Thus, from at least the 1860s, there was simmering discontent in the force over conditions of service, and especially pay. This discontent subsequently spilt over on several occasions into organised protests and public demands for improvements. In each case discontent was brought to the boil when the RIC was called upon to police major outbreaks of public and political disorder. Pitting Irish Catholic policemen against

43 In his memoirs, Andrew Reed, who did much to encourage promotion from the ranks, nevertheless acknowledged that promotion to such senior positions was often a matter of patronage. On his arrival at the depot as a cadet in 1859 he had noted that the important position of adjutant was held by T.M. Brownrigg, the son of the then inspector general, Sir Henry Brownrigg (1858–65). When Sir Henry retired, his son was immediately promoted assistant inspector general. Subsequently, Q.J. Brownrigg served from 1853 till 1894, retiring as a county inspector, while H.G. Brownrigg, who joined the force in 1890, was a senior district inspector by 1919. Presumably these men were four generations of the same family, serving in senior positions for nearly a century. Reed, *Recollections*, pp 40–1, 13–14.

Irish Catholic Nationalists, land agitators, impoverished tenant farmers, striking trade unionists or Republican guerrillas had the effect of bringing into sharp focus for the police their conflicting loyalties. Overall it is remarkable how loyal the RIC remained in the face of sometimes intense popular hostility. But, when the men felt that their officers and the government were not reciprocating their loyalty, then their faith in their superiors, and even in themselves, faltered. Not until the Anglo-Irish War did policemen abandon or turn against the RIC in significant numbers, but in 1882 and again in 1907 groups of policemen breached regulations, defied their officers and demanded improved conditions. In 1882 their defiance was largely successful, but in 1907 it was not.

The police 'agitation'[44] of 1882, which lasted for two weeks in late July and early August, grew out of the Land War and was greeted with a good deal of sympathy among both politicians and the press. The Land War made enormous demands upon the RIC; demands that extended over more than three years. Large numbers of men were required to police Land League meetings, evictions and sales of distrained goods; constables had to protect landlords, agents and bailiffs; and they had to investigate attacks on landlords and their property. At times the police clashed with angry crowds and were abused, stoned or beaten. The RIC was vilified in particular for its role in facilitating evictions. But there is evidence that some policemen, coming as most of them did from similar small farming families to those being evicted, sympathised as much, if not more, with the evictees rather than the evictors.

Head Constable Thomas Fennell, who served in Co. Mayo during the early 1880s, claimed fifty years later in his memoirs that many RIC men 'had their eyes opened' during the Land War. They 'found themselves the chief instruments employed to keep in subjection their kith and kin in the interests of the enemies of the faith and freedom of their country'.[45] While there are reasons to question Fennell's retrospective reading of events, there is no doubt that Land War policing was difficult and often extremely unpleasant for RIC men. Dublin Castle certainly worried at times that the

---

44 This discussion draws heavily upon an article by Bill Lowe, and I have used his term 'agitation' to characterise what occurred. While the police authorities did employ the word 'mutiny', it is clear from Professor Lowe's account that the RIC did not mutiny or go on strike in 1882. While still carrying out their duties, they agitated by means of meetings and publicity for improved pay and conditions. Lowe, 'The constabulary agitation of 1882', pp 37–59. 45 Fennell, *The Royal Irish Constabulary*, p. 90.

morale of the force was being damaged by the additional burdens placed upon it.[46] These extra duties came on top of all the many routine tasks that were already required of the police. Men from the reserve and the extra force were employed extensively, but large numbers of constables from the counties also had to be sent, often at short notice, long distances, for extended periods to undertake dangerous duties.

Policemen certainly did not relish dangerous and demanding duties, but what especially angered them was the way they were treated by their superiors. If they were despatched considerable distances on special duties, they had to pay for their own transport and, if transport was hard to come by, they could be forced to walk for many hours in all weathers. Accommodation and food were frequently inadequate. Most officers did not consider it their responsibility to organise facilities for the men under their command; that obligation they left to their head constables or sergeants. But this could mean the men having to pay inflated prices for inadequate food and to sleep on straw in damp barns and derelict houses for weeks on end.

Difficult duties and poor working conditions increased the long-standing discontent felt by RIC men over pay and allowances. In fact in 1881 a vice-regal committee had recommended that policemen be compensated for extra expenses entailed in policing the Land War since 1879. But nearly twelve months later, in July 1882, this money had still not been paid and policemen were beginning to lose confidence that it would ever be forthcoming. During 1882 500 of them resigned.

In a sense the RIC authorities and the government had only themselves to blame for the agitation of 1882. The discontented policemen did not complain about their duties; they complained about their pay and allowances. Specifically they demanded a pay increase of 10s. per month, a lodging allowance for married men living outside barracks, an accommodation allowance for men serving away from their barracks, immediate payment of the promised grant approved in 1881 and improvements to pensions.[47] This was not a mutiny or even a strike. The police were not saying that they would not undertake duties in connection with the Land War; they just wanted to be better recompensed for the added demands being placed upon them. Yet the police authorities responded

---

46 E.A. Muenger, *The British military dilemma in Ireland: occupation politics, 1886–1914* (Lawrence, KS, 1991), p. 91. 47 Lowe, 'The constabulary agitation of 1882', p. 42.

very negatively at first, accusing the men of mutiny and reminding them that, in the army, the penalty for mutiny was death.

The agitation began in the William Street barracks in Limerick city, where on 28 July a group of some eighty sub constables held a meeting at which there were threats of resignation if pay, allowances and pensions were not improved. News of the event spread rapidly. The meeting was reported extensively and relatively sympathetically in the press over the next few days. On 2 August the Limerick policemen drew up a 'circular' setting out the demands listed above and telegraphed copies to hundreds of barracks around the country. Messages of support poured in; 180 men met in Cork and 160 in Belfast to endorse the Limerick circular. The press – Conservative, Liberal and Nationalist – was in rare agreement that the government had brought this problem upon itself by failing to address justified and long-standing grievances among the Irish constabulary. Questions were asked in parliament. The government was certainly alarmed, but its response was confused at first. The agitation presented it with a quandary. Ministers were aware that discontent was widespread in the RIC and the press had demonstrated that there was general public sympathy for the policemen's plight. But the Irish executive was anxious that the government should not be seen to be yielding to pressure; they feared that such a perception would make it impossible in future to maintain police discipline during times of crisis. The chief secretary, G.O. Trevelyan, informed the lord lieutenant, Earl Spencer, on 7 August that 'submission should precede redress' – but he meant submission by the RIC not by the government.[48]

On 4 August Clifford Lloyd, an English-born RM with limited Irish experience, had addressed the William Street men and he was followed the next day by the inspector general, Colonel Robert Bruce. Both Lloyd and Bruce employed threats and bullying tactics, but failed to intimidate the dissident constables. Another influential RM and a former RIC inspector, Henry Blake, took a similar line, advising Spencer in writing on 5 August that the government must not 'yield to the demands put forward' as this would give the men 'an undue sense of their power' and encourage similar tactics in the future. Blake recommended that the government call the men's bluff: let them resign and replace them with the

48 Quoted in ibid., p. 44.

army in the short term and, in the longer term, with new recruits, of which there was a plentiful supply.[49]

But the government disregarded Blake's advice, much to his annoyance, and opted for an essentially conciliatory policy. On 10 August Spencer promised the immediate appointment of a committee of enquiry into RIC grievances and the following week the government began distribution of the money approved in 1881 to recompense policemen for expenses incurred during the Land War. The committee, which reported in 1883, brought about some improvements. There were pay rises of 1s. per week for recruits and between 2s. and 4s. for long-serving men; a lodging allowance of 1s. a week was introduced for married men with at least ten years' service living outside barracks; boot money of 6d. per week was also introduced; the distance travelled in order to qualify for an allowance was reduced; policemen's wives were permitted to take up certain types of employment, although this required official approval in each case; pay stoppages during illness were done away with; men were permitted to enter public houses when off duty; and they could also fish in their leisure time. But some changes were largely cosmetic. For instance, the titles of a number of ranks were changed: sub constables became constables, constables became sergeants and sub inspectors became district inspectors. But regulations governing retirement and pensions underwent more substantive reform. A man with thirty years' service automatically became eligible for retirement, but retirements could be forced on men with twenty-five years' service. However, after twenty-five years, all retirees were entitled to the top rate of pension, which amounted to two-thirds of pay at separation. Disability pensions were introduced, as was statuary provision for the widows and orphans of serving men. The impact of these changes was soon evident with a sharp fall in resignations and, ultimately, a sharp rise in those serving until retirement.[50]

While the government largely sought to end RIC discontent with concessions, it did not altogether eschew punishment. Five of the Limerick ringleaders were dismissed from the constabulary within weeks of the ending of the agitation and several transferred. But the concessions already announced were sufficient to forestall further protests.[51] Those like Lloyd, Bruce and Blake, who feared that giving in to protest-

49 Ibid., p. 53.   50 Ibid., pp 56–8.   51 Ibid., p. 54. In his memoirs, Head Constable Fennell claimed that the rank-and-file quietly subscribed to a fund for the five dismissed constables that allowed them to immigrate to America,

ing constables would simply feed discontent and promote ill discipline, were proved to be wrong. After 1882 it was to be twenty-five years before another serious bout of unrest occurred in the RIC. Then many of the grievances were similar to those of the Land War years, but the government's reaction this time was much harsher.

THE BELFAST UNREST, 1907

By the 1890s Belfast was Ireland's largest and most industrialised city, and also probably its most bitterly divided in terms of religion and politics. The RIC had taken over Belfast policing in 1865, after the local force was criticised by a government enquiry as ineffective and sectarian.[52] But the RIC was never popular in Belfast. The city's leading businessmen, magistrates and councillors, who were overwhelmingly Protestant, resented their loss of control over policing. Ulstermen, and especially Ulster Protestants, were under-represented in the RIC and the force was perceived – correctly in fact – as largely composed of southern Catholics and directed centrally from Dublin, with little if any local input. To many northern Protestants it was a 'foreign' force. The bloody clashes between Protestants and police that occurred during the riots of 1886, discussed in Chapter 5, worsened relations that had been bad to begin with. To Unionists the RIC represented the sort of oppressive rule from Dublin that they feared would be their lot if an Irish Home Rule Bill ever got through parliament. From the outset the RIC recognised that policing Belfast raised special problems and so regulations governing the city were different in major ways from those that prevailed elsewhere.

While the RIC authorities always denied that religion played any role in appointments and promotions, with regard to Belfast they conceded that there was a policy of trying to maintain a balance between Catholics and Protestants in the city's force. A major enquiry into Belfast policing in 1906 found that there were 1,056 constables and head constables stationed in the city's twenty-six barracks, of whom 561 were Protestant and

where they all 'made good'. Such fund raising was against regulations, but the 'authorities did not interfere'. Fennell, *The Royal Irish Constabulary*, p. 29. 52 For an account of the pre-1865 Belfast police force, see Griffin, *The Bulkies*.

495 were Catholic. Given that overall at the time the RIC rank-and-file
were three-quarters Catholic, the Protestant majority in Belfast was obviously a deliberate creation. Within the city itself religion played a role in
postings. The chief clerk of the city's police commissioner told the
enquiry that more Protestants were stationed in Protestant areas and more
Catholics in Catholic parts of the city.[53]

For constables a posting to Belfast held out certain attractions. It was
RIC policy not to transfer men out of Belfast if they fulfilled their duties
satisfactorily. Even on marriage to a local woman men were allowed to
remain, unless the woman had undesirable connections: for instance, if
her family was involved in the drink trade. In 1906 half the Belfast force
was married and living in the community. Long-serving policemen with
families dreaded the upheaval and expense of a transfer and so a permanent posting was highly attractive. Policemen also valued the fact that
Belfast offered better educational and employment opportunities for their
children than did most parts of rural Ireland. The children of country
policemen, like the children of rural families generally, often had to leave
home in order to make a living. However, men were not appointed to
Belfast straight out of the depot, but only after several years' service in
the country. By that time they were presumably well aware of Belfast's
advantages. But the policy of only appointing experienced men to Belfast
reflected the fact that policing the city was not a job for 'green' recruits.[54]

If service in Belfast had clear attractions, it also carried with it major
drawbacks. Some of the discontents of the Belfast force were similar to
police grievances expressed elsewhere, but were exacerbated by conditions peculiar to the city. Pay and promotion were significant issues. The
cost of living in Belfast was higher than in rural Ireland and more men
lived outside barracks. Married men received a lodging allowance, introduced as a result of the 1882 agitation, which by 1900 was 2s. 2d. per
week, but the 1906 enquiry was told that this fell far short of rent levels
in Belfast. Constable Thomas Fennell[55] said he was paying 5s. 5d. per week

53 *Belfast Police Commission, 1906. Appendix to Report of the Commissioners. Minutes of Evidence, Appendices and Index* (Dublin,
1907), pp 2–3, 18. 54 Ibid., pp 7–8, 37, 52. 55 This is a different Thomas Fennell from the Thomas Fennell who
wrote a history and personal memoir of the RIC. This Thomas Fennell, whose service number was 49370, joined
the RIC in 1882, aged eighteen, and served until retirement in 1920. After 1896 he worked in Belfast and was promoted to the rank of sergeant in 1908. See RIC General Register (PRO(L), HO 182/26). Head Constable Thomas
Fennell, who served from 1875 to 1905 and left a memoir, had service number 41310. For his personnel record, see
Fennell, *The Royal Irish Constabulary*, pp 176–77. I would like to thank Dr Rosemary Fennell for helping me to

for a house that did not really meet his family's needs. As well as comparing themselves unfavourably to their RIC colleagues in rural areas, the Belfast men also felt that they were at a distinct disadvantage in terms of pay in comparison to the DMP – the other main urban force in the country. Whereas a head constable in Dublin received £120 per annum, his equivalent in Belfast was paid a mere £91 per annum. This differential may have made some sense fifty years earlier when Dublin was the far larger city and thus perhaps more difficult to police, but by 1900 Belfast had overtaken Dublin in terms of population. Moreover, Dublin lacked the sectarian problems that regularly made the policing of Belfast extremely hazardous.[56]

There were also particular problems connected with promotion in Belfast. Barracks were larger than in most of the rest of the country, ranging in 1906 from Ligoniel with 26 men to Mountpottinger with 113. There were thus fewer sergeants. This, combined with the fact that men served longer in Belfast, meant that opportunities for promotion were very limited. It was claimed that constables had to wait twenty-two or twenty-three years for a promotion in Belfast, whereas in other places promotion usually came after ten or twelve years. Intense competition for promotion led to bitterness and accusations of cronyism. Both Protestant and Catholic constables claimed that there was religious discrimination in promotions. Some constables won the support of local Protestant gentry, businessmen or magistrates, who lobbied on their behalf. Plainclothes men and detectives had more opportunities to distinguish themselves and thus secure promotion. So such appointments were much sought after. Senior officers were accused of patronage. When C.W. Leatham was promoted from Derry to be Belfast's chief commissioner in 1902, he brought with him several Derry constables. All were made detectives on arrival in Belfast and then swiftly promoted, ahead of longer-serving Belfast constables. This caused deep resentment in the Belfast force.[57] The failure of either the 1901 enquiry into the RIC or the 1906 enquiry into Belfast policing to institute any significant reforms suggested to many that changes were not going to come from the top, but would have to be agitated for from the bottom.

clarify this matter. Rosemary Fennell, Abingdon, to ELM, 21 April 1997 (RIC Letters, V, 213). **56** The problems of policing Belfast are discussed at length in Mark Radford, 'A trial of strength'. **57** *Belfast Police Commission, 1906*, pp 2, 27–32, 39–41, 51, 55, 60.

Police discontent came to a head in Belfast in July 1907 during a major dock strike led by Jim Larkin.[58] Policing the strike put more pressure on a force that was already seriously disaffected. Men were obliged to work longer hours and they complained that they were not properly recompensed for this. According to the regulations, policemen working more than eight hours continuously were entitled to receive one shilling extra over and above their normal pay. But from the outset of the strike the police authorities adopted a policy of relieving men shortly before they had served eight hours and then deploying them again almost immediately afterwards. Such tactics obviated the need to pay an overtime allowance. If sent to serve at some distance from their barracks, men were also denied a travel allowance in the form of tram fare. So policemen could find themselves in dangerous and exhausting situations, struggling for up to sixteen hours at a stretch to protect strike breakers from hostile dockers. For this they received no overtime pay and, indeed, were expected to expend money from their own meagre wages so as to carry out their orders.

For many Belfast policemen such treatment was unendurable. That officers, in Belfast and also in Dublin Castle, did not appreciate this is a measure of how out of touch they were with the rank-and-file. Hundreds of the city's police, amounting to nearly 80 per cent of the force, attended a number of meetings in the last week of July 1907 to air their grievances and to petition Dublin Castle for redress. They demanded in particular a pay rise and improved pension entitlements. But, under RIC regulations, no man was permitted to complain on behalf of another; nor were men allowed to sign collective letters of complaint. Thus the meetings and petitions amounted to insubordination. The editor of the *Constabulary Gazette* asserted with some justification that, when the police had a grievance, 'the Regulations induce indiscipline' for there was no adequate mechanism of redress. 'Men of high respectability and intelligence of the R.I.C.' he wrote 'ought surely to be trusted to make an application to their superior officers without fear of punishment as a consequence.'[59]

When Belfast's acting commissioner, Henry Morrell, banned meetings, many policemen ignored him; and when he attended one such meeting himself he was knocked down and eventually thrown out. The Belfast

58 Radford, 'A trial of strength', pp 149–78.   59 [Harding], *The R.I.C.: a plea for reform*, pp 2–3.

men received many telegrams from barracks around the country supporting their stand. Nationalist newspapers, traditional critics of the RIC, sympathised with their grievances, and the Unionist press, while very critical of police actions, nevertheless acknowledged that the force was seriously overworked and underpaid.

As in 1882, the RIC leadership and Dublin Castle were at first unsure how to handle the Belfast dissidents, some advocating a conciliatory approach and some a hardline one. But the uncertainty among the authorities was matched by uncertainty among the men. They desperately wanted better pay, but they did not regard themselves as strikers or mutineers; they were loyal policemen, simply demanding improved conditions of service. Having publicly aired their grievances, they did not know what further action to take. They waited for redress. This gave the authorities time to regroup and respond forcefully. Some 2,500 additional soldiers were despatched to Belfast; 11 policemen were swiftly dismissed; 203 were transferred immediately; and 70 were singled out for later transfer. That is about 30 per cent of the Belfast police force were punished for their protest. But some in Dublin Castle, including the influential under secretary, considered this far from adequate: Antony MacDonnell had wanted every man who attended an unauthorised meeting either sacked or transferred. The inspector general, Neville Chamberlain, opposed this, however, as it was simply not feasible without major disruption to the city's policing.

But some of MacDonnell's other suggestions for changes to the Belfast RIC were implemented. They formed the basis of a minute produced by the inspector general. It instructed that 'inefficient' officers and men were to be weeded out and that Belfast policemen were to be transferred on a more regular basis, that is at least every five to seven years. So, on top of the large-scale transfers of 1907, the whole of the Belfast force was to be progressively removed and redeployed. More district inspectors were to be appointed in Belfast and they were instructed to keep a much closer eye on their men with more frequent and intensive inspections. Dublin Castle clearly blamed Belfast officers for not being aware of the depth of discontent and for not forestalling their men's public protests.

Essentially, the authorities' response to the 1907 police protest in Belfast was punitive rather than conciliatory. Men were sacked, transferred or brought under stricter control. Their grievances about pay, allowances, pensions and promotion were not seriously addressed. Discontent festered; resignations rose and recruitment slumped. Whereas resignations were running at around 500 per annum in 1882, during police unrest towards the end of the Land War, they declined rapidly thereafter and were in double figures for much of the 1890s. But a steady rise set in from 1907, and by 1913 resignations had climbed back to the levels of the troubled years of the early 1880s. At the same time it was also becoming harder to attract recruits. By 1914, with Home Rule apparently imminent, which would inevitably entail major changes to policing, the attractions of RIC service were far less apparent than they had been twenty years earlier.

THE LISTOWEL, MUTINY, 1920

While what happened among the constabulary in Limerick in 1882 and in Belfast in 1907 cannot be termed mutinies, what happened at Listowel, Co. Kerry, in 1920 certainly can. The earlier outbreaks of unrest reflected discontent with conditions of service, in particular with pay, but the acts of the constables in Listowel, although ostensibly a protest about transfers, were in fact a rejection of the way the British government was using the RIC in its war against the IRA. Only fourteen men were involved, unlike the hundreds who took part in the events of 1882 and 1907, but in Listowel the men defied direct orders, appealed for IRA support and some of them, after receiving no satisfactory response to their complaints, deserted their barracks. In 1920 the authorities' reactions were also different. While a handful of men were dismissed or transferred in 1882 and a large number in 1907, the mutineers of 1920, despite their more serious offences, were not punished. The differences between the events of 1920 and those of 1882 and 1907 reflect, on the one hand, the politicisation of disaffection among the RIC during the Anglo-Irish War and, on the other, the government's weakening grip, not only on the police, but on the country as a whole.

Unlike the outbreaks of 1882 and 1907, a detailed, first-hand account of the RIC mutiny at Listowel survives, provided by its leader, Constable Jeremiah Mee. At the time, Mee wrote a partial account, the accuracy of which was challenged by some of the officers present, but shortly before his death in 1953 he published several articles about his experiences and also wrote an autobiography. The latter, in a heavily edited form, was finally published in 1975. Before examining the mutiny in some detail, it is worth describing Mee's ten-year career as a policeman, since this tells us something about the man and gives an insight into the nature of rural policing in the second decade of the twentieth century.

Mee, as we saw in previous chapters, was a small farmer's son from north Co. Galway, who joined the RIC in 1910. After six months' training at the depot, he was posted early in 1911 to a small, rural barracks at Kesh in Co. Sligo. He enjoyed his time at Kesh and received the news of his transfer in August 1913 to Collooney, also in Sligo, 'with a heavy heart'. In summing up policing at Kesh, he wrote:

> In my two and a half years at Kesh I had practically forgotten that I was a policeman and I had learned much that many policemen miss. It was true that our sergeant had broken every regulation of the police code but he substituted instead the finest code of all, a Christian outlook towards his fellow men. In the barracks all were treated as equals and this created a wonderful atmosphere. During the two and a half years not one prisoner had entered our lock-up and that at a time when intoxicating drink was within the reach of all. Being the driver of an unlighted vehicle at night or the owner of a cow which wandered on the public road were the only crimes which occurred in the area. This surely was a good record and speaks volumes for the people of that district.[60]

Mee's account of the peaceful, undemanding life at Kesh barracks is fairly typical of the experiences of many policemen in rural Ireland in the years before 1914.

Collooney's barracks was in a town and was the headquarters of a district inspector. Thus, instead of the three or four men who had lived in Kesh barracks, it housed more than a dozen men. Mee did not enjoy the more formal and regimented life there, although his duties were hardly onerous, as there had been no 'serious crime' in the town or district for some twenty years. But the bad-tempered head constable in charge of the barracks, who was not on speaking terms with the novice

60 Gaughan (ed.), *Memoirs of Constable Jeremiah Mee*, p. 31.

district inspector, insisted on rigid adherence to the regulations. Mee quickly applied for a transfer to another small Sligo rural barracks, this time at Geevagh, and there again he found a relaxing life more to his taste.[61] But, after less than eighteen months, he was on the move once more, being transferred to Ballintogher, where he spent nearly three years. He largely enjoyed this posting as well and made life-long friendships with three local national school teachers. But with the outbreak of war in August 1914, Mee, who at age twenty-five was very fit and the only single man at the barracks, came under pressure from his district inspector to volunteer for the army. Mee took considerable interest in the progress of the fighting and was not opposed to Irishmen volunteering for the British army, but he had no wish to do so himself. He knew he could not be forced to join by his inspector, but realised that his refusal would be noted as a black mark on his record.[62]

In June 1918 he was transferred to Grange in north Sligo, before in July 1919 being posted out of Sligo altogether, to Listowel in Co. Kerry. At Grange he began to notice a more reticent attitude towards the RIC; the people were not openly hostile, but there were not the same relaxed relations that he had experienced in his previous rural postings. Shortly after arriving at Grange, he alienated his superiors further by joining the Police Union, that is the Irish branch of the National Union of Police and Prison Officers, which had been established by Sergeant Thomas J. McElligott of Trim, Co. Meath, earlier in the year. We shall discuss this union later, but Dublin Castle refused to recognise it and McElligott was forced to resign from the RIC in May 1919, after which the union went into swift decline.[63]

Mee's account of his career prior to 1920 portrays a policeman who largely enjoyed his work and had developed some firm friendships with fellow constables and even with several of his sergeants. He had little respect for the petty-fogging regulations of the constabulary's *Code* and officers he clearly regarded as largely useless and likely only to cause trouble. He was also obviously concerned about the deteriorating political situation in 1918 and 1919 and the impact this was having on the RIC.

61 Ibid., pp 32–7. 62 Ibid., pp 44–6. 63 Ibid., pp 54, 62–3, 243–75. I would like to thank Gerard McElligott for allowing me access to his father's papers, which, as well as correspondence, include lists of members of the Police Union numbering about 4,300. Sergeant McElligott went on to head an organisation for resigned and dismissed RIC and DMP men, which lobbied the Free State government for financial assistance in the 1930s. Copies of these papers are now in the Garda Síochána Museum, Dublin Castle. Gerard McElligott, Castleknock, Dublin 15, to ELM, 19 July 1990 (RIC Letters, I, 40)

When he was posted south in July 1919 away from the relative calm of Sligo, he even contemplated resignation. He enjoyed life outside his job as well, participating in a variety of sports, cycling regularly for pleasure and, whenever he could, attending race meetings, parties and dances.

The young constable who Mee presents us with in his memoirs seems to have been somewhat on the lazy side, not especially ambitious in terms of his career, rather more keen in fact on making friends and just having a good time. He certainly took an interest in politics and his sympathies were Nationalist, but he also felt a strong sense of loyalty to his fellow constables. Mee was hardly a dedicated policeman, but at the same time he did not appear a likely mutineer either. His account of his career before 1919 suggests a lively, young, unattached man in his twenties, enjoying for the first time the opportunities for pleasure that life away from home, with time on his hands and some money in his pocket, afforded. In this respect, he was probably a fairly typical young constable. So why, after less than twelve months in Listowel, did Mee lead the only mutiny in the long history of the Irish constabulary?

Listowel barracks was a district headquarters and so it was the base of a district inspector, as well as housing a head constable with between 16 and 18 sergeants and constables. It was not the sort of small, quiet rural barracks that Mee obviously preferred. Yet, at the time of Mee's arrival in July 1919, the area was still relatively peaceful. Mee noted, for instance, that day patrols of RIC men still went out without arms, and his first major job was connected with a long-standing dispute over land. He and three other constables spent four months in late 1919 on protection duty at Rattoo House, eight miles from Listowel, where the landlord's agent had been wounded in a recent shooting.[64]

But the situation deteriorated markedly early in 1920. While his time at Rattoo had been largely untroubled, two months after his departure, in March 1920, the IRA attacked the land agent in a Rathkeale hotel killing one of his RIC escorts and seriously wounding the other. Mee had worked at Rattoo with the 'inoffensive' sergeant who was killed. The police at Listowel were 'horrifed' by the attack, as they regarded protection duty as having 'nothing whatsoever to do with politics'. Men 'who had hitherto been indifferent or even ambivalent with regard to the polit-

64 Gaughan (ed.), *Memoirs of Constable Jeremiah Mee*, pp 69–73.

ical situation now hardened their hearts against Sinn Fein and the I.R.A.' At the same time public hostility towards the RIC was growing and the police were being effectively ostracised.[65] Mee praised the efforts of his district inspector and head constable to maintain the 'uneasy peace' in the Listowel district by not reacting in an aggressive manner.

Yet, while some developments during 1919/20 were tending to cement RIC loyalty, others had the very opposite effect, undermining RIC morale and the men's faith in their superiors and the government. Mee singled out for mention the replacement in January 1920 of Sir Joseph Byrne as inspector general by Sir Thomas Smith. Byrne, an experienced soldier, had filled the post since August 1916. He was the first Catholic appointed to head the RIC and was popular among the rank-and-file. His abrupt departure and replacement by Smith, who had joined the RIC as a cadet in 1882 and was widely regarded as an Ulster Unionist sympathiser, caused considerable unease in the force. A large number of delegates from the RIC in Leinster met in the depot on 11 January 1920 to protest at Byrne's dismissal. As Mee put it: 'With the Republican army striking at our front and a "loyal" Northerner at our back we now found ourselves in a most unenviable position'.[66]

It was in January 1920 too that Black-and-Tans began being posted as reinforcements to RIC barracks. In March two were assigned to Listowel and soon after transferred, in charge of a sergeant and with a young RIC constable, to a police hut at Newtownsandes (now Moyvane). Mee was despatched to join them in May. The small hut, which had been in existence since the Land War and was situated in an untilled field, was extremely uncomfortable, being hot in summer and cold in winter. The Black-and-Tans, when not sleeping, spent most of their time drinking and on one occasion amused themselves by shooting up the sergeant's bedroom-cum-office. Finding the situation unbearable, Mee and the other constable feigned illness and were sent to the Listowel workhouse hospital. The remaining constables at Listowel barracks refused to replace them and, as a consequence, the hut had to be abandoned. It was burnt down shortly afterwards by the IRA. Mee claimed that this act of defiance 'proved to the R.I.C. at Listowel that their strength lay in unity' and prepared them for the crisis that they were to face in June.[67]

65 Ibid., pp 73–5. 66 Ibid., p. 79. 67 Ibid., pp 86–91.

On 16 June orders arrived at the barracks for the immediate transfer of fourteen constables to various isolated stations in parts of south and west Kerry. Only three men were to remain, aside from officers, and the barracks was to be taken over the following day by the military. This reflected a new policy of strengthening larger barracks with soldiers and reinforcing some smaller and vulnerable barracks with more policemen. That night the fourteen constables met in the barrack dayroom and determined to resist their transfers. Some wanted to resign, others to appeal to their superiors. Mee, who in a sense was the most junior of the group having been at Listowel for less than a year, portrays himself as putting their problems into a political context. Rather than just focusing on the difficulties and dangers of the transfers, Mee argued that the men had to look to the longer term and 'select whether we are going to be on the British side or the Irish side, since neutrality will be out of the question'. But then he went on to point out that whichever side won, the RIC would suffer. Therefore it was best that they made 'a stand against being involved in the conflict'. His fellow constables agreed that they should refuse to hand over the barracks to the military and, at the same time, they elected Mee as their spokesman. Mee then telephoned the county inspector at Tralee and informed him of their decision.[68]

Early the following day the county inspector arrived and tried to persuade the men to accept their transfers, but without success. On the morning of the 19th several vehicles appeared in front of the barracks carrying large numbers of soldiers, plus, not only the county inspector, but also General Sir Henry Tudor, who the previous month had been appointed police advisor to the viceroy, Colonel G.B.F. Smyth, the divisional police commissioner for Munster and Colonel W.S.B. Leatham, the divisional commissioner for Dublin. What happened between the constables and their senior officers in the dayroom, and in particular what Smyth exactly said to them, is a matter of some controversy. Mee claimed Smyth told them that martial law was shortly to be declared, which would allow the RIC to shoot suspicious characters on sight, and that if mistakes were made and innocent people killed, then 'this cannot be helped ... The more you shoot the better I will like you, and I assure you that no policeman will get into trouble for shooting any man'. He also

68 Ibid., pp 94–5.

suggested that there was a covert policy in existence of killing Sinn Féin prisoners. After Mee's account was reported in the press, Smyth denied its accuracy, but when he was assassinated by the IRA a month later in Cork, it was generally assumed that this was in retaliation for his speech to the constables in Listowel barracks.[69]

Neither Smyth's bluster nor Tudor's attempts at reasoning could persuade the constables to accept their transfers. After the officers left on the 19th, no further action was taken and the constables were simply left in control of the building in what Mee termed a 'state of passive mutiny'. With the support of three others, Mee then secretly sent an account of the events at Listowel, via a local priest, to the IRA's headquarters in Dublin. But much to his disgust the IRA did not respond. It is worth noting that Mee did not inform the majority of his comrades that he had made contact with the IRA; he said he feared that his actions might 'be construed as treachery'. If Mee did not trust his followers, it appears that they soon lost confidence in him as well. After three weeks with no action being taken by either the RIC or the IRA, Mee wrote that they were beginning to feel 'as isolated as lepers in a leper-colony'.[70] He suggested that they leave the barracks and return to their homes, thus publicly severing their links with the RIC – in other words, that they desert. But only four of the thirteen other constables were prepared to follow him in this drastic step.

As well as contacting the IRA, Mee had also made efforts to put the Listowel constables' case before their fellow policemen and the public by means of the press. But, again, he was disappointed. Mee attributed the failure of the RIC rank-and-file to rally in support of their cause to the fact that the force had been granted a substantial pay rise in June. He termed this 'bribery' and, indeed, the rise did stem the rapidly increasing numbers of RIC men who were resigning – although only for a few months.[71]

But Mee was also convinced that the Republicans had missed a major opportunity in not trying to subvert the RIC. 'Had Sinn Fein', he wrote 'at that time [1920] devoted a tenth of the energy to canvassing support from within the R.I.C. as they did to the attacking of police-barracks, a happier chapter could be written about that period.' He argued that Sinn Féin should have supported the Police Union and the Listowel Mutiny, as

69 Ibid., pp 104, 297–301.   70 Ibid., pp 99, 113–15, 117.   71 Ibid., p. 116; Charles Townshend, *The British campaign in Ireland, 1919–21*, (London, 1975), p. 209.

these were symptomatic of deep discontent within the force. When it didn't, he concluded that Sinn Féin simply did not understand the strength of feeling among the police. Fr Gaughan, the editor of Mee's autobiography, commented in a footnote that Mee was unrealistic to suggest that the RIC could have been won over to the Republican cause and he quoted David Neligan in support of his opinion. But this is one of many examples of Gaughan's tendency to quote selectively and misleadingly.[72]

Neligan was a DMP detective, or G-man, who worked secretly for Michael Collins during 1919–21. In his memoirs, published in 1968, he did write, as Gaughan pointed out, that Collins had become discouraged about the prospect of subverting the RIC when the Police Union collapsed in 1920. But, in fact, Neligan himself made very plain that he disagreed with Collins in this and, like Mee, he was strongly convinced that greater efforts should have been made to win policemen over. It is worth quoting him at length to refute Gaughan's inaccurate representation of his opinions.

> Sinn Fein blundered where the R.I.C. was concerned. Many of those poor devils were married with families, generally large ones, and had no resources apart from their pay. A vigorous propaganda was directed at them with the object of making them resign, but no effort was made by anybody to provide alternative employment or to help them to return to civilian life. The result was that they could see nothing ahead but starvation. So literally they stuck to their guns and fought their own countrymen – to the last. I am well aware that our [Sinn Fein's] war-chest was far from overflowing in those days, but some effort, even to pay their fares abroad, should have been made. Instead, that terrible weapon, the boycott, immensely cruel, was used against them ... Naturally such treatment filled them with hatred and bitterness. They acted as the eyes and ears of the Black and Tans and fought strenuously for their British masters.[73]

As an Irish policeman himself, even if serving in a different force and committed to the Republican side, Neligan could not help but feel sorry

72 Gaughan (ed.), *Memoirs of Constable Jeremiah Mee*, pp 79, 80–1, n. 20.   73 David Neligan, *The spy in the castle* (London, 1968), pp 80–1.

for the plight of the RIC. They were drawn from a 'good class of people' he wrote, but found themselves standing 'in the road of a revolution'. It was impossible he felt 'to withhold sympathy from those men in this terrible predicament. God alone knows how they suffered'.[74] Some RIC men, Neligan acknowledged, did actively help the Republican cause,[75] while many turned a blind eye to IRA activities or just quietly resigned. Whether more could have been won over as Mee and Neligan obviously believed is a moot point. Collins was not convinced, although the introduction of the Black-and-Tans and the Auxiliaries during 1920 demonstrated that the British government was no longer confident of the effectiveness or even the reliability of the police. But, in the end, Mee's efforts at Listowel to sow rebellion among the RIC and form an alliance with the IRA failed comprehensively.

In some respects Mee's failure was indicative of the more general failure of all RIC dissenters. There was clearly persistent discontent within the constabulary over conditions of service, in particular pay, pensions and promotion, while in 1920 political grievances were very evident. Men voiced their dissatisfaction regularly before committees of enquiry, and in 1882 and again in 1907 this discontent developed into organised, public protest campaigns. But the protestors were always a small minority and, moreover, were essentially moderate in their demands and in the tactics that they employed. Governments, though naturally alarmed at indications of RIC disaffection, in the main had little trouble in extinguishing outbreaks of defiance. Ring leaders were dismissed, groups of malcontents were broken up by transfer and individual members disciplined through demotion and fines. Sometimes small concessions were made – although never enough to suggest that organised protest was effective.

An ex-sergeant in his memoirs, published in 1886, commented on the 'curious and extraordinary' fact that, although discontent in the RIC was extensive and, indeed, 'unexampled in any other kindred organization in the great Empire', yet 'the hateful strike', which was so characteristic of other police forces, was unknown until the recent crisis of the Land War. Before then, according to Michael Brophy, dissatisfied men 'always followed the rule of legally withdrawing from their contract with the

74 Ibid., p. 81. 75 RIC assistance was often vital to the Republican cause. For some examples, see T.G. McMahon (ed.), *Pádraig Ó Fathaigh's War of Independence: recollections of a Galway Gaelic Leaguer* (Irish Narratives, Cork, 2000), pp 24, 27, 66, 85.

Government, by resigning their appointments and seeking in a foreign land the bettering of their condition, and, by so doing, making room for others of their young countrymen to try their fortune in the service'. The government, for its part, 'reciprocated this fair dealing' by allowing men who had not succeeded abroad to re-join if they so wished.[76] One has only to look at the dramatic leaps in resignations and retirements during periods like the early 1880s and the early 1920s to appreciate that Brophy had a point. Resignation and emigration were far easier options for dissatisfied policemen than were attempts to change conditions from within the RIC.

A barrister, who occasionally represented officers and men in dispute with their superiors, succinctly summed up his general advice in two words: 'knuckle under'. His experience of 'many such disputes' showed him 'that no matter who was right or who was wrong, the inferior always came to grief badly. A superior will never admit any error.' To illustrate his point J.A. Curran mentioned the case of two constables he had represented, who were being prosecuted for assaulting a civilian. He knew both would be convicted and sentenced to long prison terms, and he informed them of this fact, although they were out on bail and had friends abroad. Naturally they fled and some time later Curran received his fee of two guineas in a letter from America.[77] Like Brophy, Curran took for granted that policemen at odds with the RIC, for whatever reason, were better advised to emigrate than to attempt to fight the force. If, as is likely, Brophy and Curran reflected the attitudes of most policemen, then it is not surprising that few protests, strikes or mutinies occurred, and that those which did occur were not notably successful.

76 Brophy, *Sketches of the Royal Irish Constabulary*, pp 40–1. 77 Curran, *Reminiscences of John Adye Curran, K.C.*, p. 70.

CHAPTER SEVEN

The barracks and constabulary family life

During its existence, probably 80,000 Irishmen joined and served in the Force until pensioned. If these men had not joined the R.I.C., most of them certainly would have emigrated. Seventy thousand of them at least married 70,000 Irish girls, many of whom, too, would have settled in other countries. These men and women reared families averaging five or six children each and on the whole contributed to the population of the country, probably half a million people. Their salaries and pensions were spent in the country. Their children were as Irish, *even more so than the majority*.[1]

During the years from 1822 to 1922, as ex-Head Constable Thomas Fennell says above, tens of thousands of Irishmen served in the constabulary, many of whom would otherwise have emigrated. Fennell probably under estimates their numbers, but, as he implies, the constabulary was far larger than even this substantial group, for intimately involved in many aspects of police life were the wives and children of constables and officers. Some wives and children actually lived in police barracks. But, even those who did not were profoundly influenced by the job that their husbands or fathers were engaged in. The rules and regulations that so minutely governed all aspects of the constabulary extended to families and domestic life, dictating, in particular, where wives and children should live and, especially, how they should behave. The RIC considered that men were never really 'off duty', reflected in the fact that they had to wear uniform at all times, and so their personal lives were open to official scrutiny and direction, almost as much as their working lives. In this chapter we shall consider the constabulary family and especially what life was like for men and also for women and children in barracks.

1 Fennell, *The Royal Irish Constabulary*, p. 107.

FINDING A WIFE

Before looking at policemen's wives and also their children, it is important to remember that during much of this period there were restrictions
on how many men could marry and also on whom they could marry.
Such restrictions appear not to have been rigidly enforced prior to the
consolidation of the constabulary in 1836. Recruitment was going on
actively during the 1820s and many of those employed as policemen were
at least ten years older than the recruits of the post-Famine era. Given
the high rates of marriage prevailing in Ireland before 1845, this meant
that most recruits were already married. Clearly marriage was not then
the bar to joining the constabulary that it became after 1836. Exactly how
many of the early constables were married is difficult to determine, but
some evidence suggests that the proportion was substantial.

In October 1828 the newly appointed inspector general of Munster,
William Miller, conducted a half-yearly tour of inspection and submitted a report on the state of the force in his province to the chief secretary in Dublin Castle. In the five counties he toured Miller found that
between 60 and 75 per cent of constables were married and most had two
to three children. The average age of constables, depending upon the
county, ranged from twenty-eight to thirty-three years. Miller complained
in particular that some men were 'too advanced [in] years' and 'puny [in]
body frame' to be fit for constabulary duties. He was obviously seeking
to rectify this state of affairs, however, for he informed the Castle that
of the sixty-eight appointments he had made so far in 1828 'all [were]
young men' with an average age of twenty-three years. And, after listing
other reforms he was introducing, he concluded:

> The grand clog upon the Establishment will be found to be the
> Women and Children. Heretofore the Barracks have been inun-
> dated with them; and every thing that is untidy and filthy is the
> consequence. I am using my best endeavours to discourage
> Marriage among the Members of the Establishment, the evils of
> which, as they bear upon the efficiency of the Constables, I have
> already pointed out, as strongly as I could, to the Government.[2]

2 W. Miller to Lord F. Leveson Gower, Oct. 1828 (NAI, Outrage Papers 1828 II 584).

Miller was a former army officer and in his report he made clear his opinion that what was 'most desirable in a Constabulary Officer' was 'experience in the art of controlling men which is obtained by Military Service'. Miller reflected the culture of the British army; and the army severely curtailed marriage throughout the nineteenth century.[3] As we have seen, although the number of constabulary recruits with military experience declined markedly after 1836, nearly all inspectors general were former senior army officers and a military culture prevailed in the RIC's officer corps. Restrictions on marriage were a clear indication of the paramilitary character of the Irish police; equally, the easing of such restrictions reflected a move away from the force's military roots.[4] Yet there remained a profound tension between the exercise of military discipline and the enjoyment of family life.

Marriage was never totally banned by the constabulary, but recruits had to be single after 1836 and marriage was only possible after seven years' satisfactory service. Even then constables had to seek permission from senior officers to marry and that permission might not be forthcoming. From the 1830s up to the 1860s the constabulary aimed to have no more than 20 per cent of the rank-and-file married. Therefore, if a county inspector found that this proportion of his force was married already, he was obliged to refuse further applications until existing numbers had declined. This could mean a long wait for a constable and his intended bride.

Clandestine marriages were contracted, but the surviving evidence, which admittedly is not plentiful, suggests that these were not very common. For instance, in the four months June–September 1848, of 105 men dismissed from the force only three were sacked for 'marrying without leave'. Clandestine marriages were still being entered into in the early 1870s, but again there were few and by this time culprits were being 'discharged' rather than 'dismissed'.[5] It is possible that some men were able to keep such unauthorised unions secret, but this would have been difficult given the degree of control exercised over policemen's lives and the lack of privacy afforded by barrack accommodation.

3 Trustram, *Women of the regiment*, pp 29–49.   4 For a discussion of these roots, see Malcolm, 'From light infantry to constabulary'.   5 Names of Members of the Constabulary Rewarded, Dismissed, Disrated and Fined, 1848–1872 (Garda Síochána Museum, Dublin Castle, M169). Men discharged could leave with some or even all of their pensions, but not men who were dismissed.

The 1860s were years of heightened discontent in the constabulary over pay and conditions. The restriction on marriage was one of the many grievances aired at the time. That the RIC responded is evident from the fact that reference to the 20 per cent limit, which had appeared in the first and second editions of the *Code*, was dropped from the third edition published in 1872. And subsequently the proportion of married policemen rose substantially. From around 20 per cent of constables in 1837–70, it jumped to 40 per cent during the 1870s and was over 43 per cent in 1881–1900.[6] That the marriage rate doubled rapidly after the lifting of the limit is an obvious indication of how many constables had been frustrated in their desire for marriage. From being a force in which few were married, the RIC after 1870 quickly became a force in which nearly half of men were married. Most of the unmarried were the more recent recruits, that is constables in their twenties; the married were the more experienced constables, the sergeants and head constables aged over thirty. Thus for the final half century of its existence, unlike the thirty years from the 1830s to the 1860s, most of the senior rank-and-file of the Irish constabulary were married men with children.

Yet, despite this major change, the organization and also the culture of the RIC still operated to a large extent on the assumption that men were single. Wives and children always fitted somewhat awkwardly into police life and, as we shall see, there was a concerted effort to keep them out of sight. A flavour of the rather ambivalent attitude toward marriage prevailing in senior police and government circles is evident in the report of the 1882 enquiry into the RIC.

> There is no necessity for encouraging marriage in a force exclusively filled by Irishmen, and remarkable for its high moral standard. It is undesirable to take any step that would hasten marriages or make them more numerous than at present. But, while bearing this in mind, it is wise to recognise the fact that the great body of men of advanced service will be married, and to admit, that it is not only useless, but dangerous, to discourage marriage, at a suitable age, in a force that takes between twenty-five and thirty years of life.[7]

6 Lowe and Malcolm, 'Domestication', pp 38–9. 7 *Report of the Committee, 1883*, p. 5.

So, while it was 'useless', indeed, perhaps 'dangerous', to discourage marriage, nevertheless, it was 'undesirable' to encourage it – and probably unnecessary due to the 'high moral standard' of Irishmen.[8]

Constables found their wives usually during their first or second posting, when they had been in the force for seven to ten years. Unfortunately, little information survives as to how men met their future wives or as to why women accepted marriage proposals from constables. There are scraps of evidence, however, and on the basis of these an account can be constructed, even if it is a trifle speculative in parts.

An interesting letter survives, written in 1883 by James Scott, a farmer living near Castlepollard, Co. Westmeath, to his son, Stephen, a sub constable serving in Anniscaul, Co. Kerry. James comments that he has read in the newspapers that a 'great deal of the restrictions is being taken off' the RIC and men are being granted boot money and lodging allowances. Stephen is not married, but James hints that, given his improved circumstances, he may well be contemplating marriage.

> ... when you do mediate on changing your life you wont [sic] make little of your family by gaining a low mean family and as Police Men now a day is thought more of then formerly they need not be ashamed to pay there [sic] addresses to any respectable party. But no more on that subject only when you are on that intent you have plenty of respectible [sic] acquaintances at home here that you can pick out a companion out of and as you can leave the force now after 25 years service with 42 pounds pension for a sub [constable]. [I]t is very nice. I am afraid the police will pick up all the fine respectible [sic] young girls and leave none for the poor ... farmers.[9]

James appreciated that, with the Land War over and police conditions of service improving, sub constables like his son had become attractive marriage candidates – far more attractive at the time than farmers.

James was looking at marriage from an economic, not a romantic, point of view; and it is probable that many women and their families saw

8 That Irish policemen had high moral – read, sexual – standards, especially as compared to their English counterparts, was a point made during debates over the introduction and policing of the Contagious Diseases Acts in Ireland in the late 1860s. Elizabeth Malcolm, '"Troops of largely diseased women": VD, the Contagious Diseases Acts and moral policing in late nineteenth-century Ireland', *Irish Economic and Social History*, xxvi (1999), p. 10.   9 James Scott to Stephen Scott, 6 June 1883 (NLI, MS 33062)

marriage similarly. Certainly, by 1914, when police pay had fallen behind that of comparable jobs and the RIC was having trouble in recruiting men, constables were complaining of the difficulty of securing wives. One head constable remembered that 'not so long ago ... Police had no trouble getting wives ... But times are changed now. Police prospects and financial standing have dwindled'. Courting policemen were 'reminded of [their] poverty in many parlours' and fathers were likely to 'hasten [their] departure with the boot'. Even if a constable did secure a bride, his prospects were not necessarily improved: 'If he is a strong, determined man, willing to starve, he may marry.'[10]

In 1883 it was clear that James Scott would have preferred his son to marry a 'respectible [*sic*] young' woman from the local area – one presumably known to the family in Westmeath – rather than a Kerry woman. But most constables did marry women from areas to which they were posted, so police marriages were unlike many of the 'matches' arranged by rural families during the post-Famine era.[11] It would seem that the woman's family had more say in the alliance than the man's. But as policemen were immediately transferred upon marriage, brides found themselves swiftly removed from the proximity of their families. Thus it is probably fair to say that police marriages were conducted more in isolation from extended families than were most other rural marriages of the period. This fact is worth keeping in mind when considering the *camaraderie* that existed among policemen and among police families. In part this may have developed as a substitute for the family ties that policemen and their wives were denied by the policy of posting them to counties where they had no 'connections', to use the Personnel Register's term.

It is hard to generalise about the outcome of police marriages, but there is a good deal of evidence suggesting that, despite considerable difficulties, many turned out happily. Most policemen who have left memoirs paid fulsome tribute to their wives, and the children of police marriages also frequently praised their mothers for managing the demanding role of policeman's wife. Unfortunately, wives themselves have left far fewer records of what they felt about their husbands and the very trying

10 *RIC Magazine*, May 1914, pp 198–201. 11 Much has been written about post-Famine marriage practices. See, as examples, R.E. Kennedy, Jr, *The Irish: emigration, marriage and fertility* (Berkeley, CA, 1973); David Fitzpatrick, 'Marriage in post-Famine Ireland' in Art Cosgrove (ed.), *Marriage in Ireland* (Dublin, 1985), p. 116–31; T.W. Guinnane, *The vanishing Irish: households, migration and the rural economy in Ireland, 1850–1914* (Princeton, NJ, 1997).

domestic circumstances that police service imposed. But one interesting letter survives, which includes a long poem, written in 1899 by Ada
Shiel, the wife of Constable William Shiel. William was stationed at a
police hut in Glenro, near Corofin, Co. Clare, while Ada was in hospital
undergoing an operation to correct varicose veins. She was concerned
that he would be lonely without her and wrote:

> I'll end this lengthy letter which I hope may find you well
> Enjoying health and plenty, in the Hut or rather cell
> When next week I do go home we'll have a lengthy talk
> I'll take you for a long patrol to show you I can walk
> Goodbye my dearest Willie, heave a loving sigh
> We'll meet again in Corofin [in] the sweet Bye and Bye
> I think you'll hardly know me so lively shall I feel
> Farewell my Willie darling, Ada Sheil.[12]

Constables could not be posted to the counties where they had been
born and, as we have seen, they could not stay in counties where their
wives had family. Marriage thus entailed automatic transfer. In 1883 this
rule was softened somewhat when a circular decreed that, where practi-
cable, men should be sent on marriage to neighbouring counties.[13] So a
woman marrying a policeman knew that she would have to leave, not
only her family, but also the county in which she had grown up. Shortly
we shall look closely at life for women in barracks. Obviously though,
being the wife of a policeman was not an easy task. Young wives were
isolated from their families and friends, and also, if they lived in barracks, from the new communities where they were obliged to take up residence. If there were other police wives living in or near the barracks,
then they could have offered valuable support and advice. But sometimes
a wife might find herself as the only woman in a small remote barracks,
a long way from home and with little or no female companionship.

The *Constabulary Gazette* regularly published a 'Women's Page ...
Conducted by "The Mater"'. The 'Page', which in fact ran to several
pages, included recipes, advice on entertaining and competitions for children. But the 'Mater' was not only concerned with the promotion of

12 Ada Shiel to William Shiel, Oct. 1899 (Goulden Papers, TCD Library, MS 7378/4). 13 Transfer on Marriage,
9 May 1883 (RIC Circulars, 1883–1900, NLI, IR3522 R3).

motherhood and domesticity. The 'Women's Page' also published letters from policemen's wives airing common problems and grievances. Early in 1900, for example, there was a correspondence from wives about the problems of living on a constable's pay of £5 a month. Questions addressed included in what circumstances a doctor should be called in case of illness, given the expense, and whether a servant – 'a little girl' – should be employed.[14] In a discussion of policemen's daughters, 'The Mater' acknowledged that, while 'some girls find their true sphere in the home … there are others who can be spared from the home duties and wish to be independent'.[15]

But 'The Mater', while opening her – or, more likely, his – page to discussions of the grievances of policemen's wives and the employment opportunities of policemen's daughters, also included more conventional and patriarchal reflections on women – reflections that very much promoted conventional middle-class values of the time. After the discussion of living expenses referred to above, a piece appeared by 'Bachelor' setting out the attributes of 'The Ideal Wife' – by implication, the ideal constabulary wife. His condescending view was that she 'need not necessarily be very learned; but she must be fairly intelligent, discreet, and common-sense [*sic*]. Virtuous in every sense, she shall possess that modesty of deportment, as well as speech, so indispensable to the true woman.' The letter continued at some length extolling the virtues of women who made the home 'as cheery and attractive as possible', were 'more disposed to excuse than magnify the faults' of their husband, paid him 'that deference which is his due' and bore 'reverses with Christian-like fortitude'.[16] This letter probably reflects fairly accurately what the RIC authorities considered desirable in a policeman's wife. Perhaps some wives lived up to these exacting standards, but many probably did not.

DOMESTIC LIFE IN AND OUT OF BARRACKS

The RIC's book of rules and regulations, known as the *Code*, contained detailed instructions on how life in barracks was to be conducted.[17] From

---

14 *Constabulary Gazette*, vii, 2 (7 April 1900), p. 59. 15 Ibid., vi, 16 (13 Jan. 1900), p. 498. 16 Ibid., vii, 2 (7 April 1900), p. 60. 17 Unless otherwise indicated, the following discussion of life in barracks is based upon the barrack regulations listed in *Standing rules and regulations for the government of the Royal Irish Constabulary* (4th ed., Dublin,

time to time such instructions were modified by official circulars. The *Code* and the circulars not only regulated the lives of policemen, but also the lives of their wives and children. They thus provide us with a fascinating picture of the highly regimented and rather claustrophobic regime that prevailed in the over 1,400 police barracks scattered throughout post-Famine Ireland.[18]

After the 1860s head constables or sergeants in charge of barracks were increasingly married as, indeed, were many senior constables. If married, the policeman in charge of the barracks was to be allotted a sitting room, as well as a separate bedroom. One bedroom was meant to suffice for the sergeant, his wife and his children to the maximum of four.[19] The distribution of married accommodation within a barracks was ultimately, however, under the control of the county inspector. He, or the district inspector, was also obliged to inspect the sergeant's quarters regularly. Some wives, however, did not appreciate such intrusions. One angry sergeant's wife complained to the *Constabulary Gazette* asking: 'What have those officers got to look at? There is not one article of public property allowed into married quarters; those limited apartments are dearly paid for; and what on earth is the object of surprise inspections to them except to render irksome the life of the unfortunate married woman?'[20] From 1882 barrack accommodation was not free; men paid the same fixed rent for it throughout the country, which by 1900 for constables was one shilling per week. This meant that single constables paid £2 12s. per annum for what was usually little more than a bed in a dormitory with three or four other men and the right to eat at a table with the same men.

The RIC preferred to have men living in barracks, but when there wasn't sufficient room, the county inspector could authorise men and their families to live outside. For the men though this was on a rotating basis, with periods of outside residence limited to three months at a time. In 1883 a lodging allowance of 1s. per week, increased in 1902 to 2s., was granted to married men with more than ten years' service whose families

1888), pp 70–85, 991–5. 18 A collection of plans and specifications for barracks are to be found in the Irish Architectural Archive, Dublin (Office of Public Works: Drawings List, Files C and D). These help with visualising the layout and interior spaces of barracks. I would like to thank Professor W.J. Lowe for sending me copies of photographs he took of the outside of a number of former RIC barracks in the early 1990s. 19 It would be an interesting exercise to analyse, if possible, the numbers of children that married policemen, and especially sergeants, had. Did the limit of four children permitted to reside in barracks act as a check on family size? 20 Quoted in [Harding], *The R.I.C.: a plea for reform*, p. 83.

could not be housed in barracks.[21] This sum was paid nationwide, although the cost of lodgings varied considerably as between rural and urban areas.

Outside accommodation had to be close to the barracks and had to be approved as adequate by the district inspector. It had to be kept as clean as the barracks and men living outside barracks followed the same timetable as men in barracks. Head constables or sergeants were instructed to visit outside accommodation periodically to ensure these rules were being followed. It was made clear to married men living out of barracks with their families for short periods that they were enjoying a 'privilege', which would be withdrawn if it was abused. Life away from barracks probably offered more privacy and perhaps more space and comfort, but men were still on duty and had to observe barrack routines. In keeping with this, up until the 1880s, they were forbidden to take in lodgers even if they had a spare room and were in need of the income.[22]

All constables had to take turns serving as barrack orderly, which was an onerous job. This was one of the reasons men could not live outside small rural barracks permanently. Barrack orderlies were not permitted to leave the building and were responsible for it at night and while the rest of the men were on patrol or engaged in other duties. In other words, it was a twenty-four-hour a day job. The orderly had to attend to any one calling at the barracks with a complaint; he had to ensure that no prisoners escaped; he recorded the departure and return of patrols; he checked and secured the weapons; he was obliged to maintain the fire in the dayroom and, if the barrack servant was absent, to keep the barracks clean and cook the men's meals. At night he was officially on guard, although allowed to sleep in the dayroom.[23] As most rural barracks only contained four to six men, orderly duty had to be rotated regularly and no man could escape it. Given the demands of orderly duty, it is perhaps not surprising that failure to carry out this duty properly figures significantly in lists of men dismissed, disrated or fined.[24]

Keeping the dayroom clean and tending the fire there in the winter were important responsibilities, for the dayroom was to the policeman

21 Lodging Allowance to Married Men, 9 May 1883 (RIC Circulars, 1882–1900, NLI, IR3522 R3). 22 This rule was eased in 1883, when wives were also permitted to work, but only in jobs approved by the RIC. *Report of the Committee of Inquiry*, 1883, p. 5. 23 *RIC Magazine*, July 1915, pp 278–81. 24 For a discussion of some of these cases, see Chapter 8.

'as the hive is to the bee, as the roost is to the hen'. It was the heart of the barracks and the RIC would not rent a house unless it had space suitable for use as a dayroom.[25] An article published in *The RIC Magazine* in 1915 described a typical dayroom in some detail. It began with the comment: 'No other room leaves such an impression of hardness and harshness on the mind.' The door to the room was reinforced and heavy to move.[26] On the back of the door hung 'copies of the Register of Criminals dating back four generations ... the fuel and light board ... the mess book ... extracts from the "Hue and Cry" ... and, above all, a board containing a list of the public property in that room'. The room contained a fireplace, a table 'of the hardest wood, bound at the corners with iron', and several wooden forms for seats. The orderly usually sat at the dayroom table with pen and ink recording the activities of the day in the barrack diary. On the walls of the room were a clock over the fireplace, various noticeboards listing the men and the sergeant's children and a shelf containing copies of the *Code*, circulars and acts of parliament. There was also an arms rack, with space for six weapons, and a map of the sub district. No comfortable chairs, flowers, table clothes or pictures were permitted.[27] The room was kept deliberately bare, bleak and functional. It was the space in which policemen ate their meals and relaxed, but it must have reminded them that, while doing so, they were still on duty.

Wives living in barracks were not expected to enter the dayroom, but sometimes in a small barracks the room was impossible to avoid. Wives could cook their family meals in the communal kitchen where the barrack servant prepared meals for the single men, but this might involve them passing through the dayroom. They were also permitted to cook in their sitting room, provided this did not 'interfere with the cleanliness of the barrack'. If the county inspector found that it did, then he could withdraw the 'privilege'. Married men could mess with the single men, who were obliged to eat together downstairs in the dayroom, or upstairs

25 Most barracks were rented, but some appear to have been purpose built. In 1840 Inspector General Duncan McGregor set out detailed specifications for constabulary barracks. They were to have two upstairs rooms for sleeping; a downstairs hall and 'lock up'; plus a kitchen and day room. See Specification of a House to be Built and Used as a Barrack, 24 Dec. 1840 (NAI, CSORP 1840/116866). 26 Doors and windows of barracks were strengthened and sometimes fortified in the wake of the Fenian Rising of 1867 and during the Land War of the early 1880s. For lengthy correspondence between the RIC and a local landlord concerning the strengthening of barracks in Co. Sligo in 1867, see NLI, O'Hara Papers, MS 20,348/2, 3, 4. 27 *RIC Magazine*, Oct. 1915, pp 363–6.

with their families. But the sergeant was to report any married man he thought was not being adequately fed by his wife and whose work was suffering as a consequence.[28] Men in such circumstances could be discharged as unfit.

Divisions between ranks were maintained in relation to wives. For instance, the wives of head constables or sergeants in charge of barracks were forbidden to cook for or look after the men. But, if the barracks could not find a suitable female servant, then the wife of a constable could fill this role. Families of head constables or sergeants were permitted to employ their own servant, in addition to the barrack servant, but she had to be either married or, if single, elderly 'so as to prevent any appearance of impropriety, or grounds for scandal'. If any dispute arose between a family servant and the barrack servant, this was to be reported immediately by the sergeant in charge to the district inspector.

The barrack servant was an important figure, especially for the younger, single constables, as it was she who cooked and cleaned for them and often acted as a mentor. She lit the fires in the morning, made the tea, filled the lamps, scrubbed the tables and forms; she cooked for the single men, washed and mended their clothes. Before an inspection by the district or county inspector, she had to clean the barracks thoroughly. She did not live in the building, but spent long days there. In a humorous article, published in the *RIC Magazine* in 1912, Sergeant Thomas Dolan of Bodyke, Collane, Co. Clare, characterised her as 'a tall, raw-boned woman, with considerable strength of character, and more or less of a beard – generally more'. According to Dolan, it was she who would take a new recruit aside and 'in a confidential whisper, inform him as to the sort of "ship" to which he was sent'. It was she who would explain the 'various aspects of the sergeant's temper' and how to address his wife so as to win her approval. Dolan warned young constables against offending the barrack servant for she 'could work a baneful influence on his career by going upstairs to the sergeant's wife'. According to Dolan, sometimes the cooking of the barrack servant was atrocious, yet, although the men paid her wages, it was very hard to remove her if she did not want to leave.[29] Despite being written in a light and amusing vein, the article

28 A Belfast head constable, complaining about married men's pay before the 1882 enquiry, claimed that on parade he could tell the married and single men apart, as the married men were 'not so well fed as the single men'. *Report of the Committee of Inquiry*, 1883, p. 20. 29 *RIC Magazine*, Feb. 1912, pp 111–15.

exhibits considerable hostility towards the barrack servant, portraying her as an incompetent or a tyrant, and frequently a combination of both.

The RIC's barrack regulations attempted to define narrowly the spaces that wives could occupy and the roles they could fill. Generally their realm was upstairs, in the sitting room and bedroom, not down-stairs in the dayroom and office where the work of the barracks took place, although they could have access to the downstairs kitchen. Female servants had more freedom of movement downstairs, but their activities were strictly prescribed. In a sense wives were expected to be invisible in the barracks. Their names did not appear in the dayroom and they did not have access to the 'public property'. Wives and children, for instance, were not to use any of the bedding or furniture provided by the RIC, but to supply their own. Women were not to hang their clothes to dry in any of the public spaces in the barracks. Indeed, all clothes of married women 'must be kept in their boxes or presses'. Nor does there appear to have been any 'sanitary accommodation' for women in barracks. They could not 'utilise the closet in common with the men and prisoners', so they and their daughters had to use a 'receptacle'. However, as one sergeant's wife complained, 'where this receptacle has to be conveyed through the men's day-room [for emptying] it is an outrage on common decency'.[30] No woman of a 'quarrelsome disposition' was to be tolerated in barracks, nor any whose conduct was not 'perfectly sober, quiet and respectable'. Wives were permitted to engage in a trade or business out-side the barracks, but the type of enterprise had to be approved, not just by the county inspector, but by the inspector general himself.

While allowing more men to marry and permitting families to live in barracks, at the same time, the RIC tried to restrict women's freedom of movement and action both within and without barracks. Contact between young wives and single constables was an especially sensitive matter – and this sensitivity extended to female children.

New constables were generally in their late teens or early twenties. At their first posting they could find themselves living under the same roof, in fairly cramped conditions, with the teenage daughters of the sergeant in charge. The bringing together of young men and women in this way was a source of great concern to the RIC authorities. Regulations decreed that once girls reached the age of fourteen they were no longer allowed to reside

30 [Harding], *The R.I.C.: a plea for reform*, p. 82.

in barracks, although they could visit. But, if their father was a widower, even visits were not permitted. This policy of excluding teenage girls from barracks was a source of much complaint. Men pointed out that suitable accommodation for their daughters was often difficult to find and also expensive; that separating girls from their families at this age exposed them to moral dangers; and that they were frequently obliged to escort their daughters home from barracks at night, after a long day's work.[31]

When children were living in barracks, policemen and their wives were expected to supervise them closely. They were held responsible for any 'uncleanliness' caused by their children. The county inspector had to authorise the presence of children in barracks and a list of the children's names and ages, plus the date of authorisation, signed by the parents was to hang in a 'conspicuous' place in the dayroom. It was to be updated 'on the first day of every year'. Children not on the list were not allowed in the barracks, unless brought in by policemen in the course of their duties. Women and children were obliged to 'strictly' observe barrack regulations and could be removed if there was any complaint about 'irregularity or lack of cleanliness'. Women who did not keep themselves and their children 'respectably clad' were also liable to expulsion.

If policemen were expected to provide models of respectable behaviour for the communities that they worked in, it is obvious that their wives and children were expected to do likewise.

LEISURE ACTIVITIES

Policemen's lives were dominated to a substantial extent by their jobs, but there were opportunities for leisure and recreation. As most constables came from rural backgrounds and many had worked on family farms before joining the police, some were keen to continue raising animals and crops while serving in country barracks. By doing so they could of course reduce their food bills. As with all other aspects of police life, however, farming and gardening were minutely regulated by the *Code*. Constables were not allowed to keep animals in or around the barracks. This included dogs and cats as pets,[32] horses for riding and poultry, pigs or

31 *Report of the Commissioners*, 1873, p. 20. 32 Sergeants in charge did, however, sometimes keep pets, especially dogs. Learning to get along with the sergeant's dog was often an issue for young constables. See the *RIC Magazine*, Dec.

cows. But, as we have seen, the regulations were not always observed to
the letter. An undated poem survives in the Goulden Papers written by
an anonymous constable lamenting the demise of his pet jackdaw. Below
are extracts from its thirteen verses, which offer a fairly typical example
of the standard of much constabulary poetry.[33]

> In a mountainy station both cosy and dry
> No peeler in Ireland so happy as I
> And I envied no man from Moville to Portlaw
> While my favourite bird lived – my pet jackdaw
> . . .
> But our new Chief came on inspection that day
> And said 'Caps must be straight and hair cut away'
> Ye Gods! When Jack heard him it was the last straw
> And it broke the proud heart of my pet jackdaw
>
> He is dead, he is dead, no more will he come
> Flying down the boreen to welcome me home
> 'Mong his wild native hills with the honours of war
> I remorsefully buried my pet jackdaw.

With the permission of the county inspector, married men were
allowed to keep two pigs and poultry for their family's consumption on
land not exceeding one quarter of a statute acre within a quarter of a
mile of the barracks.[34] In remote barracks, where it was hard to procure
milk, married men with families or the single men as a group could keep

1913, pp 39–41. For a humorous handwritten story, in which the sergeant's dog proves to be a better detective than
his master, see 'The R.I.C. and detective Dan', n.d. (Goulden Papers, TCD Library, MS 7378/17). 33 'A barrack
pet', n.d. (Goulden Papers, TCD Library, MS 7378/9). The composition of poetry was clearly a popular pastime
among constables. One of the best-known police poets was Head Constable Jack Keily, who joined the force in
1875 and died of pneumonia in Kildare barracks in 1905, aged forty-eight. For his obituary, see *Nenagh Guardian*,
30 Dec. 1905. A selection of his poems was republished by the Nenagh Historical Society on the seventieth anniversary of his death: see, *Sergeant Kiely: a wordsnare broadsheet* (Nenagh, 1975). Among these is a long verse letter to his
friend, Sergeant Thomas Waldron, who followed his father into the RIC and served from 1872 to 1898. The letter
describes Keily's transfer from Tralee to Nenagh in 1887. I would like to thank Patrick Waldron, Thomas' grandson, for providing me with this information. Patrick Waldron, Rathmines, Dublin 6, to ELM, 1 Aug. 1990 (RIC
Letters, V, 171). 34 A circular on married men living in barracks, issued in 1891, permitted them with the county
inspector's approval to keep poultry for their own use at the barracks, so long as they provided adequate coops.
31 March 1891 (RIC Circulars, 1882–1900, NLI, IR3522 R3).

a cow or goat, so long as there was proper stabling for the animal and the men themselves paid for its grazing. Unmarried constables were forbidden from holding land, but the RIC was more accommodating as regard barrack gardens. These were permitted, even encouraged, although carefully apportioned between the different ranks. In a barracks where a district inspector was resident, he was entitled to five shares in the garden; a head constable held three shares; married constables could have two shares each; and single constables one share. A married man with a garden away from the barracks was not entitled to a share in the barrack garden.

In 1912 Ivon H. Price, a district inspector since 1891, who pursued a controversial career in Crime Branch Special and later rose to be an assistant inspector general (1920–2),[35] wrote an article in the *RIC Magazine* on 'Gardening in the R.I.C.' While stating that [e]very man should have a hobby and there is no more delightful and healthy hobby than gardening', Price chose to emphasise the more 'practical' advantages of gardening for RIC men.

> There is a constant cry as to the difficulty of getting employment, especially by Constables retiring in the prime of life after 25 years' service … If every Constable retiring at 45 years of age had a practical knowledge of plain fruit, vegetable and flower-growing, such as could be acquired during half his leisure hours in the Force, he could easily double his pension. He could do this either as a working gardener, or far better still, as a tenant of a small house, with one acre of land situated within reasonable distance of a good town.[36]

Price himself owned a garden covering an acre that had been laid out thirty years earlier by his father. It produced about £60 worth of fruit, vegetables and flowers each year. While conceding that head constables or sergeants in charge of barracks had little if any spare time, Price suggested that constables had three or four hours spare every day and advised strongly that at least one hour be devoted to gardening or studying gardening. But he did concede that transfers tended to discourage garden-

35 For Price's career in political and military intelligence, see O'Halpin, *The decline of the Union*, pp 103–4, 110, 114–16, 128–32, 137, 160, 250. Price left Ireland in 1922, as his life had been threatened, and died in England in 1931. 36 *RIC Magazine*, April 1912, p. 188.

ing, as men were not inclined to put great efforts into gardens that they would eventually have to abandon. Nevertheless, he continued to stress the development of gardening skills as an important preparation for retirement. 'There is no man so boring to himself and to others as a pensioner with nothing to do and no hobby.'[37]

As well as encouraging gardening, the RIC also encouraged sports among its men. We have already seen that many officers enjoyed hunting and fishing with the local gentry; and team games, such as cricket, were sometimes played against the officers of regiments stationed in the district.[38] But the rank-and-file also engaged in team and individual sports. In June 1897, for instance, the Co. Kerry constabulary held its annual 'Athletic and Cycling Tournament' in Tralee. There were some twenty-five events, including shot put, long jump, flat and hurdle races, separate bicycle races for RIC men and for pensioners and a tug-of-war between the Kerry and Limerick constabularies – which Kerry won.[39]

Of course sports had practical benefits as far as the RIC authorities were concerned, as obviously did gardening. It was vital for men to remain fit, so that they were able to walk long distances, run swiftly[40] and ride a bicycle well. They needed also to be physically strong. The sports that were most encouraged developed these attributes.

On occasion barracks also hosted dances for their men and the local community. For instance, at New Year in January 1900 the Dromod barracks in Co. Leitrim held a dance that began at 9.00 p.m. and 'continued without a break' until 7.00 a.m. As well as waltzes, polkas, quadrilles and mazurkas, there were jigs, reels and hornpipes. The 'thirsty souls' who attended were supplied with 'all classes of liquors and beverages', and at 2.00 a.m. a buffet supper was served. The dance took place in the large, upstairs dormitory, 'the floor of which was waxed like a sheet of glass'. The barracks was decorated with 'berried holly and ferns', the RIC arms in laurel leaves, plus portraits of the Queen and the Prince and Princess of Wales. The dance was organised by the head constable, the acting

37 Ibid., p. 189. 38 One former officer, commenting that Ireland around 1900 had some of the best and cheapest sport to be found anywhere, devoted almost an entire chapter of his memoirs to an account of his favourite sporting experiences, taking in horse racing and betting, tennis, cricket, soccer and salmon fishing. Gregory, *The house of Gregory*, pp 171–90. 39 *Constabulary Gazette*, iii, 14 (3 July 1897), 234. 40 Fast runners were particularly prized for their ability to out run fleeing illicit distillers or petty thieves. Michael Corduff, a former RIC man, collected folklore in north Co. Mayo in 1942/3 and included stories of famous races between policemen and fleeing suspects. Irish Folklore Commission Archives, Folklore Department, UCD, MS 1243, pp 194–221. See also Henry Robinson, *Further memories of Irish life* (London, 1924), pp 44–5.

sergeant and the four constables who manned the barracks. The sergeant's wife supervised the catering. Those invited included magistrates and councillors, policemen from neighbouring barracks, the local postmaster and railway clerk. Of those attending, 46 were named in the article reporting the event. It is probably no coincidence that 25 of these were single women and most of the others named were their parents.[41] An event such as this almost certainly gave constables a rare chance to meet local girls in a relaxed, if supervised, social setting. There were opportunities to dance and to talk more freely than would have been possible when a constable was on duty.

A CHILD'S LIFE IN THE CONSTABULARY

The domestic lives of policemen can be explored, as we have seen in this chapter, through the memoirs that a number of them wrote, through a small number of surviving private and public letters from policemen's wives, through articles in the RIC's *Gazette* and *Magazine* and also through the constabulary's *Code* and circulars that governed police family life. But there is another important source of information: the autobiographies and letters of policemen's children – and even grandchildren. We shall look more closely at letters and at children and grandchildren in Chapter 9, but here we'll examine a handful of autobiographies written by children of RIC constables for the light they throw on a child's experience of constabulary life.

By the latter half of the twentieth century a number of the children of Irish policemen had risen to important positions in politics, academia, the arts, the church and the civil service. In sitting down, late in life, to write autobiographies, some reflected upon how their experiences as peelers' children had shaped their future lives and careers. And several considered the complex feelings that they still harboured for their father's decision to serve the British state in Ireland.[42]

The short story writer, novelist, editor and historian, Sean O'Faolain, was born John Whelan in Cork city in 1900, the third son of an RIC

41 *Constabulary Gazette*, vi, 16 (13 Jan. 1900), p. 500.   42 The main autobiographies used in this discussion are those of Sean O'Faolain, Patrick Shea and Denis Donoghue. This is by no means an exhaustive list of the autobiographies of RIC children, but these are all books that devote significant attention to the experience of children.

constable named Denis Whelan. O'Faolain's father came from a Catholic, small farming family near Stradbally, Queen's County (now Co. Laois). His mother, Bridget Murphy, also grew up on a small farm, near Rathkeale in west Limerick. Denis Whelan's sister, Kate, married another RIC man, Owen Boyhan, who eventually retired as a sergeant and whose children served in or married into the British army.[43]

The Whelans and Boyhans were typical of many constabulary families in that they came from a small farming background; had more than one member in the RIC; and developed connections with the army. O'Faolain appears to have been aware that his family, and his father in particular, were typical, for he wrote: 'I can only remember my father ... as a figure, almost a type, rather than a person. His own inner, private life is hidden from me completely. He is to me more of a myth than a man, a figure out of that time, out of that place [pre-1914 Cork], a symbol of childhood.'[44]

As O'Faolain went on to describe his father, Constable Whelan certainly emerges as the epitome of the RIC man. He was 'modest, pious, trusting ... upright, honest as daylight, and absolutely loyal to the Empire as only a born hero-worshipper can be'. Denis Whelan, his son reflected rather cynically — but doubtless accurately — was the 'humble but priceless foundation-stuff on which all great states and empires have raised themselves, deviously, to power and glory ...' O'Faolain was convinced that his father's 'humility was really a form of proud reverence growing out of his job'. The British military training that Irish policemen received, O'Faolain wrote, succeeded with 'poor, inexperienced young men of Catholic peasant stock', like his father. O'Faolain in fact titled the chapter in his autobiography largely devoted to his father, 'The Old Grenadier', and admitted that later he sometimes told English friends his father was a graduate of the military college at Sandhurst. As a boy, he respected and even admired his father.

> In his dark bottle-green uniform, black leather belt with brass buckle, black helmet or peaked cap, black truncheon case and black boots, my father embodied the Law. What was far more important, he embodied all the accepted and respected values and conventions of what we would nowadays call the Establishment. In

43 O'Faolain, *Vive moi!*, pp 64–70. O'Faolain's autobiography was originally published in 1963. I am using the new edition, expanded by his daughter and published after his death in 1991.   44 Ibid., pp 31–2.

simple language, his language, he considered that the highest state
in life that anyone could achieve was to be a Gentleman; and he
wanted each one of his children to grow up as a Gentleman ...[45]

While his older brothers, one of whom later joined the priesthood
and the other the British civil service, were beginning to feel torn between
loyalty to the empire and to Ireland, Sean, like his father, remained true
to England. The future Irish Republican was, as a boy, in thrall to G.A.
Henty's stories of adventure and heroism in the furtherance of empire.[46]
O'Faolain was able to present his father, and also his youthful self, with
some affection and a wry amusement, although later in life he was to
reject most of what they then held dear.

In other ways too, as Sean realised, the Whelans were typical of RIC
families. Both father and mother were intensely ambitious for their children, and intensely proud of their achievements. The RIC produced many
priests, like Augustine Whelan, and civil servants, like Patrick Whelan.
Bridget Whelan took in lodgers in order to supplement her husband's
meagre pay as a constable and from this they were able to save the money
to send Sean to university in Cork. 'This ambition for their young',
O'Faolain wrote in the 1960s, 'was a universal mark of the old RIC ...'

One of the most detailed and informative accounts of a child's life
in the RIC was published in 1981 by Patrick Shea, who during the 1960s
held senior positions in the Northern Ireland Civil Service. Unlike
O'Faolain, who had spent the first decade of the twentieth century living
over a pub in Half Moon Street, on the Cork quays, across the river from
the barracks, Shea had actually lived in barracks throughout the following decade. He remarked of himself and his brothers: 'We saw everything
that went on in the barrack and we were participants in much that did
not meet with Mother's approval.'[47]

Shea's father, who joined the RIC in 1895 aged twenty-three, was, like
Denis Whelan, fairly typical of post-Famine recruits, being the bilingual
son of a Catholic small farming family from near Kenmare in Co.
Kerry.[48] He was ambitious, eager to better himself, and his options
according to his son were either emigration or the RIC. After six months'

45 Ibid., pp 22–3. 46 Ibid., p. 25. 47 Shea, *Voices and the sound of drums*, p. 9. 48 For Head Constable Shea's personnel record, see RIC General Register (PRO(L), HO 184/30).

training at the depot in Phoenix Park, he was posted to Co. Down: first to Newcastle, then Saintfield and then Newry. He met his future wife in Newry and upon marriage in 1905 was quickly transferred to Co. Westmeath: first to Mullingar, the RIC county headquarters, and then Devlin, where his second son Patrick was born in 1908. That same year the family was moved to Athlone, and Patrick Shea's first memories were of life in the RIC barracks in Athlone. He lived there until 1920 when his father was transferred to Rathfriland, Co. Down. Within months, Shea's father was sent temporarily as head constable to Templemore in Co. Tipperary, before finally being posted in 1921 to Clones, Co. Monaghan. The family did not move to Templemore, however, as it was considered too dangerous at the time. So Shea's experiences until the age of fourteen involved barrack life in Athlone, Rathfriland and Clones.[49]

Twelve of those years were spent in Athlone. Yet Athlone was far from a typical small, rural station. The town was a major economic and transportation centre and the barrack was a large building erected around a square. It was the principal station of one of the four constabulary districts of Co. Westmeath and was the headquarters of the district inspector, James McDonnell, who was responsible for seven other smaller barracks. Its head constable, Martin Feeny, under whom Shea's father worked as one of three or four sergeants, was by 1919 the most senior head constable in the county.[50] As well as the district inspector, head constable and three to four sergeants, the barracks was manned by twelve to fifteen constables. The constables lived in the building, as did the head constable with 'his large family' and Sergeant Shea and his wife, who by 1914 had four sons.[51]

Patrick Shea's account of a young boy's life in barracks often verges on the idyllic. As he got ready for school each morning, the constables would be parading in the square before being despatched on patrol. But Patrick recollected that for much of the rest of the time the area was given over to games: handball, running, jumping and the tossing of weights. The constables competed with men from other barracks and with soldiers from the local military barracks in tug-of-war matches. They organised games for Patrick and his brothers, taught them to swim, told them stories and minded them if their parents were away. When the men

---

49 Shea, *Voices and the sound of drums*, pp 2–4, 36, 43, 55. 50 *Royal Irish Constabulary List and Directory, No. 156, July 1919* (Dublin, 1919), pp 49, 121, 124. 51 Shea, *Voices and the sound of drums*, pp 8–9.

went out once a year in summer for their required target practice, the boys tagged along. Patrick was a little shocked, however, to see some of the poorer marksmen among the constables doctoring their results.[52]

Patrick's mother worried that her sons were seeing 'too much of the seamy side of life' for their own good. They sometimes played with young army deserters being held by the police before return to their regiments. They watched 'violent madmen, roped hand and foot, being brought in and, after committal by a magistrate, taken off to the lunatic asylum at Mullingar'. The boys became familiar with the local pickpockets, thieves and drunken brawlers. And lying in bed at night they could 'hear the angry profanities of prisoners in the cells' which were just below their bedroom. Patrick recognised that in the barracks, which was surrounded by a high wall, he was 'somewhat cut off from the town', but at the same time 'life in this adult world was full of excitement and novelty and sometimes great entertainment'. The shouts of the drunks arrested on a Saturday night provided 'specially good' entertainment.[53]

But Patrick was more than just 'somewhat cut off', as he slowly began to realise after 1916. His parents were Nationalists and supporters of Home Rule, but after the police raided some local houses in search of arms he and two of his brothers were beaten up on the way to school by a crowd of boys shouting 'traitors' and 'English spies'. Up until then he admits to having 'no feeling of involvement' in the rapidly polarising political situation. After then, as the beatings continued, he realised that he was 'involved in a conflict of loyalties' and, moreover, involved 'on the side that, although not yet a minority, was losing support'.[54] But it was the side to which his father's employment committed him. Sean O'Faolain in his autobiography expressed relief that his father had retired before 1916, as he knew Denis Whelan would have served loyally, 'stubbornly, however bewildered by it all',[55] which is exactly what Patrick Shea's father did.

After the killing of two constables at Soloheadbeg in Tipperary in January 1919, which, in retrospect, came to be seen as marking the beginning of the Anglo-Irish War, there was 'incredulity and fear and horror' in Athlone RIC barracks. Patrick's father was 'silent and grim', while his mother 'could not conceal her anxiety'. As an eleven-year-old, Patrick did

52 Ibid., p. 9. 53 Ibid., p. 10. 54 Ibid., pp 18–25. 55 O'Faolain, *Vive moi!*, p. 31.

not understand the politics of the bitter guerrilla war that was develop-
ing; all he knew was that his father was in grave danger. He lay awake at
night listening for his father's returning footsteps and 'was filled with a
fierce anger towards everyone associated with the new patriotism'.[56] Those
on the Republican side he regarded as 'enemies' and he 'hated every one
of them'. With a sense of some embarrassment in retrospect, he admits:
'I was an uncompromising, unapologetic West Briton.' In Rathfriland in
1920, hearing news of the deaths of young constables who had played
with him in Athlone, he welcomed the arrival of the Black-and-Tans and
the Auxiliaries with their policy of reprisals. Shea confessed that he was
'secretly pleased that the burden of fear was spreading'.[57]

In Athlone from 1919 the barrack square 'ceased to be a place of
recreation for all and sundry'; outsiders were no longer freely admitted;
'friendships ended at the gate', which was now barred at night; the back
door leading to the river bank was locked; and the windows of out-
buildings overlooking the street were bricked up. The police and their
families were 'isolated from the townspeople' and the 'feeling of an
approaching siege grew'.[58]

Patrick Shea in relating his life as a policeman's son uses two voices.
At first we hear the naïve, carefree voice of the boy, who loved swimming
and fishing with young constables and who, despite his mother's disap-
proval, laughed at the drunks swearing in their cells during the night. But
as his life and circumstances darkened after 1916, we increasing hear the
voice of the older man looking back, reflecting on his youth through the
lens of what came afterwards and struggling to explain and justify the
actions of his father and the men of the RIC, and, indeed, his own opinions and loyalties. We shall look further at Shea's memoirs in Chapter 9
when we explore the experiences of RIC men and their families after 1922.

Another son of a Kerry-born constable published an autobiography
shortly after Shea. This was Denis Donoghue, a distinguished Irish academic and literary critic, who has pursued much of his career in the
United States. Donoghue was born twenty years after Shea, in 1928, and
so did not have first-hand experience of RIC barrack life. But his father,
also called Denis, who was from near Killarney, joined the RIC in 1913
in preference to joining the army or emigrating. While stationed as a

56 Shea, *Voices and the sound of drums*, p. 27.   57 Ibid., pp 37, 42.   58 Ibid., p. 34.

sergeant in Tullow, Co. Carlow, in 1920 Denis senior married Johanna
O'Neill. She was the daughter of an RIC man then serving in Clonmel
and one of her brothers subsequently rose to be a superintendent in the
Garda Síochána.[59] So, aside from his father pursuing policing as a career,
there was also a history of policing in Denis' mother's family; indeed, the
family eventually straddled the RIC, the RUC and the Garda Síochána.

After disbandment early in 1922, Denis' father spent five months
trying to find alternative work in Ireland and England. In this he failed,
and later in the same year he went north and joined the new RUC, in
which he served until his retirement in 1946 – first in Co. Fermanagh and
then in Co. Down. Patrick Shea's family also moved north in 1922, set-
tling in Newry, his mother's hometown, but his father did not join the
RUC, although Patrick's older brother did. Professor Donoghue says that
his father's decision to join the RUC is 'easily explained: he had no choice,
no other job was available, and the RUC could not reject his application'.[60] But this comment is somewhat disingenuous. Of Catholic RIC
men disbanded in 1922, perhaps only around 6 per cent joined the RUC.[61]
Therefore, Sergeant Donoghue's decision to do so, especially when he
had no family connections in the north, certainly requires far more expla-
nation than it is accorded in his son's autobiography.

Young Denis Donoghue grew up in the RUC barracks in
Warrenpoint, Co. Down, during the 1930s. The building itself and the
lifestyle of those who lived in it had clearly changed little, if at all, in the
transition from RIC to RUC. The barracks was surrounded by a high
wall, the gates of which could be securely locked in order to withstand a
siege. The isolation of the police – which Patrick Shea saw increasing in
the south after 1916 – was obviously still very evident in the north during
the 1930s. Within this protected enclosure, behind the barrack building,
were a parade ground and a garden 'of sorts'. Donoghue characterises the
barracks as divided in half. One half was 'given over to the official business of the police' and was centred on the dayroom. There were also two
bare, whitewashed cells in this part of the building, one for men and one
for women. Donoghue, writing nearly sixty years later, still remembered
their pungent smell of disinfectant. In a smaller room, beside the stairs,

59 Denis Donoghue, *Warrenpoint* (London, 1991), pp 8–9. For Sergeant Donoghue's personnel record, see RIC
General Register (PRO(L), HO 184/35).   60 Ibid., p. 10.   61 See Chapter 9 for further discussion of RIC men
who joined the RUC.

the barrack weaponry, consisting of rifles, revolvers, hand grenades and tear-gas canisters, was kept in a chest. Sergeant Donoghue was in charge of seven or eight full-time constables, as well as the same number of part-time men. Professor Donoghue makes plain his intense dislike of the Ulster Special Constabulary, but whether he felt the same as a child living in barracks is not at all clear.[62]

Sergeant Donoghue, his wife and four children lived in the other half of the barracks, the 'married quarters', which consisted of a parlour, a kitchen and scullery, three bedrooms, a bathroom and an outside lava-tory.[63] By the 1930s police married accommodation was obviously more spacious than that described in the late nineteenth century, when the fam-ilies of sergeants had to make do with a sitting room, only one bedroom and no separate washing or toilet facilities.

I have mentioned earlier in this chapter the attempts made by the RIC to maintain a separation between family and official quarters in bar-racks, but Donoghue takes a different view, arguing that there 'was no visible separation between the dayroom of the barracks and the sergeant's married quarters'. This lack of a distinction between the official and the domestic, he suggests, helped augment 'the image of authority' that such a large building presented to the town.[64] This may be true, but his use of the word 'visible' is important. While the domestic part of the barracks was not physically divided off, invisible barriers certainly existed, created by the police regulations we have already looked at, which sought to restrict contacts between constables and the families of sergeants.

Shea's joyous account of games played with the constables in Athlone makes plain that sergeants' sons and young constables did at times estab-lish amicable relationships. But Shea says nothing of his mother's relations with her husband's men, nor of whether they played with his younger sister. So restrictions on constables mixing with the female members of their sergeant's family were probably still in force. Donoghue, on the other hand, who is clearly far more uncomfortable with his police ancestry than Shea, never discusses the constables at all, although he lived with them as a child under the same roof. While stressing that there were no divisions between the two halves of the building, his account of life in Warrenpoint barracks, nevertheless, focuses narrowly on his parents and their quarters,

62 Donoghue, *Warrenpoint*, p. 10. 63 Ibid., p. 11. 64 Ibid., p. 13.

extending out on occasion to encompass his local church and school and his mother's family in Co. Carlow. The official half of the barracks and the men who lived there remain almost totally blank.

But Donoghue, more than Shea, was acutely conscious of the complexity of his social and class status as a Catholic policeman's son in a town that was largely Protestant. His family he calculates was lower middle class, but his father's position meant that: 'Whether we wanted this to happen or not, some authority from the RUC adhered to us in our social lives.' Yet his maternal uncle, Seamus O'Neill, who had been an active Republican during the Anglo-Irish War and rose to be a Garda superintendent in Galway, Donoghue considered to be 'far socially superior to us' because he was an officer and had been an Irish-speaking school teacher.

O'Faolain, born in 1900 and growing up in Cork city, Shea, born in 1908 and growing up in Athlone, and Donoghue, born in 1928 and growing up in Warrenpoint, all illuminate aspects of the child's life in the constabulary from somewhat different perspectives. What they most obviously have in common, however, is that, when they came to write about their childhoods, each felt the need to explore his relationship with his father especially in terms of his father's occupation as a policeman. In all cases the father is almost swallowed up in the policeman. O'Faolain's revealing comment that his father was to him more a type than an person could be applied to the pictures that Shea and Donoghue also present of their fathers. The reader has little sense of the distinctive personalities of these three men; rather each emerges as a variation on the stereotype of the loyal Irish policeman. Presumably that's how their sons perceived them. If so, then in a sense all the RIC's rigorous training and discipline had succeeded, creating men who could never take off their uniforms, either literally or metaphorically. These men who, unlike their wives and children, moved easily between the official and domestic halves of the barracks nevertheless always remained policemen, regardless of their surroundings.

CHAPTER EIGHT

Leaving the constabulary

Then the Peelers did fall, without murmur or bawl,
Then their guns and their bayonets were shattered,
How sad was their case, when their eyes, nose and face,
When their lives and firelocks were battered.[1]

On behalf of the orphans of the late Constable John McEnery, whose premature demise took place on 10th June last (after serving 34 years in the police force), leaving eight helpless children, two of whom are permanently disabled, the eldest is only 18 years, a cripple, and the youngest 4 years, we most respectfully beg to appeal to you for a contribution ... both father and mother are now dead ...[2]

There is no man so boring to himself and to others as a pensioner with nothing to do and no hobby.[3]

Policemen could leave the constabulary in one of a number of different ways. The most dramatic of these was to be killed while on duty. But many men died on duty in very undramatic ways: that is they succumbed to illness. Many more resigned, or were dismissed for a variety of disciplinary offences. Most, though, retired with a pension, after long and conscientious service. We shall look at each of these various forms of departure in turn. But it is important to note at the outset that changes in the way men left the force tell us a great deal about changes in the nature and conditions of police service. As has already been mentioned, dismissals and resignations were more common methods of departure before the Famine than afterwards, when men began to serve for longer periods and thus were more likely to retire with a pension. Upsurges in deaths, whether by violence or disease, reflect years of crisis, but chronic disease also took a heavy and unrelenting toll – although a much less publicised one.

---

1 'A New Song called the Battle of Carrickshock' (NAI, CSORP, 1832/233). 2 Letter from seven Co. Limerick constables to the *Constabulary Gazette*, xxvi, 20 (29 Jan. 1910), p. 264. 3 District Inspector Ivon H. Price, 'Gardening in the R.I.C.', *R.I.C. Magazine*, April 1912, p. 189.

DEATHS ON DUTY: VIOLENT AND OTHERWISE

Surveying the whole century from 1822 to 1922 and taking into account contemporary Irish rates of mortality and morbidity, one would have to conclude that police service was not an especially dangerous occupation. But at certain times and in certain places, Irish policemen were much more prone to death and disease than was the rest of the population. Men who died while serving in the force succumbed, in the main, either to work-related diseases of various sorts or to violence. The latter usually took the form of shooting, but sometimes involved an assault with an improvised weapon. Suicides also occurred, but were rarely documented.[4]

In a clash with a crowd, the police, being well armed, clearly had the advantage. Stanley Palmer analysed what were termed 'constabulary affrays', that is clashes between police and crowds, during the twenty years from 1824 to 1844. He concluded that 'lethal violence was one-sided', as four 'peasants' were killed for every policeman killed. Omitting the Carrickshock incident, discussed below, the ratio of deaths during these years was much higher: at fairs it was 20:1; at riots 13:1; and at elections 11:1. However, evidence suggests that police may have suffered more non-fatal injuries during clashes.[5] Most of the 'affrays' Palmer studied involved stone-throwing crowds attacking parties of police who might be attempting to break up faction fights at fairs or fights between supporters of rival candidates at elections. But 47.5 per cent of 'affray' deaths during this period occurred in the years 1830–5 and mainly reflected clashes during the so-called Tithe War.[6] Up until 1835 the constabulary was used extensively, in cooperation with or in place of the army, to protect tithe collectors and process servers, as well as goods confiscated in lieu of tithe payment.[7] This

---

4 The RIC was not anxious to publicise the issue and a constable who wrote an anonymous article in 1910 about the loneliness, monotony and lack of privacy of barrack life driving men to take their own lives was, according to his daughter, denied promotion as a consequence. Forward, by the Right, 'Suicide in the R.I.C.', *Constabulary Gazette*, xxvi, 20 (29 Jan. 1910), p. 267, included in Winifred D'A., Gurteen, Co. Sligo, to ELM, 2 Jan. 1990 (RIC Letters, II, 44). 5 A return of constabulary affrays covering the years 1831–45 gives a ratio of three civilians killed for every policeman, but the situation is very different with regard to wounding. Then, interestingly, the ratio is reversed, with 2.4 policemen injured for every civilian. Yet how reliable these figures are is open to question, as, while it might have been possible to count civilian deaths fairly accurately, it was probably far more difficult to gain data on injuries. On the other hand, given that the police had firearms and crowds were generally armed with sticks and stones, it is understandable that in a violent clash more civilians would die and more policemen would be injured. *Return relative to the Persons who have been Killed or Severely Wounded in Affrays with the Constabulary ... since 1st December 1830*, H.C. 1846 (280), xxxv, pp 1–23. 6 Palmer, *Police and protest*, pp 331–3. 7 Lord Melbourne's Whig government of 1835–40, and its

brought them into direct, and often violent, conflict with communities determined to resist tithes.[8]

In terms of the deaths of policemen while on duty, the worst single incident during the century occurred at Carrickshock, Co. Kilkenny, in December 1831. A police party of 38, guarding a process server delivering summonses to tithe defaulters, was attacked in a boreen by a crowd said to number more than a thousand. Packed together in the narrow lane, the police found it difficult to aim and fire, and were overwhelmed by showers of large stones, while being assailed with pitchforks, clubs and hurling sticks. Within minutes, 13 of the party, including their officer, and also the process server, had been beaten or stabbed to death, while 14 men suffered severe injuries. Among the crowd three were shot dead and an unknown number injured.[9]

Clashes such as this between small, armed police parties and large, angry, unarmed crowds were not unusual before the Famine. As we have seen, governments used the constabulary extensively to impose public order by controlling crowds at fairs, markets, patterns and elections. Given that heavy drinking and fighting were characteristic of such events and that all lasted for several days, conflict between police and crowds was common. In the north, both before and after the Famine, clashes between police and marchers during the months of July and August were also a frequent occurrence. But Carrickshock was unique: never before or subsequently were so many policemen killed in the one incident and never did police deaths so greatly outnumber crowd deaths.

In an interesting recent article Garry Owens has studied memories of this incident. He argues that, although it was seldom mentioned in standard works of Irish history, it remained long in the social memory

representatives in Dublin Castle, sought to make the constabulary more acceptable mainly by appointing more Catholics, especially as officers, but also by withdrawing the police from their unpopular role as the protectors of tithe collectors. Ó Tuathaigh, *Thomas Drummond and the government of Ireland*, p. 20; Malcolm, '"The reign of terror in Carlow": the politics of policing Ireland in the late 1830s', pp 59–74.   8 For an interesting account of one such clash in Co. Cork in 1830, written in Irish, see Brian Ó Cuív, 'A contemporary account in Irish of a nineteenth-century tithe affray', *Proceedings of the Royal Irish Academy*, 61 C, 1 (July 1960), pp 1–21. The author, Dáibhí Do Barra, described the police involved as 'peelers', but also as 'muca dúbha', that is 'black pigs', and claimed that they were worse than the 'Lochlannach', the Vikings. I would like to thank Dr Stephen Lalor for drawing my attention to this article. There are other examples later in the century of the police being called, in Irish, 'black men', a reference to their very dark green uniforms, or 'pig men'. See Hugh Dorian, *The outer edge of Ulster: a memoir of social life in nineteenth-century Donegal*, eds Breandán Mac Suibhne and David Dickson (Dublin, 2001), p. 287. In 1909 Robert Lynd said policemen were often known as 'saigh-diúrí dubha' or 'black soldiers'. Robert Lynd, *Home life in Ireland* (London, 1909), p. 265.   9 Palmer, *Police and protest*, pp 335–8.

of rural communities. During clashes in the 1860s with Fenians and in the 1880s with Land League supporters, RIC men were often taunted with cries of 'Carrickshock'.[10] But the incident also remained in the constabulary's institutional memory. Inspector Robert Curtis discussed it in his history of the force, first published in 1869, suggesting that the attack had been carefully planned beforehand and this was why the police had suffered such heavily casualties.[11]

While the years of the Tithe War in the early 1830s were certainly dangerous ones for the constabulary, the most lethal periods for Irish policemen were without doubt those seven or eight years which, taken together, included the Famine of the late 1840s and the Anglo-Irish War of the early 1920s. In the first instance disease was the great killer, in the second violence.

Without knowing anything about what happened to the RIC between 1919 and 1922, the statistics alone would tell a grim story. The most authoritative recent study has calculated that 493 members of the RIC and DMP died violently in 1919–22, while 18 went missing and can be presumed killed and a further 77 died as a result of accidents or mistakes connected with the fighting.[12] That gives a grand total of 588 policemen who died violently in a little over three and a half years. In addition, nearly 700 were wounded.[13] We can gain a perspective on these figures when we look at police deaths during earlier and later political outbreaks. No police were killed during the 1848 Rising and only one policeman died during the Fenian Rising of 1867. During the Belfast riots of 1886, which registered the worst death toll of any single Irish political upheaval of the nineteenth century, only one policeman was killed.[14] During the Troubles in Northern Ireland in the last third of the twentieth century, some 500 members of the RUC, Ulster Defence Regiment and Royal Irish Regiment were killed, but that was over a period of more than thirty years up to 2000.[15] One would have to go back to the 1798 Rebellion to

10 For an example, see Edward Kennedy, *The land movement in Tullaroan, County Kilkenny, 1879–91* (Maynooth Studies in Local History 55, Dublin, 2004), p. 13. A memorial was finally unveiled on the spot in 1925, which listed the names of the three civilians killed, but made no mention of the thirteen dead policemen. Garry Owens, 'The Carrickshock incident, 1831: social memory and an Irish *cause célèbre*', *Cultural and Social History*, i, 1 (2004), pp 36–64. 11 Curtis, *History of the Royal Irish Constabulary*, pp 31–2. It was also discussed at length in H.R. Addison, *Recollections of an Irish police magistrate* (London, 1864), pp 28–43. 12 Abbott, *Police casualties in Ireland, 1919–22*, pp 7, 12, 66. 13 Townshend, *The British campaign in Ireland*, p. 214. 14 Policemen were occasionally killed while on duty between 1886 and 1916, but these were rare occurrences. In 1889, for instance, District Inspector William Martin was beaten to death by a crowd at Gweedore, Co. Donegal, when he tried to arrest a local priest involved in a dispute over rents. For differing views of the incident, see Dorian, *The outer edge of Ulster*, pp 43–6; John Ross, *The years of my pilgrimage: random reminiscences* (London, 1924), pp 48–59. 15 Paul Dixon, *Northern Ireland: the politics of war and peace* (Basingstoke, Hants., 2001), p.

find a comparable violent death toll among government forces to that sustained by the RIC during the Anglo-Irish War. It is also worth noting that only 150 soldiers died during this war, although late in 1919 the Irish garrison numbered some 37,000 men.[16] This brings home the fact that the brunt of the conflict was borne by the police, and not by the army.

Between January 1919 and August 1922 14,138 men joined the RIC and 7,122 left. This is of course a massive turnover in a force that at its peak in mid-1921 numbered in total a little under 16,000. Of those who left, the largest group, 3,391, resigned, while 1,911 were pensioned. But 766 were dismissed, 503 discharged, 145 were declared medically unfit and seventy-four deserted.[17] Even accepting that most of the nearly 2,000 who retired on pensions would probably have left around this time anyway, this still means that 25 per cent of the force chose resignation and about another 10 per cent were effectively sacked. Those departing, for whatever reason, were quickly replaced and the RIC grew in size by over 50 per cent between 1919 and 1921. But the men who left were often experienced Irish policemen; those who replaced them were inexperienced and, in many cases, they were not even Irish.

The material destruction was equally impressive. Of around 1,400 RIC barracks in Ireland, 547 were destroyed between January 1919 and the Truce in July 1921, while another 388 were seriously damaged.[18] This means that nearly two-thirds of barracks were rendered uninhabitable. As we have seen, barracks were far more than just places of work. For single constables and for most sergeants and their families, they were home.

Clearly, the years between 1919 and 1922 took a terrible toll of the RIC: hundreds of men were killed, thousands left the force and vast numbers lost their homes. Nothing in its training or in its experience over more than a century could have prepared the Irish constabulary for such a cataclysm. And, as we shall see in the next chapter, the RIC's ordeal during those years left a bitter legacy on both sides that lasted for much of the rest of the century.[19]

Yet we can find as substantial – if not more substantial – police death tolls if we look beyond war, rebellion and public disorder, to disease, both in its epidemic and its endemic forms. Such deaths, however, have not

---

24. 16 Townshend, *The British campaign in Ireland*, pp 214, 43. 17 Abbott, *Police casualties*, p. 66. 18 Townshend, *The British campaign in Ireland*, p. 214. 19 For a short, but interesting, discussion of RIC reactions to the war, using interviews from the recently released archive of the Bureau of Military History, see Diarmaid Ferriter, *The transformation of Ireland, 1900–2000* (London, 2004), pp 205–9.

attracted anywhere near as much attention as have those caused by politically inspired violence. During the height of the Famine, in the three years
1847–49, nearly 600 policemen died while on duty: 224 in 1847, 150 in 1848
and 221 in 1849. This rate of police deaths was twice as high as the rate
generally prevailing between 1841 and 1914, and compares with only 133
deaths on duty during the three years, 1843–5. The number of deaths in
1847 was not to be exceeded in one year until the Anglo-Irish War more
than seventy years later.[20] Although it isn't possible to analyse the causes
of these deaths in any detail, it is clear that a significant number were due
to famine-related diseases, notably typhus and typhoid.[21]

The use of the constabulary as an information-collecting agency had
begun before the Famine – police were employed, for instance, as census
enumerators from 1841 – but the urgent need to gather information on
the state of the potato crop, and other crops, on death rates and on evictions during the late 1840s expanded constabulary responsibilities dramatically. The constabulary was also employed extensively in unpopular
duties, like protecting convoys carrying food for export, assisting at evictions and pursuing those responsible for the massive increase in petty
theft that occurred during the Famine. In addition it was the police who
had to report cases of destitution to the poor law officials; it was they
who often had to recover the bodies of the dead, arrange for inquests
and for burials.[22] It is highly unlikely that any policeman starved during
1845–9, but like priests, doctors and poor law officials, who were obliged
by their occupations to deal with famine victims, close contact led to
infection, which produced illness, which sometimes resulted in death.

In the second half of the nineteenth century violent death became
less common among the constabulary and deaths from disease never again
reached the heights of the Famine years, but work-related illness was a
perennial problem. The RIC experienced a steady attrition, especially due
to respiratory disease.

Policemen had to be out patrolling around the clock, regardless of
weather conditions. Ordinary patrols involved long hours of walking and
watching city roads or town streets or country lanes. According to the *Code*,
while on 'beat duty' in a town, a constable 'should not confine his attention

20 Lowe, 'Policing the Famine', *Éire-Ireland*, pp 66–7; Griffin, 'The Irish police', p. 859. 21 L.M. Geary, 'Famine, fever and the bloody flux' in Cathal Poirteir (ed.), *The Great Irish Famine* (The Thomas Davis Lectures, Cork, 1995), pp 74–85. 22 Lowe, 'Policing the Famine', pp 51–7.

to principal streets, but should visit all the lanes and alleys within his beat. He should not loiter or gossip, but should work his beat continuously and regularly …' Patrols at night, which had to consist of at least two men, were also instructed to be constantly on the move. They were not to proceed 'in close order', however, 'but open out, walking on both sides, and in the middle of the road …'[23] After hours of walking, trying to stay alert, men naturally returned to the barracks very tired. Given the country's damp climate, they also frequently returned wet and cold. But even worse than ordinary patrols were ambush patrols. Men on ambush patrol were specifically instructed to avoid roads and instead to 'frequently traverse the fields and bogs' and to 'conceal themselves near localities favourable to the detection of offenders'.[24] This could mean lying for hours at night in damp ditches.

Nor was there much point in constables complaining about such conditions. In 1853 thirty-three Co. Monaghan sub constables from the Castleblaney district were dismissed when they protested that they had been ordered to march the ten miles to Carrickmacross in extremely bad weather, to police a race meeting all day in pouring rain, and then to march back at night, on ambush patrol, without any food or rest whatsoever. Like later sacked RIC dissidents these constables had little choice but to emigrate. The sympathetic local newspaper which reported the incident announced that most, fortunately, had the means to emigrate to America and a few planned to try their hand at gold prospecting in Australia.[25]

A constable from Moate told the 1882 enquiry into the constabulary that he knew several young men in the Co. Westmeath force with whom he would not like to share a barrack dormitory, due to 'the coughing they have; they are certainly in the first stages of consumption, from lying out at night'.[26] That the constable was not exaggerating is demonstrated by figures compiled by Brian Griffin on the deaths of a little over 2,000 serving policemen between 1850 and 1890. In 48 per cent of cases death was attributed to bronchitis, pleurisy, tuberculosis, pneumonia, influenza, a cold, congestion or inflammation of the lungs, bronchial asthma or, more vaguely, chest or lung disease.[27] All these illnesses, and especially TB, were common among the general population as well.[28] But their rates among

23 *Standing rules and regulations*, 1911, p. 287.   24 Ibid., p. 288. See Chapter 5 for further discussion of patrolling.   25 *Armagh Guardian*, 23 Dec. 1853.   26 Quoted in Griffin, 'The Irish police', p. 182.   27 Ibid., p. 184.   28 For the TB 'epidemic' that raged in Ireland during the late nineteenth and early twentieth centuries, see Greta Jones, 'The campaign against tuberculosis in Ireland, 1899–1914' in Elizabeth Malcolm and Greta Jones (eds), *Medicine, disease*

the constabulary were disproportionately high and undoubtedly reflected unhealthy working conditions. Policemen, patrolling the streets and lanes of the poorer areas of cities and towns, where diseases like TB were rife, being often wet and cold and tired, and sleeping and eating together in cramped barracks, were very susceptible to infectious diseases. A special ward was maintained at Dr Steevens Hospital in Dublin for the constabulary. Hospital treatment was not free, however, even if illnesses and injuries were acquired in the line of duty. In 1873 constables had their pay docked ten pence per day to cover the medical expenses incurred.[29]

RESIGNATION, DISMISSAL AND DISCHARGE

In its early years the constabulary had a high turnover of personnel. Many of the men who joined the force before the 1860s clearly did not see police service as a life-long career. Equally many who joined found the rigid discipline of the force onerous and were unable to accommodate themselves to it. This reflects the fact that the Irish constabulary was a novel force, unlike anything the country had seen before. As noted in Chapter 1, the police experiments that preceded the establishment of the county constabulary in 1822 had essentially involved temporary or part-time forces. Men joining the new constabulary in the 1820s or 1830s, or even the 1840s, could well have seen the force as only a temporary phenomenon and therefore not have regarded police service as long-term employment. The idea that service in the Irish constabulary could provide a secure, full-time career extending over thirty years took time to be recognised – and to be accepted. The strict and obsessive discipline imposed by the constabulary must also have been totally unfamiliar to many of the early constables and thus not easy for them to adjust to. Men who had seen military service during the Napoleonic Wars and were accustomed to discipline had joined the constabulary in considerable numbers before the 1830s, but thereafter ex-soldiers were rare. In addition the constabulary was an unpopular force. Its use during the 1830s against tithe protestors, faction fighters and Orange marchers and during the 1840s against Famine victims had led on occasion, as discussed above, to violent and bloody clashes.[30]

and the state in Ireland, 1650–1940 (Cork, 1999), pp 158–76. 29 *Report of the Commissioners*, 1873, p. 131. 30 Although open hostility towards the constabulary declined significantly over time, the fact that the Carrickshock incident

That many of the early recruits were unhappy in the police and aspired to other employment or to emigration is therefore hardly surprising. Unpleasant duties also undoubtedly were a stimulus to resignations. We saw above that nearly 3,400 men resigned during the Anglo-Irish War; during the Famine years of 1847–9 there were 1,124 resignations. That is 375 resignations per annum, compared with only 163 per annum in the four years, 1841–4, before the Famine.[31] As discussed in Chapter 6, men who were dissatisfied with the conditions of service in the constabulary tended to resign rather than to protest or seek redress from within the force. In a 10 per cent sample of resignations during 1846–51, 75 per cent of men resigning indicated that they planned to emigrate.[32] This highlights the fact that Irish emigrants of the Famine era were not only the starving and the destitute. Clearly many men with secure jobs in the constabulary preferred the risks and uncertainties of emigration to continued employment in the police of their ravaged homeland. With new English county police forces being established during the 1840s, significant numbers of Irish policemen were able to find more congenial, and usually better-paid, employment in them.[33]

In the 1860s the average length of service was between ten and eleven years and only 23 per cent of recruits served for twenty years or more. But, just thirty years later, during the 1890s 58 per cent of recruits had careers lasting twenty years or more.[34] In this regard the Irish constabulary was not unusual. Studies of new English county and borough forces established in the 1840s and 1850s have shown resignation and dismissal rates as high and, in many cases, even higher than those of the Irish constabulary; but also a tendency for these to decline dramatically towards the end of the century as police forces became more accepted institutions and policing was recognised as a worthwhile career.[35]

of 1831 was remembered, and indeed celebrated in poems and songs for the rest of the century, is an indication that undercurrents of hatred and opposition persisted. Working-class autobiographies sometimes contain unflattering portraits of peelers, while Nationalist accounts of the years 1916–22 are often full of loathing for the police. See, as examples, Dorian, *The outer edge of Ulster*, pp 287–8; McMahon (ed.), *Pádraig Ó Fathaigh's War of Independence*, pp 17–18, 84.   31 Griffin, 'The Irish police', p. 859.   32 Lowe, 'Policing the Famine', p. 67.   33 Palmer, *Police and protest*, p. 452. For a discussion of the many Irish policemen who emigrated, not only to England, but further afield, see Elizabeth Malcolm, '"What would people say if I became a policeman?" (Ned Kelly) The Irish policeman abroad' in Oonagh Walsh (ed.), *Ireland abroad: politics and professions in the nineteenth century* (Dublin, 2003), pp 95–107.   34 Lowe and Malcolm, 'Domestication', pp 41–2.   35 David Taylor, *Crime, policing and punishment in England, 1750–1914* (Basingstoke, Hants., and London, 1998), pp 94–105.

It is difficult to gain information on exactly why men resigned as the constabulary rarely publicised its men's discontents. But, as we saw in Chapter 6, at various times there was widespread and deep dissatisfaction over conditions of service, in particular, pay, allowances, pensions and promotions. The force was more ready, however, to record why men were punished, as punishments had to be justified and documented. The Constabulary Office in Dublin Castle produced lists every four or six months detailing men rewarded, dismissed, disrated or fined. These lists, studied closely by the men, were known facetiously as 'The killed and wounded' and, according to a retired sergeant, they had 'a great effect on the *esprit de corps* of the service'.[36] An incomplete collection of these lists survives for the period 1839 to 1872. It is instructive to compare a sample of the lists from the late 1840s with a sample from the early 1870s to examine if, and how, police service had changed over nearly twenty-five years.[37]

The return for the four months of June to September 1848 is especially interesting as it covers the 1848 Rising in July, during which parties of police in Cos Kilkenny, Waterford and Tipperary repelled and dispersed groups of rebels led by William Smith O'Brien.[38] For their actions 90 constables were rewarded with promotions or chevrons, while the two officers involved, Sub Inspectors Trant and Cox, received medals and £50 each. In addition 51 other constables, not connected with the suppression of the rebellion, had their conduct 'approved', through the award of chevrons or 'favourable records' entered into their personnel files. Yet, during the same four months, 105 men were dismissed, 217 disrated and 335 fined for a variety of disciplinary offences. So for every man classed as giving outstanding service during these difficult months, four to five men were categorised as having failed to fulfil their duties adequately. Leaving out the men rewarded for their role in suppressing the rebellion, we would have a ratio 12 or 13 policemen punished for every man commended.

In 65 per cent of cases the offence committed involved 'being under the influence of drink'. Yet usually 'intoxication' of itself was not sufficient grounds for dismissal. Those sacked had in virtually all cases com-

---

36 Brophy, *Sketches of the Royal Irish Constabulary*, p. 29. 37 The following discussion is based upon the Returns of the Names of Members of the Constabulary who have been Rewarded, Dismissed, Disrated and Fined, during the Four Months ended 30th September 1848, and during the Six Months ended 31st December 1871. These returns are held in the Garda Síochána Museum, Dublin Castle (M.169). 38 For a detailed account of the role of the constabulary in suppressing the 1848 Rising, see Palmer, *Police and protest*, pp 490–501. For an account from the constabulary point of view, see Curtis, *History of the Royal Irish Constabulary*, pp 59–86.

pounded their offence. The 'previous conduct' of a number dismissed for drunkenness was listed as 'bad' or 'indifferent'. Several had become involved in fights while drunk, either with their comrades or with civilians; others had been absent from their duties; one had abused an officer; one had attempted to help a prisoner escape; while another had used 'disloyal expressions'; and one was dismissed for attempting to commit suicide when drunk. In addition two constables in charge of men who were drunk were dismissed because they had not reported, or tried to cover up, the offence. Aside from breaches of discipline committed while men were drunk, the other offences in 1848 that attracted dismissal as a penalty were marrying without permission; 'highly discreditable conduct towards a female'; using a fictitious name when joining the force; insubordination or disobeying an order; allowing a prisoner charged with a political offence to escape; playing cards in a public house; misappropriating money or police equipment; stealing cattle; not fulfilling the duties of barrack orderly; and being absent from barracks without permission.

The offences for which men were disrated or fined seem on the face of it little different from those for which men were dismissed. Again 'intoxication' was far and away the most common problem. Although in a number of cases in these lists 'intoxication' is qualified by the word 'slightly'. So it would appear that the degree of drunkenness was an issue in determining whether a man was sacked or not. But in many instances it is difficult to understand the severity of punishment. For instance, men fined included Sub Constable Patrick Malone, stationed in the east riding of Co. Cork, who illegally arrested a civilian on 26 August 1848; Head Constable Frances Bernard of Co. Leitrim, who, on 4 August, committed an 'unprovoked assault on a civilian'; and Sub Constable Patrick Leonard of Co. Kilkenny who on 25 August allowed a prisoner to escape and then got drunk in a public house. Yet Sub Constable Thomas Henderson of Co. Limerick was dismissed for being 'slightly under the influence of liquor' on 13 June. In this case no other offence and no history of bad conduct were listed.

Henderson's case, however, appears unusual. Drinking of itself seldom warranted dismissal. But becoming involved in fights after drinking clearly did, as did combining drink with any sort of political activity. This is understandable. The combination of drink, politics and violence was one that, during the 1830s and 1840s, Dublin Castle was using the constabulary to curb in Ireland, so it did not want its own men

becoming enmeshed in this dangerous triangle. Policemen were forbidden throughout the century to join any political organisation; they were
also forbidden before the 1880s to enter public houses unless in connection with their duties; and their use of violence was strictly regulated.

An examination of the lists of rewards and punishments for the second
half of 1871 demonstrates that discipline in the RIC remained tough and
that drink continued to be a significant problem. In the six months from
June to December 1871 seventy-one men were rewarded for outstanding
service, while 880 were punished for infractions of the regulations. Of
these infractions 66 per cent wholly or largely involved 'intoxication'. Thus,
as in 1848, for every man commended 12 or 13 men were punished. And the
rate of dismissals in 1871 was also on a par with that of 1848: in the former
year dismissals and discharges averaged 25 per month; in 1848 there had
been 26 dismissals per month. In 1871, like 1848, men were seldom sacked
for just being drunk. Either they had a previous history of 'bad conduct'
or 'repeated intoxication', or they had committed an offence when drunk.
Some had been found drunk on duty, either on patrol or when serving as
barrack orderly; many had left their barracks without permission and had
failed to turn up for duty; others had become involved in arguments or
scuffles with fellow constables; while several had threatened civilians with
their weapons. The link between drink and violence was as evident in 1871,
as it had been in 1848, but, interestingly, none of the dismissals in the latter
half of 1871 appears to have had any political connotations.

However, a significant minority of dismissals were not drink related.
For instance, Sub Constable John Campbell, serving in Belfast, was dismissed for deserting his beat repeatedly and being absent from his barracks twice over night. In both instances he was found the next morning
in a brothel. That he was so readily discovered suggests either that his
colleagues were aware of Campbell's predilections or that they were familiar with Belfast brothels, or perhaps both. Two sub constables, Kelly and
Moriarty, from Co. Clare were dismissed for stealing straw belonging to
their constable and setting fire to it and to furze bushes near their barracks. Presumably this was some sort of attack aimed against their superior, but Sub Constable John Daly, who was barrack orderly at the time,
was also dismissed for not preventing the theft and fire, and for trying
to cover up the incident. Orderlies and constables whose men committed serious offences were highly likely to be punished themselves for not

preventing breaches of discipline or for not reporting them.[39] Sub
Constable Samuel Pickeran from Co. Donegal was dismissed for being
drunk, but he had been drinking illicit spirits that 'he had just seized'.
One intriguing case involved a Co. Leitrim sub constable dismissed for
'[h]abitually committing an indecent nuisance in Barrack'. Sub Constable
Michael Loughran of Queen's County was dismissed for '[w]riting
anonymous letters reflecting on the conduct of his officers'.

As well as being dismissed, by 1871 men could also be 'discharged'
without a pension or with a reduced pension. Of the eighteen constables and sub constables discharged in the latter half of 1871 only one was
accused of drunkenness, but seven had given false evidence at courts of
enquiry into constabulary misconduct, three had married without permission and one had incurred debts. Another was accused of '[i]mprop-
erly unlocking a comrade's box, and taking a cake there from without his
authority'. It would appear that discharge was used for offences considered somewhat less serious than those for which men were dismissed.

A number of these offences point to a strong sense of *camaraderie* prevailing among the rank-and-file of the constabulary. Constables sometimes
tried to ignore or cover up offences committed by their subordinates, even
at the risk of dismissal. Men were reluctant to give evidence at internal
enquiries against their fellows. But stealing from a fellow constable – even
if only a cake – was probably an offence that men would report as it
breached the essential bonds of trust and loyalty existing between them.

From the 1880s, and especially when Sir Andrew Reed was inspector
general during the years 1885–1900, discipline was moderated to some
extent. Yet in the 6th and final edition of the *Code*, published in 1911, there
were still forty-two offences listed for which men could be dismissed,
discharged, disrated or fined. And the easing of restrictions was often
heavily qualified – no more so than in regard to off-duty drinking in
pubs. The *Code* conceded that policemen were 'not absolutely prohibited
from entering a public house when not on duty', but made clear that this
was a 'privilege', which if abused could be withdrawn. And it went on to
'strongly' recommend that men 'not … avail themselves of the permission to drink in public houses when off duty, except where they require

39 Before parliamentary committees of enquiry senior constables often complained that they could be punished
severely for offences committed by their subordinates, even if they had little or no control over what had occurred.
Report of the Commissioners, 1873, p. 20.

refreshment on a journey'. They were not to get into the habit of fre-
quenting pubs or hotels in their district for the purposes of drinking.
Thus, while conceding the 'privilege' of drinking in pubs to men off
duty, on the one hand, the force nevertheless 'strongly recommended'
against it, on the other. If they felt they wanted to drink when off duty,
men were advised to do so in the privacy of their barracks. Also, they
were never to accept free drink from anyone, but always to purchase their
own.[40] While in theory off-duty men could drink in pubs, in practice it
must have been very difficult for them to do so. This supposed easing of
the RIC's strict discipline was therefore more apparent than real.

RETIREMENT: ONCE A POLICEMAN, ALWAYS A POLICEMAN

Hundreds of policemen were killed in the course of duty, thousands died
of disease and thousands more were dismissed, discharged or resigned.
Yet most of those who left the constabulary between 1822 and 1922
departed quietly, peacefully and according to fixed rules: that is they
retired on a pension after serving, in most cases, for more than twenty
years. The conditions governing pensions were thus of vital interest to
most constables and to many officers as well. As we saw in Chapter 6,
along with pay and promotion, pensions were the issue about which
policemen complained most commonly before government enquiries.
The rates of pensions were of course controversial, but even more so was
the question of when exactly men qualified for a pension. How long did
they have to serve and at what age could they retire?

Before a number of select committees police witnesses argued that they
should be allowed to retire after twenty-five years' service and that retirement should become compulsory after thirty years. As recruits joined the
constabulary generally in their late teens or early twenties, this meant that
most men would have been retiring around the age of fifty. There appears
to have been a consensus of opinion among rank-and-file policemen that
after twenty-five to thirty years' service a man was 'worn out'. One Cork
constable with twenty-three years' service told an enquiry in 1872:

> my experience is that a man cannot do anything after thirty years'
> service – he is only sticking in the service for the advantage of

40 *Standing rules and regulations*, 1911, p. 276.

himself and his family. When there is a certain class of duty to be discharged, such as attending fairs, assizes, and elections, the duties of which are very arduous, those men do not go, so that other men have to take their places.[41]

As discussed above, attending fairs, assizes and elections often involved the police in controlling large, and sometimes drunken, crowds day and night for three or four days. Such duties were indeed 'arduous' as the men probably had little sleep and inadequate food during that time. Moreover, there was always the danger of riots and fighting. It was not a task for 'worn out' men.

But were policemen retiring in their early fifties, after thirty years' service, really 'worn out'? Clearly many were not, as large numbers took up other jobs after retirement. At the outbreak of World War One there were around 8,000 constabulary pensioners in Ireland, 57 per cent of whom were working.[42] The fact that more than half of retired policemen continued to work was probably due to a variety of factors. Given that policemen had to serve at least seven years before marrying, many men did not marry until they were in their thirties and were still fathering children when in their forties. Therefore, on retirement in their early fifties, significant numbers would still have had dependent children. Police memoirs and the recollections of their children attest amply to the fact that policemen were ambitious for their children, wanting them to get a sound education, to pursue a 'respectable' career, to secure a 'steady' job or to make a 'good' marriage.[43] Encouraging the upward mobility of their children was expensive and not easily funded out of a police pension.

It is quite possible also that men who were not 'worn out', but were still in good health and energetic, wanted to continue working. For thirty years these men would have led highly regimented, active and, on occasion, demanding lives. Some may have welcomed the leisure of retirement, but others doubtless were conditioned to be busy and involved. Some went back to farming; others engaged in small business, notably running public houses; still others sought employment in areas related to policing.

The writer Sean O'Faolain, whose father was an RIC constable, tells us that his uncle, Sergeant Owen Boyhan, who had three children, eked

41 *Report of the Commissioners*, 1873, p. 23. 42 *Report of the Committee inquiring into the RIC and the DMP*, 1914, pp 10, 25–6. 43 See Chapter 9 for many examples of police ambitiousness. For an interesting study of Irish social mobility that, although it deals largely with the 1960s and 1970s, makes points that are relevant to policemen of an earlier period, see Michael Hout, *Following in father's footsteps: social mobility in Ireland* (Cambridge, MS, and London, 1989).

out 'his modest pension with various unexacting jobs'. For a time he was gatekeeper at Castletown House in Celbridge, Co. Kildare, and the family lived rent free in the gatehouse. Later he was in charge of the public weigh-machine and market house in Newbridge, Co. Kildare, living first in attached accommodation and then in a house in the town. The top floor of the house was let by Boyhan to married army officers, most of whom were English and on temporary postings in Ireland.[44] In working as a gatekeeper and a supervisor of weights and measures, Sergeant Boyhan was continuing in jobs his police career would have familiarized him with. His links with the army were also consistent in this regard.

When his only son was killed in France during World War One and his wife died, Boyhan gave up work and moved to the Curragh army camp, where he lived in married quarters with his two daughters who had secretarial jobs there. Boyhan obviously had dependent children when he retired. O'Faolain also tells us that his aunt Kate, Boyhan's wife, was pretentious and always over dressed, aspiring to be a 'grand lady'.[45] It is hardly surprising then that the ex-sergeant sought out 'unexacting jobs', often with free accommodation. Presumably he had to supplement his 'modest pension' in order to meet the expenses of his wife and children.

Another policemen's son growing up in the years before 1919, who later published an autobiography and who we discussed in the previous chapter, was Patrick Shea. Although born in Co. Kerry, Shea's father, who was disbanded in 1922 with the rank of head constable, after twenty-seven years' service, settled in Newry, Co. Down, and continued to work. The head constable had met his wife, Mary McLaughlin, in Newry and so the family had relatives in the town. His son believed, however, that the move north was brought about by his father's desire for secure and well-paid employment, which was more likely for an ex-RIC man in the north at that time than in the new Free State. The Sheas had five children, all under sixteen years of age in 1922, and, like so many RIC families, were intensely ambitious on their children's behalf. As Patrick Shea recalled:

> Father had almost an obsession about security; for him the first test
> of a career was that it should be permanent and pensionable. He
> had known insecurity as a child, when his household was at the
> mercy of the climate and economic hazards affecting life on a small

---

44 O'Faolain, *Vive moi!*, pp 64–5. 45 Ibid., pp 68–9.

farm at a time when there were no government subsidies, no state
pensions for the old and no financial aid for the unemployed. The
penalty for failure was the workhouse. Small wonder that the Royal
Irish Constabulary was an attractive career for farmers' sons.[46]

The head constable was employed, until his final retirement in the late
1930s, as clerk of the petty sessions court in Newry. As his son remarked
coyly, this was 'a job in which his interest in legal processes served him
well'.[47] Although Patrick spent his career in the Northern Ireland civil
service, his eldest brother Jack followed in his father footsteps by joining the Royal Ulster Constabulary.[48]

But, even in retirement from the RIC and engaged in other employment, ex-policemen were not considered – before 1922 at least – to have
completely severed their connections with the constabulary. The 1883 act
governing pensions (46 & 47 Vic., c.14) made plain that men were
'granted' pensions on certain conditions; they did not have an absolute
right to a pension. And even when they had satisfied the conditions qual-
ifying them for a pension, they could still forfeit that pension in the
future. Men could have their pensions cancelled if they were convicted
of an indictable offence; if they knowingly associated with thieves or 'suspected persons'; or if they were guilty of any 'illegal' conduct or, indeed,
any conduct considered by the inspector general to be 'disgraceful', 'discreditable' or 'improper'.[49] The latter condition obviously gave the RIC
considerable power to regulate the lives and activities of retired policemen. More specifically, pensioners were forbidden to leave the United
Kingdom without the inspector general's permission. Serving officers and
constables were instructed to keep in 'constant communication' with pensioners, from whom they were expected to receive 'useful information
from time to time'.[50] And any pensioner who refused to give information
or assistance to the RIC could have his pension stopped.

Even after retirement then, men were expected to continue their
duties of watching and collecting information for the authorities. In this
sense, there was really no retirement from the RIC: pensioners went on
fulfilling some basic, but significant, police duties until disease or death
ended their active lives. In the case of retirees, it was a matter of, once a
policeman, always a policeman.

46 Shea, *Voices and the sound of drums*, p. 99. 47 Ibid., p. 169. 48 Ibid., p. 100. 49 *Standing rules and regulations*, 1911,
p. 296. 50 Ibid.

CHAPTER NINE

Living and dying in the shadow of the 'old' RIC

The Royal Irish Constabulary

Grandfather's at rest now, she told me
though I had seen his jaw collapse, his fingers
clutch the air; in the darkened room a priest
murmured Latin words while mother lit a yellow

wax candle; he died, a sound like draining waters
in his throat. Lilies left in jars about the room
absorbed his sickness. She had called him 'sir'
and feared him, shone the crown on the brass

buttons of his uniform, and was ashamed of him.
Sea-shells and coloured glass spell out his name;
the locked graveyard is a wilderness but his ghost
flickered for years across our lives.[1]

Although the RIC officially ceased to exist in 1922, a social history of the force that ended in that year would be incomplete, for the influence of the RIC, on its former members and their families, and on other Irish police forces, continued for decades after disbandment. As in all wars, and especially internal wars, the end of violence does not necessarily bring peace, reconciliation and harmony to those involved. Many carry the psychological, as well as the physical, scars for life. Also, after the fighting ceases, the political and propaganda wars begin over how violence should be remembered, interpreted, commemorated and, ultimately, justified; what future generations should be told at home, in school, on the hustings – and in the history books.[2] In this final chapter we shall firstly survey briefly the impact of the RIC on the forces that succeeded

---

1 John F. Deane, *Sunday Tribune*, 10 Dec. 1989.   2 An important literature on memory and commemoration began to develop in Ireland from the 1990s. See Joep Leerssen *Remembrance and imagination: patterns in historical and literary representation of Ireland in the nineteenth century* (Cork, 1996); Lawrence MacBride (ed.), *Images, icons and the Irish nationalist imagination* (Dublin, 1999); Roy Foster, *The Irish story: telling tales and making it up in Ireland* (London, 2001); Ian McBride (ed.), *History and memory in modern Ireland* (Cambridge, 2001). David Fitzpatrick's article in the latter collection dealing with commemoration and the Irish Free State is especially relevant to this chapter.

it, and then look closely at ex-RIC men and their families, for many of whom the RIC caste a long shadow over the remainder of their lives.

POLICING NORTH AND SOUTH, 1922–68

The final three or four years of the RIC's existence up to 1922, as described in the previous chapter, were traumatic. Hundreds of policemen were killed and thousands resigned or were driven from their homes. At the same time, communities in both the north and the south of the country lost confidence in the ability of the police to protect them or came to regard the police as their bitter enemies. A key aspect of the partitioning of Ireland was the creation of new and separate police forces. And a key question that the fledgling northern and southern governments faced during the early 1920s was: should their new police be modelled on, and even recruited from, the RIC or should they not? To this question the north, ultimately, answered yes and the south, apparently, answered no. And yet the connections between the RIC and its successor forces in both the north and the south were more persistent and complex than is often realised.

Initially, it was by no means predictable that the north would adhere more closely to the RIC model than did the south. As we have seen, by the early years of the twentieth century, the RIC was largely composed of southern Catholic Nationalists and, while the force had become generally accepted in the south, hostility towards it in the north remained strong. Thus when the provisional government in the south, at the instigation of Michael Collins, established a committee in February 1922 charged with the task of organising a new police force to replace the RIC, 13 out of the 20 identifiable committee members were serving or former RIC men, while a further three were members of the DMP. Of nine senior officers quickly selected to head the new Civic Guard, seven had previously served in the RIC.[3] The very first rank-and-file guard recruited was a former RIC constable. The new force was armed with RIC weapons and supplied with RIC equipment; its first manual, used until 1942, was the RIC's manual, while its first code book published in 1928 was based on the old RIC code. Gregory Allen, the most recent histo-

3 Allen, *The Garda Síochána*, pp 27–8, 218–19.

rian of the Garda Síochána, argued that: 'If it had been politically possible he [Collins] would have retained the RIC, shorn of its imperialist traditions and answerable to a native government ...'[4] But there were many who disagreed with Collins' inclination to create, in effect, a new RIC; and the most influential of these dissidents proved to be the many former IRA fighters who swiftly joined the Civic Guard.

In May and June 1922, when the new force was about 1,500 strong and barely three months old, it staged a mutiny at its training base in Kildare. The story of this mutiny has been recounted in detail elsewhere,[5] suffice it to say here that the mutineers complained in particular at the appointment of so many former RIC men to senior and training positions. The mutiny and subsequent inquiry in July, combined with the death of Collins in August, led to major changes. The Civic Guard was technically disbanded and reconstituted; most of the senior former RIC men left,[6] and the inquiry made the surprising recommendation that the force in future should be unarmed. Even more surprisingly, the provisional government accepted this recommendation. So, after more than a century of armed paramilitary policing, and in the midst of a civil war, the southern government established an unarmed, civilian police force.

In retrospect this decision has been lauded, but at the time many disagreed with it. Even those who had opposed the recruitment of ex-RIC men still essentially envisaged a police force along RIC lines. The influence of the RIC on the guards continued after the summer of 1922, but more subtly and less overtly. For instance, the new commissioner appointed in the wake of the mutiny, Eoin O'Duffy, quietly employed as civilian advisors many of the senior RIC men who had been forced out. One of his deputies, Patrick Walsh, an ex-RIC district inspector, was charged with the important task of drafting a new code. According to Conor Brady, the code that eventually emerged was 'virtually ... a transcript of the RIC code'.[7] O'Duffy also proposed to recruit and train offi-

4 Ibid., p. 13. 5 The three major monographs dealing with the history of the Garda Síochána all provide long accounts of the 1922 Kildare mutiny. See Brady, *Guardians of the peace*, pp 52–70; McNiffe, *A history of the Garda Síochána*, pp 17–24; and Allen, *The Garda Síochána*, pp 31–48. 6 McNiffe calculated that before the mutiny, of the around 1,500 guards recruited, 6.6 per cent had previously served in the RIC. Although not numerous, most were appointed to influential positions. But after the mutiny RIC recruitment fell dramatically, so that overall between February 1922 and February 1932, of 8,230 guards recruited, only 1.9 per cent had RIC experience. They were vastly outnumbered by the 73 per cent who had joined the IRA at some point, by the 23 per cent who had previously been civilians and even by the 3 per cent who had seen service in the British army. McNiffe, *A history of the Garda Síochána*, pp 33–5. 7 Brady, *Guardians of the peace*, pp 72, 74.

cers separately, as the RIC had done. However, after the training of one group of cadets in 1923, rank-and-file demands for the right of promotion into the officer grades forced the abandonment of the system.[8]

The relationship between the Garda Síochána and its predecessor the RIC is therefore complex, and has often been misunderstood. Despite the 1922 mutiny against RIC appointments, the fact that few former RIC men actually joined the guards and that the force was disarmed, the RIC nevertheless did have a profound influence on the Garda Síochána. Liam McNiffe repeatedly talks about the 'continuity' – indeed, the 'great continuity' – that existed between the RIC and its southern successor. According to him: 'Successive Irish governments, Ministers for Justice, garda commissioners and senior officers continued, either consciously or unconsciously, to adopt and adapt the traditions, regulations and mechanisms that had been used by the RIC.'[9]

But of course it was not possible, for political reasons, to acknowledge this openly in the south at the time. Instead differences had to be stressed and especially the difference between an armed and an unarmed force. That the south could be policed by a force without weapons, which had not been possible under British rule, was used as an argument to bolster the legitimacy of the southern state. Yet the Garda recruited from the same social classes as the RIC had; training occurred at the old RIC depot in Phoenix Park; in the early years ex-RIC men were employed as instructors; the Garda's training and duty manuals were all actual RIC documents or ones closely modelled upon them; guards were distributed in small groups to stations, in the same way as RIC constables had been; Garda stations were frequently old RIC barracks; the system of ranks in the guards was almost identical to the RIC system, although with different names; and, underlying all this, the duties carried out by the guards were the same as those previously undertaken by RIC constables.[10] A comparison of the RIC in the early 1920s with the Garda Síochána up to the 1950s, points to the fact that the guards developed directly out of the constabulary. Despite name and personnel charges, and even the disarming of the police, the similarities between the two organizations are far more striking than the differences.

If there was intense hostility towards the RIC in large parts of the south, especially after the advent of the Black-and-Tans, northern

---

8 McNiffe, *A history of the Garda Síochána*, p. 68. 9 Ibid., p. 171. 10 Ibid., pp 171–3.

Unionists had little affection for the force either. By the early 1920s, and indeed much earlier, they had come to regard it as a Catholic Nationalist body directed from Dublin, with little understanding of, and even less sympathy for, the interests of Ulster Protestants. As already mentioned, it represented a warning of what their lives would be like under a Home Rule parliament based in the south. Thus when IRA attacks in the north increased in 1920, Unionists set about establishing their own police force. Relying solely upon the RIC for protection against the IRA was out of the question. In September 1920 a 'special' constabulary began to be recruited, with the approval of the British government, to bolster the RIC in the north, just as at the time the Black-and-Tans were being introduced in the south for the same purpose. This force was to be divided into three sections: A Specials, who were armed, full-time policemen; B Specials, who were armed, part-time policemen; and C Specials, who were unarmed and were to act as a reserve. Members of the Ulster Special Constabulary (USC), who eventually numbered more than 24,000, were overwhelmingly Protestant; a significant number were ex-soldiers; and many belonged to the Protestant paramilitary Ulster Volunteer Force.[11]

When the RIC was disbanded in the south and replaced by the Garda Síochána early in 1922, the mainly English and Scottish Black-and-Tans left the country, rewarded with government gratuities. But in the north, when the Royal Ulster Constabulary (RUC) was created in June 1922 to replace the RIC, nearly half the new force was recruited from the USC. The Northern Ireland government decided it needed a police force numbering 3,000, one-third of whom should be Catholics. These Catholics would be recruited from the RIC. If, however, 1,000 Catholic ex-RIC men could not be found to join the RUC, then recruits would be sought among the Catholic community in the north. Yet many Unionists – some in very senior government positions – were strongly opposed to the creation of a Northern Ireland police force that was one-third Catholic. They therefore set about doing all they could to increase the Protestant proportion in the force.

By May 1924 the RUC had virtually reached its target of 3,000 members, of whom 47 per cent had formerly served in the RIC and 48 per

11 Michael Farrell, *Arming the Protestants: the formation of the Ulster Special Constabulary and the Royal Ulster Constabulary, 1920–7* (London, 1983), pp 30–54; Arthur Hezlet, *The 'B' Specials: a history of the Ulster Special Constabulary* (London, 1972), pp 1–27.

cent in the USC. At this time 23 per cent of RUC men were Catholics – well short of the 33 per cent envisaged when the force was established just two years before. Yet this figure marked the peak of Catholic membership of the RUC. It declined swiftly thereafter, being 17 per cent by 1935 and a mere 10 per cent by 1966.[12] Many RIC men joining the RUC were older than other recruits and so tended retire earlier.[13] Resigning or retiring Catholic policemen were generally replaced by Protestants, often by former members of the USC. So that well into the 1950s around half the RUC continued to be composed of ex-USC men.

That the RUC was to be a force with a pervasive Protestant, Unionist culture was signalled clearly as early as 1922/3. In order to forestall charges of political or sectarian bias, the RIC had always forbidden its members to discuss politics, to vote in elections or to join any organization, except for the Freemasons. But in July 1922 it was decided that RUC men could belong to the Orange Order, so long as they did not attend lodge functions in uniform. Policemen were also permitted to vote. In January 1923 an Orange lodge was formed exclusively for RUC men, called the Sir Robert Peel Memorial Temperance Loyal Orange Lodge. It soon had a membership of around 300, or, in other words, about 10 per cent of the RUC.[14]

Although the RUC was predominantly a Protestant and Unionist force, whereas the RIC, in terms of its rank-and-file at least, had been largely Catholic and Nationalist, in other respects the two forces were very similar. For the RUC, like its counterpart in the south, inherited most of the duties, organisation and materiel of the RIC. The influence of the RIC on the RUC was greater, partly because far more RIC men joined the RUC than joined the Garda Síochána and because the RUC adhered more closely to the RIC's paramilitary style. But both forces for decades were trained along the same lines as the RIC, followed RIC rules and regulations, did the same duties as the RIC and even lived and worked in the same buildings. As Chris Ryder has written of the RUC: 'In reality life for the ordinary RUC man closely resembled that of the RIC and changed

---

12 Chris Ryder, *The fateful split: Catholics and the Royal Ulster Constabulary* (London, 2004), p. 71. As a point of comparison, it is worth noting that the Garda Síochána was even more disproportionately Catholic, with only 1.3 per cent of members being Protestants between 1922 and 1952; and most of these had joined in the early 1920s. In the twenty years from 1932 to 1952 only about half a dozen Protestants joined the guards. McNiffe, *A history of the Garda Síochána*, p. 51. 13 Farrell, *Arming the Protestants*, p. 267. 14 Ryder, *The RUC*, pp 59–61.

little between the late 1920s and the early 1960s.'[15] Indeed, most of the RUC's commanders for half a century had RIC backgrounds. The first two long-serving inspectors general, Charles Wickham (1922–45)[16] and Richard Pim (1945–61), had both previously been officers in the RIC; Albert Kennedy (1961–9) was the son of an RIC man,[17] as was Jamie Flanagan (1973–6), the only Catholic to head the force.[18]

It was really only from the 1950s that RIC influence in terms of personnel, regulations and equipment began to disappear in both the Garda Síochána and the RUC.[19] Yet, ironically, the outbreak of the Troubles in Northern Ireland in the late 1960s saw the paramilitary model of policing, represented by the RIC, reassert itself, not only among the RUC, but eventually among the Garda as well.[20]

LIFE AS AN 'RIC MAN'S "GET"'

At the time of disbandment in 1922 the RIC totalled nearly 16,000 officers and men. Some 4,000 to 5,000 were Black-and-Tans and 1,500 Auxiliaries, few of whom remained in Ireland.[21] One Black-and-Tan, who later served in the Palestine police force (1922–6) and then in the London Metropolitan Police (1926–51), summed up the attitude of such men when he wrote many years later: 'All was coming to an end in Ireland for chaps like me ... [the RIC] was a very prestigious force in its way, and it was about to be murdered. If one was a loyalist, that is, if one was non-Irish, then one must get out. It was rather like the time the Romans left Britain, or so it seemed to us at the time.'[22] English-born mercenary police

---

15 Ibid., p. 85. 16 'Sir Charles Wickham', *Proceedings of the Royal Ulster Constabulary Historical Society* (autumn, 1996), p. 1. 17 Ryder, *The RUC*, pp 40, 79, 94. Kennedy obituary, *The Guardian*, 14 Oct. 1991. 18 Flanagan obituary, *The Guardian*, 10 April 1999. 19 Keith Jeffery, 'Police and government in Northern Ireland, 1922–69' in Mark Mazower (ed.), *The policing of politics in the twentieth century* (Providence, RI, and Oxford, 1997), pp 151–66. 20 For a discussion of the impact of the Troubles on the Garda during the 1970s, see Allen, *The Garda Síochána*, pp 193–6. 21 Bill Lowe has recently suggested that there was a significant minority of Irish-born men among the Black-and-Tans and the Auxiliaries: 20 per cent in the case of the former and 10 per cent in the case of the latter. But whether most remained in Ireland after disbandment or left isn't clear. W.J. Lowe, 'Who were the Black-and-Tans?', *History Ireland*, 12, 3 (Autumn 2004), pp 48–9. 22 Yet the wife of an English official in Palestine did not see ex-RIC men as representing a civilizing force when they first arrived, commenting in a letter: 'Our Irish Constabulary have arrived, and a rough looking lot they are. Already it's rumoured they are painting Jaffa red. They don't fit with our scheme for a morale Utopia'. Arab merchants in Jaffa agreed and responded by locking up their shops, for fear of police violence and looting. Horne, *A job well done*, pp 77, 86–7.

might have seen 1922 as marking the end of civilization in Ireland and a return to the Dark Ages, but what of the 8,000 or so Irish-born regular policemen? What happened to these men and their families after 1922? Did they enter a new Dark Ages?

Given the bitterness of the fighting, especially in 1920/1, and the level of popular hostility displayed towards the RIC, not surprisingly, many Irish-born disbanded policemen also concluded that there was no future for the likes of them in the new independent Irish state. This opinion was strengthened by the fact that the IRA continued to shoot policemen after the Truce was declared in July 1921 and even after the Treaty was signed in December and approved, narrowly, by the Dail in January 1922. The brutal killing of two long-serving RIC sergeants in Galway in March 1922 had a particularly serious impact on morale, as both men were in hospital, recovering from serious illness, and were shot dead in their beds by a masked gang.[23] In that very month – March 1922 – Dublin Castle informed the British government that the RIC was 'completely dispirited and demoralised'.[24] Although the force was formally disbanded in the south in March and in the north in May, finalising all the arrangements dragged on until August.

It was naturally an anxious time for RIC men and their families. The financial compensation awarded to disbanded men was relatively generous, but the pension still represented only a proportion of their existing salaries, and so most needed to find new employment.[25] Some, realising that their skills were transferable, sought to join other police forces. Around 1,350, including a little over 500 Catholics, joined the new RUC, while 200 initially joined the Garda. Nearly 500, about half of whom were Black-and-Tans or Auxiliaries, joined the new Palestine police force.[26] But hopes of finding secure employment in English forces were largely frustrated. With regard to the London Metropolitan Police, the Home Office made very clear that it was opposed to employing ex-RIC men. Among English police authorities generally there was a suspicion

---

23 M.P. M., ex-RIC, Gort, Co. Galway, to ELM 13 Dec. 1989 (RIC Letters, I, 34). Abbott, *Police casualties in Ireland*, p. 281. For the IRA's campaign of selective assassinations, especially aimed against ex-soldiers, see Jane Leonard, 'Getting them at last: the I.R.A. and ex-Servicemen' in David Fitzpatrick (ed.), *Revolution? Ireland 1917–23* (Dublin, 1990), pp 118–29. 24 Kent Fedorowich, 'The problems of disbandment: the Royal Irish Constabulary and imperial migration, 1919–29', *Irish Historical Studies*, xxx, 117 (May 1996), p. 94. 25 For pension details, see Award of Pensions, on Disbandment of the RIC, to Members of the Force who were Appointed Prior to 1 July 1919 (PRO(L), PMG 48/76). 26 Horne, *A job well done*, p. 77.

of the RIC because of its paramilitary style and its recent experience of guerrilla war. Such a background was regarded as inappropriate to English conditions.[27]

Dominion police forces displayed a somewhat similar attitude. Most indicated that they were not in need of recruits and, anyway, they had large numbers of their own ex-soldiers to draw upon if men were required. But prejudice and political anxieties clearly underlay some of these responses. Kent Fedorowich has noted that Toronto was not interested in Catholic ex-RIC men as its police force had long been a stronghold of Ulster Protestant immigrants. In Australia too there were worries that ex-RIC men would exacerbate sectarian tensions, which had reached new heights during the World War One over the issue of conscription.[28]

The plight of ex-RIC men was made worse by the outbreak of civil war in Ireland in the middle of 1922. This spurred the British government to take action to facilitate their emigration. If imperial police forces had snubbed Irish policemen, then perhaps dominions and colonies would be prepared to accept them as civilian settlers. Men willing to emigrate were permitted to commute their pensions into lump sums that could be used to buy property or establish businesses abroad. In the two years from early 1922 until early 1924 some 5,400 applications for commutation were received, of which 3,600 were approved. Although accurate statistics are not available, it would appear that perhaps half, or around 1,800, of successful applicants emigrated, with the majority going to Canada, Australia and the United States.[29]

Nevertheless, although many ex-RIC men joined other police forces or emigrated abroad, the majority of disbanded men remained in Ireland. The fact that most did not leave after 1922 raises a number of intriguing questions. For instance, how did ex-RIC men negotiate, what might be termed, their post-colonial lives and identities? And what of subsequent generations? How did the children and grandchildren of the Irishmen who had served and fought for Britain – not abroad against Germans, but at home against their fellow Irish – deal with their legacy while growing up in the new state? The Irish Free State, which in 1948 declared itself a republic, was intensely proud of its 'founding fathers', especially those who had fought during the Easter Rising of 1916 and, what came to be

27 Fedorowich, 'The problems of disbandment', pp 97–8. 28 Ibid., pp 100–1. 29 Ibid., p. 107.

called, the War of Independence of 1919–21. Family history and genealogy have always been important in Ireland. Put rather bluntly then, if a
grandfather, father, brother or uncle – or even, as was common, more
than one of them – had fought against the 'heroes' of the independence
struggle, how did a family deal with this apparent treachery? Should
someone enquire as to a family's role in the years 1916–23, what did a
member say? Did they hide the fact that a close relative or relatives had
served in the RIC? And, in addition to what was said in public, how did
a family deal with their history in private? What did ex-policemen say to
their wives; what, if anything, did parents tell their children? In other
words, what did families chose to remember – and to forget? The descendants of the RIC had to deal with such difficult questions, especially in
the south, for half a century after the early 1920s.

When I began to study the history of Irish policing during the late
1980s, with a colleague, Professor W.J. Lowe, we were well aware that some
ex-RIC men were still alive. Oral histories of former policemen had
already been collected by other researchers, notably J.R.W. Goulden in
the 1950s and 1960s and John Brewer in the 1980s. We were certainly keen
to find men who had not as yet recorded their recollections, but we were
also very interested in the experiences of the descendants of policemen.
We wondered what it was like for a family to be on the losing side in a
war of national independence, yet to remain in the country and, presumably, have to work out a new set of loyalties. We were also very conscious that this was an experience by no means restricted to the Irish or
to policemen, but one shared during the twentieth century by many
indigenous groups that had served foreign and colonial rulers.

In order to find answers to such questions, we set out to publicise
our work through the Irish media. As a result of these efforts, and in
particular an article by the journalist Kevin Myers in the *Irish Times* in
1989,[30] I received letters from over 200 people. The vast majority were resident in Ireland, but others were living in England, Australia, Canada, the
United States, France, South Africa, and even the United Arab Emirates.
A small number were RIC veterans, but most were the children and
grandchildren of RIC men. Many had been born before 1922 and had

---

30 'An Irishman's Diary', *Irish Times*, 9 Dec. 1989. Articles soliciting information also appeared in the *Cork Examiner*,
27 April 1990; *Belfast Telegraph*, 30 April 1990; *Donegal Democrat*, 18 May 1990; *Garda News*, May 1990, p. 21; *Clare
Champion*, 1 June 1990; and *Galway Advertiser*, 5 July 1990.

first-hand experience of the force; some had even spent portions of their childhoods living in barracks. Most only wrote to me once, but some wrote numerous times over a period of several years. A few encouraged others to write to me or put me in touch with people they thought might also be able to help. Quite a number enclosed documents, photographs and family trees. While of course interested in their RIC ancestor or ancestors, I sought especially to draw out my correspondents as to their own experiences as the offspring of the RIC.

Although it is impossible to obtain accurate figures, it would appear that many of those who left the country in 1922, to join other police forces or to emigrate, eventually returned, either permanently or temporarily. So the figures on those departing in 1922 are somewhat misleading. A number of letter writers spoke of fathers who went to England to work for varying periods, but returned to Ireland when they felt it safe to do so. One Kildare constable, who had in fact resigned from the RIC as he did not want to work with the Black-and-Tans, still considered it necessary to take his family to England for three years in 1922–5. He died in 1953 and, according to his daughter, never spoke about his police career. The little she discovered came from her mother and an older sister, who was a teenager at the time.[31]

Constable Luke D., who was from Co. Roscommon and had mainly served in Co. Galway, went to Birmingham after disbandment and worked there for some years as a night watchman. According to his daughter, he did not talk much about his police career or his time in England. He returned to Ireland at the request of his family as his father was ill and he was heir to the family's small farm. He married a local woman, who was twenty years his junior, had four children and continued farming for the remainder of his life. His only son joined the Garda, rising to the rank of superintendent.[32] While Luke D. 'did not mix much with neighbours … he loved to meet old colleagues from the force' and a 'few times every year he called on a Mr McD. who ran a pub in … Boyle. They talked about

31 Zita C., Newcastle, Co. Galway, to ELM, 25 Feb. 1990 (III, 90). 32 Another correspondent, a retired member of the Garda Síochána, whose maternal grandfather and two cousins of his father had been in the RIC, commented that 'quite a large proportion of Garda members had R.I.C. connections', including several commissioners. Other correspondents made the same point. One, who had served in the Garda from 1959 to 1990, had a grandfather who had been a head constable in the RIC. Thus, although not many ex-RIC men actually transferred to the Garda during the 1920s, it would appear that a significant number of later recruits came from families with a history of service in the RIC. Michael Q., Kilsallaghan, Co. Dublin, to ELM, 15 May 1990 (I, 17); William C., Charlestown, Co. Mayo, to ELM, 24 Jan. 1991 (V, 192).

old times'. But his daughter remembered 'being advised by my parents not to bother saying my father had served in the R.I.C. when I was going off to Dublin to work in the Civil Service, and I didn't tell my closest friends.'[33] Several correspondents commented that those who sought jobs as teachers or civil servants usually kept their RIC ancestry secret.[34]

Even if fathers remained in England, sometimes their children returned to Ireland. Sergeant John O'B. from Co. Limerick, who had two brothers in the RIC, left Ireland with his family in 1922 and spent five years in Brighton, before moving to London. His daughter says that he never worked and her mother had to make ends meet on a pension of £3 15s. per week. The sergeant's brother-in-law from Cork, who had also been in the RIC, was already settled in Brighton, where it appears a number of former Irish policemen were living. Friendships were formed with such families in Brighton and also later in London, but if anyone Irish called at the house, the children were sent out for a walk 'in case some story was told – not for us'. John O'B. died in London in 1938, but his daughter returned to Ireland and married in 1947, although the initial reaction of her future Macroom mother-in-law when presented with the marriage plans was: 'surely not an RIC man's daughter'.[35]

Two brothers from Co. Tipperary, Michael and James H., who had served in the RIC for over twenty years, left the country in 1922, not because of a vague threat, but because they were specifically ordered to do so by the IRA. Several correspondents sent copies of IRA letters, either ordering a named RIC man to leave or, in light of assistance given, guaranteeing him protection.[36] Michael and James H. went to Bristol, but returned in 1924 when 'bad feelings seemed to have died down'. Both bought farms in their native county and settled with their families, but they maintained contact with many fellow RIC veterans.[37] As we shall

33 Bernadette Q., Dundrum, Dublin, to ELM, 12 Dec. 1989 (I, 12).   34 See, for example, Desmond S., Mullingar, Co. Westmeath, to ELM, 8 Sept. 1990 (I, 19).   35 Maureen L., Berrings, Cork, to ELM, 7 May 1990 (IV, 139).   36 For instance, a letter headed 'Final Warning' from the Headquarters of the 1st Battalion, South Wexford Brigade of the IRA, dated 10 May 1922, ordered Bryan D. of New Ross '(a late member of the R.I.C) ... to leave the South Wexford Brigade area immediately'. According to Bryan D's grandson, he did not leave New Ross, as the signer of this 'Final Warning', 'had been brought into the world by my grandmother [who was a local midwife] and she was quite capable of sending him back whence he came'. Stephen L., Arbour Hill, Dublin 7, to ELM, 19 June 1990 (IV, 123). On the other hand, a letter from the Headquarters of No.1 Brigade, 3rd Northern Division of the IRA, dated 15 May 1922, announced that Thomas S. of Co. Sligo, while serving with the RIC in Belfast, had 'been in touch with our men and ... many times rendered us service at his own personal risk. We therefore request that he be treated with the utmost respect whereever [*sic*] he may wish to reside in Ireland'. Thomas G., Tullaghan, Co. Leitrim, to ELM, 23 May 1990 (IV, 149).   37 Carmel H., Tullow, Co. Carlow, to ELM, 16 Feb.

see, what today would be termed 'networking' was a feature of the lives of many ex-RIC men.

Another RIC constable from west Cork, Patrick D., who had joined the force in 1913, emigrated to England in 1922 and worked in Manchester, but his wife remained living with his parents in Cork. Later he worked for a time in Buffalo, New York, before returning to Ireland permanently in 1927 with the money to buy a farm in his native county. Patrick D. too appears to have maintained contacts with old comrades. According to his son, a number of ex-policemen like his father helped train the part-time Local Defence Force established in 1940 to defend neutral Ireland during the 'emergency' of the Second World War.[38] At his death in 1974 his children decided to include 'ex RIC' in his newspaper death notices, 'because we knew how proud he was of his service with the RIC'.[39]

Even those who joined other police forces in 1922 did not necessarily totally sever their ties with Ireland. A Cork policeman, who was appointed to the RIC in 1920 aged twenty, joined the Palestine police briefly after disbandment, but soon returned to Ireland, where he married, and was by 1925 serving in the Birmingham city force.[40] There he was killed in a traffic accident in 1935, while on duty. This man's father had been an RIC sergeant in Kilkenny, while his wife, from Co. Wexford, had both a father and uncle in the force. The uncle, who was a sergeant in King's Co. (Co. Offaly), was shot dead by the IRA in November 1920.[41]

Others who joined the Palestine force served much longer, but quite a few returned to Ireland on retirement, usually during the 1940s. It is not possible to number these men exactly, but the following are typical examples of them. Gerald F., born in 1886, a graduate of Trinity College, Dublin, was appointed an RIC district inspector in 1911 and served as a major with the Royal Dublin Fusiliers during the war before rejoining the RIC in 1919. At disbandment he joined the Palestine police and helped

1990 (III, 100). This correspondent, who specifically asked that I not name her RIC ancestors, also enquired: 'In these days of peace and reconciliation is there a danger that your book will arouse old feelings of animosity among people who are now good friends?' I hope this much-delayed work will allay her understandable fears. 38 For another correspondent whose father served in the RIC and later helped train the Local Defence Force, see Francis H., Virginia, Co. Cavan, to ELM, 8 Feb. 1990 (II, 66) 39 John D., Churchtown, Dublin 14, to ELM, 14 Nov. 1992 (III, 105). 40 The chief constable of Birmingham had himself seen service in the RIC and thus may have been more willing to appoint ex-RIC men after 1922 than were the heads of other English forces. Fedorowich, 'The Problems of Disbandment', p. 98. 41 Robert H., Summerhill, Co. Meath, to ELM, 20 Feb. 1990 (III, 94). For an account of the shooting of Sergeant Henry Cronin in Tullamore, see Abbott, *Police casualties*, p. 140.

recruit other ex-RIC men for the force. In Palestine he reached the rank of assistant inspector general before his retirement in 1939. He then took up farming in Co. Wicklow and died at Greystones in 1982. Michael McC., born in 1892, joined the RIC as a district inspector in 1910 and served in the Leinster Regiment until 1919. He too returned to the RIC and in 1922 went to Palestine. Appointed deputy inspector general in 1943, he retired to Ireland in 1945. Patrick H., from Co. Cork, served in the Irish Guards during the war and joined the RIC in 1920. He went to Palestine in 1922 and by 1945 was a commissioner of prisons there. On retirement he returned to his home county and died at Glanmire in 1975.[42]

But most ex-RIC men never left Ireland at all, although many struggled to find new jobs or make ends meet on a limited pension, which sometimes forced them to move around the country. The following story is fairly typical. Thomas R. (1881–1962), born on a west Cork farm, joined the force as a constable in 1906, as did his younger brother, James. His daughter wrote that Thomas R. had never been out of his home county nor handled money before he came to Dublin for training at the Phoenix Park Depot. He was posted to Co. Kerry, where he met his wife. They married, despite the fact that her family was opposed; not because he was in the RIC, but, as they were Protestants, they objected to the fact that he was ten years older than his bride and also that he drank alcohol. Thomas R.'s marriage led to his transfer to Belfast, which was a bit of a shock to his wife who had always lived on a farm.

On disbandment, Thomas R. was offered promotion and a job in the RUC, but he refused and sought to make ends meet on a pension of £153 2s. 9d. per annum, supplemented by part-time work on farms in the vicinity of Bangor, where the family had moved from Belfast.[43] But influenza killed two of his young daughters and burdened the family with heavy

---

42 One of the longest and most varied careers undertaken by an ex-RIC man was that of Michael O'R. (1895–1981). Born in Dublin, he served in the Royal Flying Corps during World War One, in the RIC (1920–2) and the Palestine police (1922–44). He commanded the Cyrenaica police in liberated North Africa in 1944, served as a senior police officer in British-occupied Germany (1945–50) and then became commissioner of police in Kenya, before retiring in 1954. He never resettled in Ireland though, living in Minorca and then in London until his death. I would like to thank Edward Horne, the author of a history of the Palestine police, for supplying me with this information. Edward Horne, Barton on Sea, Hampshire, to ELM, 18 Aug. 1990 (V, 162). 43 Another correspondent, whose grandfather from Co. Leitrim served in Belfast from about 1895 until disbandment, commented that many ex-RIC men from the south, who did not join the RUC, nevertheless stayed in Belfast, so that 'even up to the early 1960s it was quite common to see small groups of tall elderly men with brogues gathering after mass outside Catholic churches all over Belfast. They were distinctive because of their height and military bearing and they towered over the rather stunted city dwellers'. John R., Belfast, to ELM, 2 Jan. 1990 (II, 56).

medical bills. This forced them to leave Bangor and return to their families' farms in Cork and Kerry. In 1925, however, Thomas R. was offered a job managing a quarry by an acquaintance in Bangor and so the family headed north again. Nevertheless, according to his daughter, he continued to take summer jobs on farms and in gardens. He had injured his leg in a cycling accident while on duty in Kerry and always walked with a limp. Farm and garden work was often painful, but, aside from the much-needed income and produce that such work yielded, his daughter wrote that he loved to grow vegetables. He often reminded his children that his grandmother had survived the Famine in Cork by growing vegetables.[44]

Families who had a number of members in the RIC were often able to support each other in the difficult years after 1916. Cecil A. King, the son of an RIC man from Co. Roscommon, was born in 1908 while his father was serving in Co. Sligo. One of ten children, Cecil King went on to work as a journalist and newspaper editor in Cos Londonderry, Donegal, Tyrone and Sligo from the 1920s to the 1970s, and published his memoirs in the 1980s.

His father was one of five brothers from a large family who had joined the RIC as an alternative to emigration. According to King, his extended family was a close-knit one. While conceding that many reproached those who joined the RIC, King wrote: 'I never felt myself in disgrace through being the son of an R.I.C. man, though many a time I and other members of the King family had pro-British mud thrown at us ...' Fortunately, however, his teachers, though 'openly sympathetic with the "cause"', protected he and his brothers from bullying at school by older boys. According to King, the 'I.R.A. made repeated overtures to my father to resign from the force, but he refused, preferring fear of death by a bullet to the alternative – a life of abject penury and a brand of cowardice'.

But as his father was caught up in ambushes, had comrades killed and the family was boycotted,[45] tension increased and the 'King home had become a place of dread, as more and more pressure was exerted on my father to "get-out"'. When his barracks at Collooney was attacked, Sergeant King was warned beforehand by the IRA and decided to stay

---

44 Annie S., Cork city, to ELM, 29 Dec. 1989 (II, 54). 45 In April 1919, referring to the RIC, as 'spies in our midst' and 'the eyes and ears of the enemy', Eamon de Valera called for policemen to be 'ostracised socially by the people of Ireland'. For the effectiveness of this campaign against the RIC, see Paul Leonard, '"Spies in our midst": the boycott of the Royal Irish Constabulary, 1916–21' in Philip Bull, Frances Devlin-Glass and Helen Doyle (eds), *Ireland and Australia, 1798–1998* (Sydney, 2000), pp 313–20.

home that night. But for 'the King family, it was a night of terror, the ill effects of which remained for quite a while, especially where my mother was concerned'. When offered promotion to district inspector, though with a transfer to a more dangerous district, Sergeant King refused. Clearly he was negotiating an extremely difficult and dangerous path.

Cecil King tended to down play the problems of the period, commenting, in an under statement, that an RIC career at the time 'wasn't an enviable existence'. But what was especially important for him was the fact that the force 'prized the Christian way of life and put a special value on family responsibilities'. And he went on to ask if any 'other section of the Irish community contributed more to the social advancement of their time, or fostered more religious vocations, than did these men who endured the intolerance of so many'. In every diocese in the country and in all the 'lay professions', according to King, were to be found 'sons of R.I.C. homes'.[46] Other correspondents too stressed the moral values and discipline of RIC families and the fact that many priests, nuns, teachers and civil servants, working in and for the new Irish state from the 1920s onwards, were children of RIC men. It is clear that, for King, being part of an extended RIC family was a source of strength, and helped him to deal with attacks on the force in 1919–22 and the criticism of it later.

Other correspondents too wrote of the importance of family connections. Joan O'B., for example, had a father, two uncles, and five second cousins in the force. All remained in Ireland after 1922, except for one cousin who joined the Singapore police. Her father, Justin, who had served for twelve years in Manor Street station in Waterford city before disbandment, helped set up an association of ex-RIC men to lobby the British government for better pension benefits, especially for the widows of the RIC. Thus she grew up as part not only of an extended RIC family, but also having contact with a large group of former policemen. Joan O'B. and one of her brothers joined the Irish civil service and came across 'many, many ex R.I.C. men's children in the Civil Service (in the higher echelons, I might add)'. Such extensive contacts made Joan O'B. 'very proud' of her RIC associations and she relished meeting the children and grandchildren of former policemen, which she did in many 'organisations ... that give outstanding service to our country'.[47]

46 Cecil A. King, Ballyshannon, Co. Donegal, to ELM, 5 June 1990, enclosing Cecil A. King, *Memorabilia: musings on sixty-odd years of life as a newspaper man* (n.p., [1989]), pp 12–15, 20–4 (IV, 151). 47 Joan O'B., Phibsborough, Dublin

Yet other children of the RIC, who grew up in the south of Ireland after 1922, were less proud. Serving with Constable Justin O'B. in Manor Street, Waterford, was a sergeant named Joseph Brown, later Browne. The two men were close friends and when Joe Browne's fourth child and second son was born in 1915, he asked his friend Constable O'B. to be the godfather.[48] Browne, who was from Co. Galway and had joined the force in 1891, was the child of an RIC sub constable, as was his wife, Mary Cooney, from Co. Mayo. The couple were married in 1905, while Browne was serving in Mayo, and he was thereupon transferred to Waterford city where he worked until his retirement in 1918, aged forty-five, with a pension of approximately one pound a week.

The family's life after Browne left the police proved to be difficult and often tragic. For a short period they lived in Derry, where both parents worked in the shirt industry. But they were unable to make ends meet and support a growing family that eventually numbered nine children. In 1919 Browne appears to have gone to England, for there he joined the National Society for the Prevention of Cruelty to Children (NSPCC). In 1920 he returned to Ireland as a district inspector for the NSPCC and was posted to Athlone. Browne's predecessor in the job had been an ex-RIC man, as was his successor. Obviously the NSPCC considered that the skills acquired by policemen were appropriate qualifications for their Irish inspectors. But the Browne family, like so many Irish families of the period, succumbed to the ravages of tuberculosis. Joseph Browne died from TB in 1927, as did his wife in 1929, and three of their children. But Constable O'B.'s godson, although contracting the disease and being very ill, survived. He was Dr Noël Browne, later, and controversially, to be Irish minister of health in first Inter-Party government.

Dr Browne published an autobiography in 1986, which was a best seller in Ireland. In that he described his difficult childhood movingly and in some detail. He did not include, however, the information that his father – and, indeed, both his grandfathers – had seen service in the RIC.[49] This was no careless omission. Browne's biographer, John Horgan, says that the Gill and Macmillan editor working with him on the book

---

7, to ELM, 25 Feb. 1990 (III, 88). **48** Ibid. **49** Noël Browne, *Against the tide* (Dublin, 1986), pp 1–2, 13–14. Browne described his father touring his NSPCC district during the early 1920s on a bicycle, serving court orders on families, giving evidence in court and on occasion being threatened and assaulted – all of which sounds very similar to RIC work.

suggested he should discuss his father's twenty-seven years in the RIC. Browne responded forthrightly by writing the word, 'No', in the margin of her letter. Horgan speculates as to the reasons for this obviously deliberate omission. He points out that for a politician in the Republic during the mid twentieth century family ties to those who had policed Ireland on behalf of the British were a political liability. Browne refused as late as the 1980s to write about his father's RIC service, yet this fact was widely known and had been used against him by political opponents since his first entry into Irish politics in the late 1940s. Horgan mentions Seán MacEntee in particular, a leading Fianna Fáil hardliner, who referred disparagingly to Browne's parentage, describing him on one occasion as an 'RIC's man's "get"',[50] while at other times he implied that Browne was pro-British and anti-Nationalist. Browne never responded publicly to such jibes and insinuations, and he presumably was only continuing in this long-standing silence when he refused to mention his father's RIC career in his otherwise outspoken autobiography.[51] However, as we shall see, Browne was not the only Irish public figure to omit mention of an RIC father in an autobiography.

Children who had fathers killed or injured while on duty had an especially difficult legacy to deal with. One correspondent, whose father was a sergeant killed in Co. Fermanagh in 1920, wrote that his mother 'did not speak much about the R.I.C.' and did not 'keep in touch with other R.I.C. families'. She died only five years after her husband and the letter writer was brought up by an aunt in the Free State and 'didn't feel part of a group associated with the R.I.C.' But the raid on the barracks, in which the unarmed sergeant had been fatally wounded, was planned by an ex-constable, who had joined the IRA, and facilitated by a former comrade serving in the barracks under the sergeant.[52] That the sergeant's widow did not maintain contacts with the RIC is perhaps understandable, given the circumstances of her husband's death.

50 The strict definition of the word is, the offspring of an animal, but it was used loosely as a synonym for the less acceptable term, bastard.   51 John Horgan, *Noël Browne: passionate outsider* (Dublin, 2000), pp 1–21.   52 Leslie L., Downings, Co. Donegal, to ELM 10 April 1990 (I, 1). Sergeant Samuel Lucas, who later died in a Belfast hospital, was wounded during a raid on his barracks at Tempo, Co. Fermanagh, in October 1920. Abbott, *Police casualties*, pp 136–8. For information on the ex-constable who planned the raid, see Gaughan (ed.), *Memoirs of Constable Jeremiah*, pp 201–2, 283–5. Lucas, who was a Presbyterian from Co. Tyrone, had joined the RIC at the late age of twenty-two, probably because of family problems, and had served twenty-two years by the time of his death. RIC General Register (PRO(L), HO 184/30, p. 108).

The fact that a number of RIC men worked secretly for Michael Collins or passed information to local IRA units undoubtedly created a great deal of distrust and resentment within the force.[53] One correspondent, growing in Co. Tipperary during 1919–21, was not related to the RIC and remembered 'peelers' children' being bullied at school. She also recollected meeting an elderly man years later in Belfast, who said that he had served in the RIC in Tipperary during those years. He lamented all 'the fine lads' he had seen killed and complained bitterly that many of their officers were 'in league with the bloody Sinn Feiners, sending us out to our deaths'.[54]

Children were particularly sensitive to threats aimed at their fathers and to injuries inflicted upon them. We saw previously how the young Patrick Shea worried when his father went out on patrol at night and how he came to hate those whom he perceived as threatening his father's life. An anonymous correspondent wrote, bitterly:

> My father was shot as he left the church unarmed – after Mass and Holy Communion. Some of the local 'heroes' had the nerve to tell my mother that the bullets were not meant for him but for others who were with him. Some comfort! Thank God I do not remember the incident but I have no doubt atal [*sic*] that I was psychologically damaged by it, and by the absence of my father in hospital for nine or ten months.[55]

Like Shea, this correspondent's political views were shaped by her father's career as a policeman and especially by the dangers he had endured between 1916 and 1922. She noted that her mother's family had 'disowned' her for 'marrying a British uniform' and that her parents suffered 'ostracism' after 1916. They were both, however, according to their daughter, 'conscientious, upright, ambitious and hard working people'. But their 'lives were blighted by the course of Irish history'.

As well as fathers killed, injured or threatened, another trauma that clearly had a deep and lasting impact upon children was bullying at school. As we have seen, Patrick Shea in his autobiography reported that

---

53 For the memoirs of an IRA intelligence officer, who hated the RIC, and yet successfully recruited a number of RIC men to act as informers, see McMahon (ed.), *Pádraig Ó Fathaigh's War of Independence*, pp 24, 27, 66, 85. 54 Elizabeth P., Fethard, Co. Tipperary, to ELM, 17 Dec. 1989 (I, 32). 55 Anonymous, Tralee, Co. Kerry, to ELM, 10 Dec. 1989 (I, 26)

he and his brothers were beaten up by classmates outside their national school in Athlone. Shea's older brother, Jack, recalled in a letter written in 1990 that, aside from fights on the way home, in the school itself 'the other children teased us and passed derogatory remarks about the police, calling them traitors and English spies'.⁵⁶ Others suffered even more humiliating experiences. One correspondent, whose maternal grandfather had been promoted from head constable to district inspector during 1920 and posted to Belfast, told of what happened to his mother and her brother while they stayed during this period with their mother's relatives in Malahide, Co. Dublin. Both children attended national schools in the town. Jack McL., aged nine, 'received a severe beating from a gang of his classmates', while his sister Nora, aged ten, 'had a more subtle treatment meted out to her'.

> One day unknown to her some of her classmates pinned a large number of Union Jacks behind the lapels of her overcoat, in the cloakroom. On the way home from school in the evening, they began to taunt her about her RIC connection; and when a good level of hostility had been fomented the perpetrators rushed up and turned back Nora's lapels to reveal the Union Jacks. This resulted in a similar fate to that of her brother Jack.⁵⁷

Another correspondent suffered at school for his father's RIC background, even though he was not born until 1932, ten years after disbandment. During the 1940s he attended Christian Brothers' schools, which were characterised, according to him, by 'gung-ho republicanism with a glorification of every minor skirmish and a lionisation of the participants as [C]hristian patriots'. He, 'by defination [*sic*], was not part of this'. But

> [y]ou weren't just neutral, you were projeny [*sic*] of the enemy, you were suspect, your father had taken the saxon shilling, you were anathema. I don't mean to dramatise things or indicate that my time at school was totally unhappy but a sense of an unremitting and residual guilt was extant and undoubtedly contributed to trauma.⁵⁸

56 Jack Shea, Newry, Co. Down, to ELM, 30 May 1990 (IV, 136).   57 Ronan B., Dublin 13, to ELM, 28 Dec. 1989 (II, 45).   58 Timothy O'H., Monaghan town, to ELM, 18 Dec. 1989 (II, 48).

The writer confessed to 'torn loyalties' and great difficulty in reconciling the account of the events of 1916–21 presented to him at school with what he knew of his father at home. Other correspondents mentioned a similar conflict when growing up in the thirty years after 1922 as the children of the RIC, but few expressed it more powerfully.

> [W]as your father a bad man who was a spy, an oppressor of his people, possibly an accessory to the imprisonment or murder of his people? Yet you knew him in the house, [and] he was upright with a code of decency, honesty and probity which was accentuated by the very fact that he was a policeman.[59]

This correspondent's father, Timothy H., who died in 1961, in fact had had a very distinguished career in the RIC. He joined in 1907 and was posted to Co. Monaghan. In 1916 he was promoted a sergeant and married a local woman, as a result of which he was transferred to the Cookstown district of Co. Tyrone. He represented Ulster sergeants before the 1919 enquiry into pay and conditions, and in 1920 was made head constable major at the Phoenix Park Depot. This was the most senior non-officer position in the force and meant he was in charge of training rank-and-file recruits. In 1921 he was promoted into the officer corps and despatched to Co. Kerry as a district inspector, his predecessor having been killed. According to his son, Timothy H. loathed the Black-and-Tans. After 1922 there was 'no ambivilence [*sic*] in [his] loyalty to the new state or any predilection to residual loyalties to the ancien regime'.

> My father was, in a sense, apolitical, and that sense of service permeated his make-up. Yet he was a proud man and very proud of having been an R.I.C. man and he never ducked beneath the parapets when any question of his association came up. He was very Irish, he approved of the country ruling itself, maybe not in the way it happened. I don't think that men like himself really knew or understood what happened to them ... He was, I suppose, like most policemen essentially loyal to the force and to his comrades and to its rigid code of honour and conduct, and he retained contact in an active way with his former comrades for many years of his life.[60]

59 Ibid.　60 Ibid.

Family networks were obviously important within the RIC, as already discussed, but family networks also linked the RIC to the RUC, the Garda Síochána and, even, to the IRA, in complex and sometimes problematical ways. One letter writer had a father and two other close relatives who had served in the RIC. The father, Charles M., from Co. Sligo, whose own father and uncle had preceded him in the constabulary, joined in 1905 and was disbanded in 1922, aged thirty-six, with the rank of sergeant. He subsequently joined the RUC, rising to the rank of head constable, before being retired as medically unfit in 1941 and dying three months later, early in 1942. Charles M. had two sisters, both of whom were active supporters of the Nationalist movement, plus a half sister, who was a nun, and a half brother, who joined the Garda during the 1920s and served for thirty years. One of Sergeant Charles M's Nationalist sisters was the writer Mary Colum (1885–1957), who was active in Dublin cultural circles before emigrating to the United States with her husband, Padraic, in 1914. In her autobiography, the first seventy-five pages of which were devoted to her childhood, she talked a great deal about various family members – the book was dedicated to her maternal grandmother – but managed not to mention her father or brother at all, let alone the fact that both were policemen.[61] Her nephew remarked: 'I would not be at all surprised to read that we are a typical Irish family of that period ...' Typical might be something of an exaggeration, but there were certainly some RIC families whose members included active supporters of the IRA, plus men who served simultaneously in the RUC and the Garda Síochána.[62] Preventing such conflicting loyalties from tearing a family apart sometimes necessitated diplomatic silences.

As a child, Denis Donoghue, later a professor of literature in Dublin and New York, experienced such silences in his own family. As discussed earlier, Donoghue's father, also called Denis, like Mary Colum's brother

---

61 Although not mentioning her family's strong links to the RIC, she did discuss Irish people who worked for the British government, conceding that 'government jobs with a pension were the great prizes' and suggesting that 'one found ... some of the most ardent devotees of Irish freedom and separatism in the government services ...'. Mary Colum, *Life and the dream* (New York, 1958; rev. ed. Dublin, 1966), p. 65. Tom Barry, in his famous autobiography recounting his exploits with the IRA during the War of Independence, made clear that he had served in the British army during World War One, but he too failed to mention the fact that his father was in the RIC. Attempting to explain why he had joined the army aged seventeen, he complained that his upbringing and education meant he 'knew no Irish history and had no national consciousness'. Tom Barry, *Guerilla days in Ireland* (Dublin, 1949), p. 2.   62 Colm M., London, to ELM, 29 Jan. 1990 (III, 81).

Charles, was a Catholic sergeant in the RIC, who joined the RUC after 1922 and served into the 1940s. Both sergeants had close relatives who had been in the RIC, but both also had close relatives in the Garda. Whereas Mary Colum had a half brother in the Garda, Denis Donoghue had a maternal uncle, who had supported the Easter Rising and been imprisoned afterwards. In his autobiography, Donoghue, unlike Colum, did allude to the tensions that arose when the one family contained within it RIC, RUC, Garda and IRA members and supporters. Fortunately Sergeant Donoghue of the RUC 'liked' his brother-in-law, Superintendent O'Neill of the Garda Síochána, 'well enough and respected the range of his education'. But it 'was silently agreed that we would talk of domestic matters, not of politics'. When the two families visited each other:

> ... domestic matters, schooling, health, the cost of living, and the problem of acquiring an education and getting ahead in the world filled the available space. My mother, between policemen and a rebel brother, kept her own counsel. She was gifted in that respect.[63]

Doubtless, there were many women, and also men, who learned to keep their own counsel in the decades following the violent partition of Ireland. Donoghue noted that his father too was not very forthcoming about his past: 'Apart from giving me the bare details of his early life, my father didn't engage in reminiscence ... he didn't bask in gone times or occasions. He was grimly related to the present tense ...'[64] Many correspondents reported similar experiences: fathers, and sometimes mothers as well, who were obviously reluctant to talk about their pasts. In quietly excising her RIC relatives from the account of her childhood published in the 1950s, Mary Colum was not untypical; just as Denis Donoghue was not untypical in the 1990s when he chose to be somewhat more open about the stark political divisions that had existed in his family during the first half of the twentieth century.[65]

---

63 Donoghue, *Warrenpoint*, p. 27. 64 Ibid., p. 15. 65 As discussed earlier, even as late as the mid 1980s, Noël Browne had refused to write about his family's RIC links. An RIC background was much less of a liability by then, but Browne had first established the habit of not referring publicly to his father's career during the 1940s, when it certainly was a liability for an aspiring politician. One correspondent, whose father had resigned from the RIC and served for a time in the Garda, remarked upon the 'republican ethos' under de Valera that characterised the 1930s and 1940s and was openly hostile to ex-RIC men. According to him, '[e]ven in the 1960s a Fianna Fail member

The common RIC background of both the Garda and the RUC could lead to tension, but it could also produce a sense of comradeship. One correspondent's grandfather had served in the RIC for thirty years, retiring about 1911. Yet, when his father, Andrew E., joined the force in 1920, it was apparently at the instigation of Michael Collins, and while in Belfast he supplied Collins with intelligence information. He resigned subsequently and joined the IRA and then in 1922 the Garda, in which he served until 1954. His son wrote that, despite his rather 'chequered career' in the RIC, Andrew E. nevertheless 'often expressed admiration' for the force. While stationed near the border in Cos. Cavan and Monaghan after 1922, he and Garda colleagues would get together 'with some of the RUC for a few drinks' and 'join in singing both rebel and orange songs'.[66] Given that many ex-RIC men who joined the RUC appear to have been stationed in south Cos Down and Armagh, it is possible that a factor underlying this fraternisation between the Garda and the RUC was a shared background of service in the RIC before 1922.

While many ex-RIC men maintained contact by letter, met occasionally over drinks and socialised at former colleagues' funerals,[67] others actually settled near each other. As we have seen, Brighton and London had significant communities of retired Irish policemen. But there were also communities in Ireland itself. Many of the Belfast RIC, although from the south, apparently chose to stay after 1922 in and around Belfast. Parts of Dublin too were favoured retirement locations. One correspondent, whose ex-RIC father had worked in England for a number of years before returning to Ireland in the late 1920s, recollected from his childhood during the 1940s that areas of 'the north side of Dublin city had a great many residents who had served with the RIC'. His family's local doctor was the son of an RIC district inspector from Killarney.[68] Others settled in Northern Ireland.

Portstewart in the first half of the twentieth century – as today – was a small, pleasant seaside resort on the north coast of Co.

of Roscommon County Council saw nothing untoward in referring to a former Dail Deputy as "the son of a Tan". The Deputy's father had been a member of the R.I.C.'. Francis H., Virginia, Co. Cavan, to ELM, 8 Feb. 1990 (II, 66). 66 Andrew E., Templeogue, Dublin 6, to ELM, 30 April 1990 (I, 18). 67 For a description of 'tremendous' RIC funerals in Sligo during the 1930s, see Bernard McD., Sligo town, to ELM, 10 Dec. 1989 (I, 30). 68 William O'B., Blackrock, Co. Dublin, to ELM, 13 Dec. 1989 (I, 29). This correspondent, like many, emphasised his father's 'thirst for education'. According to him, for ex-RIC men, 'the education of their children was their major priority in later life'.

Londonderry. It became after 1922 a haven for retired policemen, firstly from the RIC and later from the RUC.

One correspondent, whose father retired to Portstewart in 1922 and served as a justice of the peace there, forwarded extracts from a brief account of his career that he had written himself. Head Constable McC., a Methodist, had joined the RIC in 1892, served in Co. Londonderry where he met his wife and was promoted sergeant in 1901 and transferred to Co. Roscommon. Further transfers to Cos Monaghan and Tyrone followed, with promotion to head constable in 1915 and a transfer to Co. Galway. But after 1919 Galway became a dangerous area. Three men under his command were killed; the barracks in which he lived was destroyed; and he had to send his family north 'to be safe'. In 1921 he was transferred to Bessbrook in Co. Armagh. He was 'glad' to leave Galway, but Bessbrook 'was out of frying pan and into the fire' as 'there was nothing but murders and ambushes'. His wife 'took very ill there'.[69] Clearly retirement in 1922 came as a relief to Head Constable McC. after all the dangers he had faced in Galway and Armagh during the previous three years, and he doubtless enjoyed his more relaxing life as a part-time magistrate in Portstewart.

Another correspondent, who had no RIC family links but grew up in Portstewart during the 1920s and 1930s, was fascinated by the ex-policemen who congregated there.

> The[y] took the money at the time of disbandment and not been [*sic*] overly welcome in the West and South where they had their roots settled in Portstewart where their bones now rest in Agherton grave yard. They played a bit of Golf and fished around the rocks and most of them slept with a Webely [*sic*][70] under their pillow. I was asked once when I was 21 to put 'Pennys' in and close the eyes of one who had just made the big trip. Well I lifted the pillow and under it was the gun. I broke the barrel and sure enough it was loaded in every chamber.[71]

---

69 T. Mitchell, Portstewart, Co. Londonderry, to ELM, 21 and 28 May 1990, enclosing extracts from an unpublished memoir written by her father (IV, 153).   70 A Webley .45 revolver, containing six rounds, was a weapon used by British military and police forces, including the RIC, from the 1880s until the 1960s.   71 Phil C., Carrickfergus, Co. Antrim, to ELM, 15 April 1990 (I, 2). I would like to thank this correspondent for drawing my attention to a novel based loosely on the experiences of one former RIC and RUC man he knew who settled in Portstewart: David Martin, *The Road to Ballyshannon* (London, 1981). For a short account of this man's career, see

RIC men who had joined the RUC in 1922 also, on retirement during the late 1930s and 1940s, settled in Portstewart. This letter writer remembered one who had been with District Inspector O.R. Swanzy, when he was shot by the IRA in Lisburn, Co. Antrim, in August 1920,[72] and who, 'till the day he died when walking took three steps and then looked over his shoulder to see if there was anyone coming with a gun. Many a time I watched him.'[73] Whether the anxiety evident among ex-RIC men in Portstewart, as described by this correspondent, was a legacy of their experiences during 1919–21 or whether it also reflected Northern Ireland life under Stormont rule isn't altogether clear. Although correspondents writing from the south certainly spoke of hostility and prejudice, only one mentioned ex-RIC men there maintaining personal weapons.[74]

Belfast, as already mentioned, became another centre for ex-RIC men in the north. Some had been serving there already, but others moved there from the south. F.F. Rainsford, who later joined the Royal Air Force and rose to the rank of air commodore, was the son of the county inspector for Mayo and later Leitrim. He was at school in Dublin during 1919/20 and, in his memoirs, published in 1986, he recalled restrictions on school outings, hearing the sound of gunfire and the fact that his maths master kept a gun in his desk. But life in prosperous south Dublin was secure compared to his parents' experiences living in a large house just outside Carrick-on-Shannon. While he was home on holiday in 1920, the house was raided by IRA men, who stole several of his father's shotguns. The county inspector was, perhaps fortunately for him, not at home at the time, and young Rainsford hid under the bed sheets.

His father retired in the middle of 1920; he was then sixty-one and had served in the RIC for thirty-eight years. Leitrim 'being no place for a retired senior RIC officer to live', the family moved to Belfast. But County Inspector Rainsford was from the south, as was his wife, who had a brother serving as a district inspector, and his children had all been

Joe Rawson, 'Sergeant Herbert Houston McKenzie, RIC and RUC', *Proceedings of the Royal Ulster Constabulary GC Historical Society* (Spring 2005), p. 6. 72 Michael Collins was convinced Swanzy had led the party that killed Tomas MacCurtain, the lord mayor of Cork, in March 1920. With the help of RIC men working for the IRA, Swanzy was traced to Lisburn and shot as he left a church there. His killing sparked widespread rioting in Lisburn and Belfast, which resulted in twenty-two further deaths and prompted the first use of special constables to reinforce the RIC in the north. Abbott, *Police casualties*, pp 113–5. 73 Phil C., Carrickfergus, Co. Antrim, to ELM, 15 April 1990 (I, 2). 74 'I and two other RIC children found a cache of revolvers and ammunition about 1940 in a RIC house. We were disarmed by the Guards after a Wild West shoot out [that] left the ... Tennis Club full of bullet holes.' Bernard McD., Sligo town, to ELM, 10 Dec. 1989 (I, 30).

born there. He had served for four years in Co. Antrim during the 1880s, but thereafter his whole career was spent in the south, and, indeed, much of it in the west. His son records that they 'were really sorry to be leaving Connaught. We had enjoyed a very pleasant life there until the last year or two and we knew almost nobody in the North'. Moreover, their departure was hasty and their journey to Belfast not uneventful.

> We left in a hurry, leaving most of our belongings behind … We travelled on one of the old single track Irish light railways. It was probably the 'Slow, Late and Never Certain', which was our name for the Sligo, Leitrim and Northern Counties Railway. When we reached the Ulster border the train was stopped by a large number of the 'B' Special Constabulary, some of them sitting on top of haycocks with their rifles pointed at the train. We were there quite a while and wondered if life was going to be like this in Belfast …[75]

Rainsford's parents considered it not 'wise' to send him back to his Dublin school, although he had enjoyed himself there. His sisters, one of whom was also at school in Dublin and the other studying at Trinity College, Dublin, were restricted to Belfast as well. Even more than sixty years later, Rainsford's disappointment and dislocation were still very evident: 'I myself felt that the world had almost come to an end when we had to go, almost as refugees, to what was then called the "Black North", leaving behind all our friends in the South'.[76] For the son of a county inspector, this flight to a virtual foreign land was clearly a bitter experience.

Another centre for ex-RIC men in the north appears to have been Newry. One correspondent had a father from Co. Louth who had joined the RIC about 1910. Three of his brothers and a cousin were also in the force. He served mainly in Co. Down and on disbandment returned to farming in the south with one of his brothers. But this did not prosper in the depressed years of the 1920s and early 1930s, so he moved to Newry, where he had served for a time, married a woman he already knew there and became registrar of the Catholic cemetery. His son wrote that there were a number of ex-RIC men and their families in Newry, work-

75 F.F. Rainsford, Hereford, to ELM, 18 Oct., 1 Nov., 20 Dec. 1991 (V, 167), enclosing F.F. Rainsford, *Memoirs of an accidental airman* (London, 1986), pp 3–5. For County Inspector Rainsford's career, see RIC General Register (PRO(L), HO 184/45, p. 302). 76 Rainsford, *Memoirs*, p. 5.

ing as estate agents, customs officials, court officers and as small farmers in the vicinity of the town. Patrick Shea's father was clerk of petty
sessions in Newry at this time. RIC 'families were closely knit and supported one another' and also the families of RUC men. But the townspeople 'inclined towards republicanism [and] were always suspicious of
the RIC and their families'.[77]

Significant numbers of the ex-RIC who joined the RUC appear to
have been posted to border areas with large Catholic populations.[78] Denis
Donoghue's ex-RIC father served, as we have seen, in the RUC in
Warrenpoint, just over the border from Co. Louth. Another correspondent, whose father was also an ex-RIC man serving in Warrenpoint
during the 1920s and 1930s, remarked that: 'the R.U.C. sergeants in so
many south Down towns were Catholics and had all served in the R.I.C.'
Most were from the south, especially Co. Kerry. The writer felt that, as
families, 'we were isolated[,] not quite accepted by either Catholic or
Protestant'. Her mother, who had eloped from her home in Co. Armagh
in 1920 to marry her father, was 'rather pitied by her family'. Families of
the Warrenpoint RUC 'visited other R.U.C. families in neighbouring
towns, especially at Christmas'. Like so many other correspondents, this
woman commented on her father's 'eagerness for education'. She was surprised to find that, despite the fact he had not gone beyond national
schooling, when stationed on Achill Island, Co. Clare, in 1915[79], he had
bought copies of Thomas MacDonagh's history of Irish literature and
John D'Alton's history of Ireland. He was equally 'ambitious' for his children and 'no expense was spared on our education, perhaps because of a
desire to excel and be accepted'.[80]

While finding further employment was clearly an imperative for most
ex-RIC men, for some, like many who settled in Portstewart, it was not.
Men who would have retired anyway around 1922 or who were single or
who, though married, did not have pressing family responsibilities, sometimes chose to survive on their pensions.

A few invested wisely and were able to supplement their pensions by
dividends. John D., a Mayo Catholic, who joined the RIC as a constable

77 Patrick H., Derry, to ELM, 2 May 1990 (I, 4).   78 One correspondent, who had a father and uncle in the
RIC, both from the Aran Islands, wrote that her father joined the RUC in 1922 and served till 1951, spending
much of that time as a sergeant in south Armagh. Mary K., Naas, Co. Kildare, to ELM, 10 Nov. 1990 (V, 187).
79 As MacDonagh's book was only published in 1916, after his execution, the constable must have bought it then
and not in 1915.   80 Margaret O'C., Glenageary, Co. Dublin, to ELM, 6 Jan. 1990 (II, 61).

in 1902, was promoted a head constable in 1917 and then in 1920 was made a district inspector. He served at the depot in Dublin in 1920 and in Belfast in 1921, before being disbanded in August 1922, aged forty, with a pension of nearly £380 per annum.[81] According to his son, John D., 'like many of his fellow members [of the RIC,] ... was interested in stocks and shares and had sufficient income from investments, combined with his pension, to live in relative comfort for the rest of his life'. In 1926 he married a woman twenty-three years his junior and they went on to have five children. They bought a house in the comfortable north Dublin bayside suburb of Clontarf, and John D., like so many farmers' sons, devoted himself to gardening and managing an allotment. Like other ex-policemen, he also enjoyed sports, especially cycling, swimming and walking. He maintained contact with former comrades, until his death in 1960, and 'never missed the funeral of a "Member", as he called them, if he could help it'. John D. had been a Home Ruler and, according to his son, he 'accepted the disbandment of the Force and the formation of the new State without bitterness or complaint'. But he avoided politics, and 'placed a lot of importance on education and was constantly urging us children to do better at school'.[82]

Others did not seek further employment perhaps because their experiences during 1919–21 made further work impossible. John D., a district inspector born in west Cork, who had joined the RIC around 1890, was another of those long-serving Catholic sergeants or head constables hurriedly promoted into the ranks of the officer corps in the final years of the force's existence. His maternal grandson, who remembered him from the 1950s fondly, described him as 'a good-natured, unintellectual, rather easy-going and even lazy man ... an addict of old ballads and nineteenth-century popular verse. Tom Moore and Robert Burns he had off by heart in huge amounts'. He had been a champion cyclist during the 1890s and a tug-of-war enthusiast, and maintained a passion for Gaelic football throughout his life. During 1919–21 he was stationed in Co. Galway and his loyalties were deeply torn. He was a Home Ruler and 'his attitude to the British was "they paid you a fair wage"'. But he 'knew the local IRA "lads" personally' and his grandson says that IRA men 'would contrive

81 RIC General Register (PRO(L), HO184/47, p. 121).   82 Owen D., Clontarf, Dublin 3, to ELM, 12 April 1991 (IV, 126) Like many other policemen, John D. was also a keen reader and an 'avid diary keeper'. He wrote a fictionalised account of his RIC service during 1919–21, but unfortunately destroyed it before his death.

to have themselves arrested by regular RIC like himself, for fear the Tans would kill them out of hand'. He also knew Michael Collins. Yet fellow RIC men were being killed by the IRA, which produced in John D. a 'chronic condition' of 'political schizophrenia'.

After 1922 John D. did not seek further employment, but lived on his pension, although 'his daughters felt ... that he could have made more of himself and not thrown so much burden on the shoulders of his wife, who heroically held everything together in classic Cork lower middle-class style'. Nevertheless, his pension paid for two of his daughters to study at University College, Dublin. His grandson was convinced that the 'demise of the RIC broke something in him, and he lost the will to work', preferring instead to escape into 'gardening, listening to the radio, and compiling scrapbooks of old love and patriotic ballads culled from *Ireland's Own*, like somebody out of Myles [na Gopaleen]'. In terms of his own life, his grandson wrote that, living in Dublin, he personally felt 'no shame for having an RIC man in the family' – 'never thought about it!' – but, at the same time, he pointed out that his father's family from Co. Sligo had been in the IRA.[83]

The fact that many Irish families contained members who fought on different sides during the years 1916–23 has generally been presented in negative terms: families were divided and this created hatred at the time and lasting bitterness thereafter.[84] Certainly, as Denis Donoghue's autobiography reveals, during the 1930s and 1940s families divided in this way had to exercise a good deal of restraint if arguments and rifts were to be avoided. Yet, perhaps oddly, this very division could have advantages, especially in later decades for the children and grandchildren of such families. In a sense, they were able, with hindsight, to choose sides or even, if they wished, to straddle both sides. Many letter writers, in making the point that their family's RIC links were not a problem for them, at the same time mentioned familial connections to the IRA. They had the luxury therefore of privileging whichever aspect of their ancestry they felt most comfortable with, or of creating a personally satisfying retrospective reconciliation of opposing parties.

83 Tom G., Dundrum, Dublin 14, to ELM, 10 Feb. 1990 (III, 104). 84 Sometimes, however, the fact that policemen had family connections with the IRA could literally be a lifesaver. One correspondent's family was supported in Sligo town by an uncle, who was an RIC district inspector, after the death of their father, a doctor, in 1921. According to this correspondent, his uncle was a loyal and strict policeman, but his aunt had relatives who supported the IRA, and she 'received many a tip-off from her relatives, which saved my uncle's life'. Thomas A. D., North Circular Road, Limerick, to ELM, 16 March 1990; 29 June 1990 (III, 114).

One correspondent, commenting 'we children of the RIC are a shy lot' and that to 'remain silent was a natural instinct', nevertheless indicated that a family's history could be manipulated to suit particular situations: 'It was no lie to say that they were out in 1916 — but omit to say on which side'.[85]

Many officers, like constables, left Ireland permanently or temporarily; some, as we have seen, moved to the new Northern Ireland; but some remained. Some lived off their pensions, but others pursued totally new careers. District Inspector William B. (1877–1948), who had joined the RIC in 1901 and by 1919 was serving as musketry instructor at the Phoenix Park Depot, left Ireland in 1922 for London, where he enrolled, aged forty-five, as a medical student at St Thomas' Hospital. He graduated in 1928 and practised as a doctor for fifteen years in Bedfordshire in the south of England.[86]

The children of Catholic officers, like the children of Catholic constables, shared in the stigma after 1916 of being the offspring of the RIC. One Catholic district inspector's daughter, whose father had joined the RIC in 1906 and served in Cos Mayo and Armagh, described a rather isolated childhood, living in a house outside of town, 'driven in each morning [to school] and collected in the afternoon', and not mixing with the other children. Inspectors' children 'didn't meet with children of the same rank [because of distance] and didn't mix with those of lower ranks [because of class]'. Like the children of many officers stationed in rural districts, this correspondent was eventually sent to boarding school 'quite young'. She remembered being 'just one of the children' before 1916, but thereafter while none 'of the children actually said anything to me ... attitudes had changed and I was out of things. Not so my brothers in their boarding school — boys gave them a hard time'. Her family, she wrote, were nevertheless, 'always proud of our father and made no secret of this connection with the R.I.C.'. But her husband had been a member of the IRA, although he 'always spoke about my father and his career with respect'.[87]

In 1974, as we have seen, the children of one ex-RIC man decided very publicly to acknowledge his police background by referring to it in his

85 Bernard McD., Sligo town, to ELM, 10 Dec. 1989 (I, 30).   86 Eily B., Harpenden, Hertfordshire, to ELM, 30 Jan. 1990 (II, 80).   87 Maura C., Thomastown, Co. Kilkenny, to ELM, 21 June 1990; to W.J. Lowe, 4 May 1990 (IV, 130).

newspaper death notice.[88] But death notices – given the lack of formal monuments to the RIC in Ireland[89] – had already begun to play a role in commemorating the force. January 1969 marked the fiftieth anniversary of the killing of constables James McDonnell and Patrick O'Connell at Soloheadbeg in Co. Tipperary by a group of Irish Volunteers, led by Seán Treacy and Dan Breen.[90] Subsequently, this ambush came to be seen as the first clash in the Anglo-Irish War or War of Independence. On 21 January 1969, the day of the attack, a notice appeared in the Births, Marriages and Deaths column of the *Irish Times*, under the heading 'Roll of Honour'. As well as being in 'proud memory' of the two constables, the notice also commemorated 'all their gallant comrades of the old R.I.C. killed in the execution of their duty, 1919–21. "Faithful unto death"'.[91]

Survivors and descendants of the RIC had begun to use the word 'old' in order to distinguish between professional Irish-born policemen and the English and Scottish Black-and-Tans and Auxiliaries,[92] just as the IRA of the 1919–21 period would become known by many after 1970 as the 'old' IRA to distinguish it from the new Provisional IRA. In both cases, 'old' implied tradition and honour, and, more than that, legitimacy and acceptance. The small word 'old' was thus of great significance for it signalled a re-writing of history in which most of the atrocities of the years 1919–21 were, rightly or wrongly, laid at the door of the 'Tans' and 'Auxies'. The conflict was in fact sometimes misleadingly called the 'Tan War'.[93]

Ironically, the descendants and supporters of the 'old' RIC and the 'old' IRA were largely in agreement on this interpretation. Both found it

---

88 John D., Churchtown, Dublin 14, to ELM, 14 Nov. 1992 (III, 105).   89 There are memorials to the RIC in London: at Brompton Oratory, Westminster Cathedral, unveiled in 1937, and St Paul's Cathedral, unveiled in 1939. The latter two plaques were set up at the instigation of an association of ex-RIC officers, which met annually in London from 1923 until the mid 1950s. The minutes of its committee are in the Goulden Papers, TCD Library, MS 7371–2. I am not aware of any public memorial in Ireland, although there are memorials in churches and graveyards to individual members of the RIC. *Belfast Newsletter*, 27 May 1939; *Irish Times*, 26 March 1992. J.V. Ballantine, Belfast, to ELM, 15 Oct, 1992 (IV, 127); Lieutenant Commander Niall Brunicardi, Fermoy, Co. Cork, to ELM, 29 April 1991, 28 March 1992 (II, 58).   90 Dan Breen, *My fight for Irish freedom* (Dublin, 1924; rev. ed., Tralee, 1964), pp 43–65; Abbott, *Police casualties*, pp 30–33.   91 *Irish Times*, 21 Jan. 1969. The correspondent who sent me this clipping, commented: 'In more recent times thinking people do not look on Soloheadbeg as noble but few are prepared to condemn it'. William C., Thurles, Co. Tipperary, to ELM, 13 Feb. 1990 (III, 110). James Gleeson noted in 1962 that 'the majority of the Irish people condemned the shooting as wanton', but he personally disagreed with this assessment. James Gleeson, *Bloody Sunday* (London, 1962), p. 47.   92 The earliest example of the term 'old RIC' I have found occurs in a poem, 'The Boys of the Old R.I.C.', written by a sergeant about the visit of King George V to Belfast in June 1921, to open the new Northern Ireland parliament. See Raymond Orr, 'The police guard of honour', *Proceedings of the Royal Ulster Constabulary GC Historical Society* (spring 2005), pp 1–2.   93 For some interesting thoughts on both the name and the nature of this 'war', see Peter Hart, *The I.R.A. at war, 1916–23* (Oxford, 2003), pp 62–4.

convenient to see their sides as noble combatants and to ignore a great deal of evidence of murder and torture by all the protagonists. A professional historian might deplore such a mis-reading of the past, but, on the other hand, she must recognise that present Irish generations are in search of reconciliation after the long and bloody Troubles of the latter part of the twentieth century. The renewed interest in the RIC in recent years, the willingness of the descendants of policemen to acknowledge their ancestry and the readiness of Irish people more generally to accept those who worked for the British state during the period of the Union is surely a welcome development, in terms of the past, but especially of the future. One can only applaud the fact that the RIC is returning to the Irish public memory, even if such memories remain determinedly selective.

Bibliography

PRIMARY SOURCES

UNPUBLISHED

Irish National Archives, Dublin
Chief Secretary's Office, Registered Papers
Crime Branch Special Papers
Outrage Papers
National Library of Ireland, Dublin
Official Diary of County Inspector William Burke, RIC, 1865–72
Comerford Transcript
Larcom Papers
O'Hara Papers
RIC Circulars, 1882–1900
Trinity College, Dublin, Library
J.R.W. Goulden Papers
Barrack Journal, Coleraine, Co. Londonderry, 1838/9
Minutes of the RIC Ex-Officers Association, 1923–56
University College, Dublin
Archives of the Irish Folklore Commission
Irish Architectural Archive, Dublin
Office of Public Works, Drawings List: RIC Barracks
Garda Síochána Museum, Dublin Castle
Names of Members of the Constabulary Rewarded, Dismissed, Disrated and Fined, 1848–1872
Papers of Sergeant William Devery, RIC
Public Record Office of Northern Ireland, Belfast
Patrol Diary, Moy, Co. Tyrone, 1833–9
Patrol Diary, Stewartstown, Co. Tyrone, 1844–7
Memoir of District Inspector John Regan, RIC and RUC
Royal Ulster Constabulary Museum, Belfast
Tom Heslip Papers
Public Record Office, London
Home Office Papers: RIC General Register, 1816–1922
Paymaster General's Office Papers: Award of Pensions on Disbandment of RIC
Treasury Blue Notes, 1892–3, 1920–1: RIC
John Rylands Library, University of Manchester
Tynan Papers: Recollections of Sir David Harrel, 1926
Author's Collection
RIC Letters, Volume I (Correspondents 1–40); II (41–80); III (81–120); IV (121–60); V (161–213)
RIC photographs and documents

Private Collections

District Inspector E.J. Kerin: Personal Journal, 1874–84

Sergeant Thomas J. McElligott: Letters and Police Union Membership Lists

Constable Jeremiah Mee: Memoirs and Newspaper Articles

Inspector General Sir Andrew Reed: Recollections of My Life, 1911; Extracts and Reminiscences, 1885–1900; Diary, 1879–81; Letters, 1876–85

Sub Inspector W.D. Rooke: Constabulary Journal, 1859–64

Constable Denis Shields: Police Notebook, 1869

PUBLISHED

Parliamentary Papers

Report from the Select Committee on Orange Lodges in Ireland, H.C. 1835 (377), xv

Third Report from the Select Committee on Orange Lodges, Associations or Societies in Ireland, H.C. 1835 (476), xvi

Minutes of Evidence taken before the Select Committee of the House of Lords, appointed to enquire into the State of Ireland, since the Year 1835, in Respect of Crime and Outrage, H.L. 1839 (486–III), xii

Return Relative to the Persons who have been Killed or Severely Wounded in Affrays with the Constabulary … since 1st December 1830 …, H.C. 1846 (280), xxxv

Report of the Select Committee on Outrages (Ireland) …, H.C. 1852 (438), xiv

Report of the Select Committee … appointed to consider … extending the Functions of the Constabulary in Ireland to the Suppression or Prevention of Illicit Distillation, H.L. 1854 (53), x

Report of the Commissioners of Enquiry into the Irish Constabulary, H.C. 1866 (3658), xxxiv

Report of the Select Committee on Westmeath, &c. (Unlawful Combinations), H.C. 1871 (147), xiii

Report of the Commissioners appointed … to enquire into the Condition of the Civil Service in Ireland on the Royal Irish Constabulary, [C 831], H.C. 1873, xxii

Return of Outrages reported to the Royal Irish Constabulary Office from 1 January 1844 to 31 December 1880, [C 2756], H.C. 1881, lxxvii

Report of the Committee of Inquiry into the Royal Irish Constabulary, [C 3577], H.C. 1883, xxxii

Belfast Riots Commission 1886. Report of the Belfast Riots Commissioners. Minutes of Evidence and Appendix, [C 4925–I], H.C. 1887, xviii

Royal Irish Constabulary. Evidence taken before the Committee of Inquiry, 1901, [Cd 1094], H.C. 1902, xiii.

Belfast Police Commission, 1906. Appendix to Report of the Commissioners. Minutes of Evidence, Appendices and Index (Dublin, 1907),

Report of Committee of Inquiry into the RIC and DMP, [Cd 7421], H.C. 1914, xliv

Report of the Vice-Regal Commission on Re-Organisation and Pay of the Irish Police Forces, [Cmd 603], H.C. 1920, xxii

Constabulary Rules, Guides and Manuals

Belfast police manual: compiled for the use of the Royal Irish Constabulary Force serving in the town of Belfast (Belfast, 1888)

Dagg, George, *The road and route guide for Ireland of the Royal Irish Constabulary* (Dublin, 1893)

Depot standing orders 1846 (Dublin, 1847)

Drill book compiled for the use of the Royal Irish Constabulary from the infantry drill book, 1905 (Dublin, 1906)

A manual of drill for the Constabulary Force of Ireland (Dublin, 1859)

Reed, Andrew, *The Irish policeman's manual* (2nd ed., Dublin, 1883)

——, *The Irish constable's guide* (4th ed., Dublin, 1907)

——, *The liquor licensing laws, Ireland* (Dublin, 1889)

Milling, J.C., *The R.I.C. A.B.C.: police duties in relation to acts of parliament in Ireland* (Belfast, 1910)
The Royal Irish Constabulary manual; or Guide to the discharge of police duties (3rd ed., Dublin, 1882; 4th ed., Dublin, 1888; 6th ed., Dublin, 1909)
[Shaw Kennedy, James] *Standing rules and regulations for the government and guidance of the Constabulary Force of Ireland* (Dublin, 1837)
Smith, Joseph, *A hand-book of police duties* (2nd ed., Dublin, 1896)
The standing orders and regulations for the conduct and proceeding of the chief constables and other constables of the county ... (Dublin, [1825])
Standing orders and regulations for the government and guidance of the Dublin Metropolitan Police ... (Dublin, 1889)
Standing rules and regulations for the government and guidance of the Royal Irish Constabulary (3rd ed., Dublin, 1872; 4th ed., Dublin, 1888; 6th ed., Dublin, 1911)
Rules and regulations for the control and management of the finance department of the Royal Irish Constabulary (3rd ed., Dublin, 1874; 4th ed., Dublin, 1892)
Wynne, Owen, *A pocket summary of the law of evidence* (Dublin, 1891)

Periodicals
Constabulary Gazette
Irish Times
Proceedings of the Royal Ulster Constabulary Historical Society
Royal Irish Constabulary Directory and List
Royal Irish Constabulary Magazine

Books and articles
Addison, H.R., *Recollections of an Irish police magistrate* (London, 1864)
Anderson, Robert, *Sidelights on the home rule movement* (London, 1906)
Anonymous, *Tales of the R.I.C.* (Edinburgh and London, 1922)
Ball, Stephen (ed.), *A policeman's Ireland: recollections of Samuel Waters, RIC* (Cork, 1999)
Barry, Tom, *Guerilla days in Ireland* (Dublin, 1949)
Blake, H.A., 'The Irish Police', *The Nineteenth Century*, ix, 48 (Feb. 1881), pp 385–96
Bodkin, M.M., *Famous Irish trials* (1918; new ed., Dublin, 1997)
Breen, Dan, *My fight for Irish freedom* (1924; rev. ed., Tralee, 1964)
Brophy, Michael, *Sketches of the Royal Irish Constabulary* (London and New York, 1886)
Brownrigg, H.J., *Examination of some recent allegations concerning the constabulary force of Ireland, in a report to his excellency, the lord lieutenant* (Dublin, 1864)
Colum, Mary, *Life and the dream* (1958; rev. ed., Dublin, 1966)
[Croker, John], *The Croker inquiry: miscarriages of justice exposed. Brief pamphlet* (Dublin, 1877)
Crozier, F.P., *Ireland for ever* (London, 1932)
Curran, J.A., *Reminiscences of John Adye Curran, K.C.: late county court judge and chairman of quarter sessions* (London, 1915)
Curtis, Robert, *History of the Royal Irish Constabulary* (2nd ed., Dublin, 1871)
——, *The Irish police officer: comprising the identification, and other tales* (London, 1861)
Donoghue, Denis, *Warrenpoint* (London, 1991)
Dorian, Hugh, *The outer edge of Ulster: a memoir of social life in nineteenth-century Donegal*, eds Breandán Mac Suibhne and David Dickson (Dublin, 2000)
Dunlop, Eull (ed.), *Robert Dunlop (RIC) of Clough, County Antrim: reminiscences (1825–75) of a Northern boyhood, followed by service in County Longford and County Kildare, before retirement in Belfast* (Ballymena, 1995)
Elrington, M.C., *A constabulary officer's reasons for resigning* (Dublin, 1872)

Fennell, Thomas, *The Royal Irish Constabulary: a history and personal memoir*, ed. Rosemary Fennell (Dublin, 2003)

Gaughan, J.A. (ed.), *Memoirs of Constable Jeremiah Mee, R.I.C.* (Dublin, 1975)

Green, G. Garrow, *In the Royal Irish Constabulary* (London and Dublin, n.d.),

Gregory, Vere, *The house of Gregory* (Dublin, 1943)

Hall, S.C. and A.M., *Ireland: its scenery, character, &c.* (3 volumes, London, n.d.)

Hart, Peter (ed.), *British intelligence in Ireland, 1920–1* (Irish Narratives, Cork, 2002)

Head, Francis, *A fortnight in Ireland* (London, 1852)

Headlam, Maurice, *Irish reminiscences* (London, 1947)

Kickham, Charles J., *For the old land: a tale of twenty years ago* (Dublin, 1886)

Leatham, C.W., *Sketches and stories of the Royal Irish Constabulary* (Dublin, 1909)

Lloyd, Clifford, *Ireland under the Land League: a narrative of personal experiences* (Edinburgh and London, 1892)

Lynch-Robinson, Christopher, *The last of the Irish R.M.s* (London, 1951)

Lynd, Robert, *Home life in Ireland* (London, 1909)

McMahon, T.G. (ed.), *Pádraig Ó Fathaigh's War of Independence: recollections of a Galway Gaelic leaguer* (Irish Narratives, Cork, 2000)

Marx, Karl and Engels, Frederick, *Ireland and the Irish question* (Moscow, 1971)

Montgomery, J.W., *Mervyn Grey; or, Life in the Royal Irish Constabulary* (Glasgow and London, [c.1875]),

Neligan, David, *The spy in the castle* (London, 1968)

O'Brien, R.B., *Dublin Castle and the Irish people* (Dublin and Waterford, 1909)

——, *Thomas Drummond, under secretary in Ireland, 1835–40: life and letters* (London, 1889)

Ó Cuív, Brian, 'A contemporary account in Irish of a nineteenth-century tithe affray', *Proceedings of the Royal Irish Academy*, 61 C, 1 (July 1960), pp 1–21

O'Faolain, Sean, *Vive moi!: an autobiography*, ed. Julia O'Faolain (London, 1993)

Robinson, Henry A., *Further memories of Irish life* (London, 1924)

Ross, John, *The years of my pilgrimage: random reminiscences* (London, 1924)

Sergeant Kiely: a wordsnare broadsheet (Nenagh, 1975)

Shaw Kennedy, James, *Notes on the battle of Waterloo, with a brief memoir of his life and services* (London, 1865)

Shea, Patrick, *Voices and the sound of drums: an Irish autobiography* (Belfast, 1981)

Street, C.J.C., *The administration of Ireland, 1920* (London, 1921)

Thynne, Robert, *Story of a campaign estate; or, the turn of the tide* (London, 1896)

Williams, R.H. (ed.), *The Salisbury-Balfour correspondence, 1869–92* (Cambridge, 1988)

Winter, Ormonde, *Winter's tale* (London, 1955)

Yates, Lionel and Goodhart, Honor, *The eclipse of James Trent, D.I.* (London, 1924)

SECONDARY SOURCES

Abbott, Richard, *Police casualties in Ireland, 1919–22* (Cork, 2000)

Akenson, D.H., *The Irish education experiment: the national system of education in the nineteenth century* (London and Toronto, 1970)

Allen, Gregory, *The Garda Síochána: policing independent Ireland, 1922–82* (Dublin, 1999)

Anderson, D.M. and Killingray, David (eds), *Policing the empire: government, authority and control, 1830–1940* (Manchester, 1991)

——, *Policing and decolonisation: nationalism, politics and the police, 1917–65* (Manchester, 1992)

Augustein, Joost, *From public defiance to guerrilla warfare: the experience of ordinary volunteers in the Irish war of independence, 1916–21* (Dublin, 1996)

—— (ed.), *The Irish revolution, 1913–23* (Basingstoke, Hants., 2002)

Ball, S.A., 'Policing the Land War: official responses to political protest and agrarian crime in Ireland, 1879–81', unpublished PhD thesis, University of London, 2000

Ballantine, John V., 'The life and times of the R.I.C.' [fourteen articles], *Police Beat* (April 1981 to Aug. 1982)

Bartlett, Thomas, 'An end to moral economy: the Irish militia disturbances of 1793', *Past and Present*, 99 (1983), pp 41–64

——, and Jeffery, Keith (eds), *A military history of Ireland* (Cambridge, 1996)

Barry, Sebastian, *The whereabouts of Eneas McNulty* (London, 1998)

Bayley, D.H., 'The police and political development in Europe' in Charles Tilly (ed.) *The formation of national states in Western Europe* (Princeton, NJ, 1975), pp 328–79

Beames, Michael, *Peasants and power: the Whiteboy movements and their control in pre-Famine Ireland* (Brighton, 1983)

Bennett, Richard, *The Black and Tans* (London, 1959)

Blackstock, Allan, *An ascendancy army: the Irish yeomanry, 1796–1834* (Dublin, 1998)

Bonsall, Penny, *The Irish RMs: the resident magistrates in the British administration in Ireland* (Dublin, [1997])

Bourke, Angela, *The burning of Bridget Cleary* (London, 1999)

Bowden, Tom, *Beyond the limits of the law: a comparative study of the police in crisis politics* (Harmondsworth, 1978)

——, *The breakdown of public security: the case of Ireland, 1916–21, and Palestine, 1936–9* (London and Beverly Hills, 1977)

Boyle, Kevin, 'Police in Ireland before the Union: I; II; III', *Irish Jurist*, new series, vii (1972), pp 115–37; viii (1973), pp 90–116; viii (1973), pp 323–48

Bracken, Noreen, 'The demise of the Royal Irish Constabulary, c.1919–24', unpublished MA thesis, University College, Dublin, 1987

Bradshaw, Brendan, 'Nationalism and historical scholarship in modern Ireland', *Irish Historical Studies*, xxvi, 104 (Nov. 1989), pp 329–51

Brady, Conor, *Guardians of the peace* (Dublin, 1974)

Breathnach, Seamus, *The Irish police from the earliest times to the present day* (Dublin, 1974)

Brewer, J.D., 'Max Weber and the Royal Irish Constabulary: a note on class and status', *British Journal of Sociology*, 40, 1 (March 1989), pp 82–96

——, *The Royal Irish Constabulary: an oral history* (Belfast, 1990)

——, and Magee, Kathleen, *Inside the RUC: routine policing in a divided society* (Oxford, 1991)

Brewer, John and Styles, John (eds), *An ungovernable people: the English and their law in the seventeenth and eighteenth centuries* (London, 1980)

Bridgeman, Ian, 'Policing rural Ireland: a study of the origins, development and role of the Irish constabulary, and its impact on crime prevention and detection in the nineteenth century', unpublished PhD thesis, The Open University, 1993

——, 'The Constabulary and the criminal justice system in nineteenth-century Ireland' in Ian O'Donnell and Finbarr McAuley *(eds) Criminal justice history: themes and controversies from pre-independence Ireland* (Dublin, 2003), pp 113–41

Broeker, Galen, *Rural disorder and police reform in Ireland, 1812–36* (London and Toronto, 1970)

Brown, Stephen (ed.), *Ireland in fiction: a guide to Irish novels, tales, romances and folk-lore* (new ed., Dublin and London, 1919)

Browne, Noël, *Against the tide* (Dublin, 1986)

Campbell, Fergus, *Land and revolution: nationalist politics in the west of Ireland, 1891–1921* (Oxford, 2005)

Carroll, P.J., 'Notes for a history of police in Ireland' [fourteen articles], *Garda Review* (Jan. 1961 to Feb. 1962)

Clark, Sam and Donnelly, J.S. Jr (eds), *Irish peasants: violence and political unrest, 1780–1914* (Manchester, 1983)

Clarke, J.R., RIC history [twenty-three articles], *Constabulary Gazette* (Feb. 1979 to Nov. 1982; July 1986 to June 1987)

Cochrane, Nigel, 'The policeman's lot is not a happy one: duty, discipline, pay and conditions in the Dublin Metropolitan Police, c.1833–45', *Saothar*, 12 (1987), pp 9–20

——, 'The policing of Dublin, 1830–46: a study in administration', unpublished MA thesis, University College, Dublin, 1984

——, 'Public reaction to the introduction of a new police force: Dublin, 1838–45', *Éire–Ireland*, xxii, 1 (Spring 1987), pp 72–85

Coleman, Anne, *Riotous Roscommon: social unrest in the 1840s* (Maynooth Studies in Local History 27, Dublin, 1999)

Conley, Carolyn A., *Melancholy accidents: the meaning of violence in post-Famine Ireland* (Lanham, MD, 1999)

Connolly, S.J., 'Violence and order in the eighteenth century' in P. O'Flanagan, P. Ferguson and K. Whelan (eds) *Rural Ireland: modernisation and change* (Cork, 1995), pp 42–61

Cramer, James, *The world's police* (London, 1964)

Critchley, T.A., *A history of police in England and Wales* (London, 1967)

Crossman, Virginia, *Politics, law and order in nineteenth-century Ireland* (Dublin, 1996)

——, 'Preserving the peace in Ireland: the role of military forces, 1815–45', *Irish Sword*, xvii, 69 (1990), pp 261–72

Cullingford, Elizabeth, 'Colonial policing: *The Steward of Christendom* and *The whereabouts of Eneas McNulty*', *Eire-Ireland*, xxxix, 3/4 (2004), pp 11–37

Curtis, L.P., *Coercion and conciliation in Ireland, 1880–92: a study in conservative unionism* (Princeton, NJ, 1963)

Daly, M.E., 'Review article: historians and the Famine: a beleaguered species', *Irish Historical Studies*, xxx, 120 (Nov. 1997), pp 591–601

D'Arcy, Fergus, 'The Dublin police strike of 1882', *Saothar*, 23 (1998), pp 33–44

Davis, J.A., *Conflict and control: law and order in nineteenth-century Italy* (London, 1988)

Dawson, N.W., 'Illicit distillation and the revenue police', *Irish Jurist*, new series, xii (1977), pp 282–94

Delany, V.T.H., *Christopher Palles* (Dublin, 1960)

Denman, Terence, *Ireland's unknown soldiers: the 16th (Irish) Division in the Great War* (Dublin, 1991)

Desmond, Liam, *With the constabulary in Roscommon* (Midleton, Co. Cork, n.d.)

Donajgrodzki, A.P. (ed.), *Social control in nineteenth century Britain* (London, 1977)

Duggan, G.C., 'The Royal Irish Constabulary' in Owen Dudley Edwards and Fergus Pyle (eds) *1916: The Easter Rising* (London, 1968), pp 91–9

Duggan, J.P., *A history of the Irish army* (Dublin, 1991)

Emsley, Clive, *Crime and society in England, 1750–1900* (London and New York, 1987)

——, 'The English bobby: an indulgent tradition' in Roy Porter (ed.) *Myths of the English* (Cambridge, 1992), pp 114–35

——, *The English police: a political and social history* (Hemel Hempstead, 1991)

——, *Policing and its contexts, 1750–1870* (London, 1983)

Fanon, Frantz *The wretched of the earth*, trans. Constance Farrington (London, 1965)

Farrell, Michael, *Arming the Protestants: the formation of the Ulster Special Constabulary and the Royal Ulster Constabulary, 1920–7* (London and Sydney, 1983)

Fedorowich, Kent, 'The problems of disbandment: the Royal Irish Constabulary and imperial migration, 1919–29', *Irish Historical Studies*, xxx, 117 (May 1996), pp 88–110

Ferriter, Diarmaid, *The transformation of Ireland, 1900–2000* (London, 2004)

Finnane, Mark, 'A decline in violence in Ireland? Crime, policing and social relations, 1860–1914', *Crime, Histoire et Sociétés/Crime, History and Societies*, i, 1 (1997), pp 51–70

——, *Police and government: histories of policing in Australia* (Melbourne, 1994)

—— (ed.), *Policing in Australia: historical perspectives* (Sydney, 1987)

Fitzpatrick, David, 'The disappearance of the Irish agricultural labourer, 1841–1912', *Irish Economic and Social History*, vii (1980), pp 66–92

——, 'Marriage in post-Famine Ireland' in Art Cosgrove (ed.), *Marriage in Ireland* (Dublin, 1985), pp 116–31

——, *Politics and Irish life, 1913–21: provincial experience of war and revolution* (Dublin, 1977)

Foucault, Michel, *Discipline and punish: the birth of the prison*, trans. Alan Sheridan (London, 1977)

Frame, Robin, 'The judicial powers of the medieval Irish keepers of the peace', *Irish Jurist*, new series, ii (1967), pp 308–26

——, 'Military service in the lordship of Ireland, 1290–1360' in Robert Bartlett and Angus Mackay (eds), *Medieval frontier societies* (Oxford, 1989), pp 101–26

Fulham, G.J., 'James Shaw-Kennedy and the reformation of the Irish constabulary, 1836–8', *Éire-Ireland*, xvi, 2 (summer 1981), pp 93–106

Gallagher, Ronan, *Violence and nationalist politics in Derry City, 1920–3* (Maynooth Studies in Local History 52, Dublin, 2003)

Garnham, Neal, *The courts, crime and the criminal law in Ireland, 1692–1720* (Dublin, 1996)

——, 'How violent was eighteenth-century Ireland?', *Irish Historical Studies*, xxx, 119 (May 1997), pp 377–92

Garvin, Tom, *Nationalist revolutionaries in Ireland, 1858–1928* (Oxford, 1987)

Gatrell, V.A.C., 'Crime, authority and the policeman-state' in F.M.L. Thompson (ed.), *The Cambridge social history of Britain, 1750–1950* (Cambridge, 1990), iii, pp 243–310

Gibbons, S.R., *Captain Rock, night errant: the threatening letters of pre-Famine Ireland, 1801–45* (Dublin, 2004)

Gleeson, James, *Bloody Sunday* (London, 1962)

Glob, P.V., *The bog people: Iron-Age man preserved*, trans. by R. Bruce-Mitford (London, 1969)

Goffman, Erving, *Asylums: essays on the social situation of mental patients and other inmates* (New York, 1961),

Gray, John, *City in revolt: James Larkin and the Belfast dock strike of 1907* (Belfast, 1985),

Griffin, Brian, *The Bulkies: police and crime in Belfast, 1800–65* (Dublin, 1997)

——, 'The Irish police: love, sex and marriage in the nineteenth- and early twentieth-centuries' in Margaret Kelleher and James Murphy (eds), *Gender perspectives in nineteenth-century Ireland: public and private spheres* (Dublin, 1997), pp 168–78

——, 'Religion and opportunity in the Irish police forces, 1836–1914' in R.V. Comerford et al (eds), *Religion, conflict and coexistence in Ireland: essays presented to Monsignor Patrick J. Corish* (Dublin, 1990), pp 219–34

——, 'The Irish police, 1836–1914: a social history', unpublished PhD thesis, Loyola University of Chicago, 1990

Griffith, Kenneth and O'Grady, T.E., *Curious journey: an oral history of Ireland's unfinished revolution* (London, 1982)

Guinnane, T.W., *The vanishing Irish: households, migration and the rural economy in Ireland, 1850–1914* Princeton, NJ, 1997).

Gurr, T.R., *Rogues, rebels and reformers: a political history of urban crime and conflict* (Beverly Hills, CA, and London, 1976)

Farrell, Sean, *Rituals and riots: sectarian violence and political culture in Ulster, 1784–1886* (Lexington, KY, 2000)

Hand, G.J., *English law in Ireland, 1290–1324* (Cambridge, 1967)

Harries-Jenkins, Gwyn, *The army in Victorian society* (London and Toronto, 1977),

Hart, Peter, *The I.R.A. and its enemies: violence and community in Cork, 1916–23* (Oxford, 1998)

——, *The I.R.A. at war, 1916–23* (Oxford, 2003)

Harvey, A.D., 'Who were the Auxiliaries?', *Historical Journal*, xxxv (1992), pp 665–9

Hawkins, Richard, 'An army on police work, 1881–2: Ross of Blandensburg's Memorandum', *Irish Sword*, xi, 43 (winter 1973), pp 75–117

——, 'Dublin Castle and the Royal Irish Constabulary (1916–22)' in Desmond Williams (ed.) *The Irish struggle, 1916–26* (London, 1966), pp 167–81

——, 'The "Irish model" and the empire: a case for reassessment' in Anderson, D.M. and Killingray, David (eds), *Policing the empire: government, authority and control, 1830–1940* (Manchester, 1991), pp 18–32

Heaney, Seamus, *North* (London, 1975)

Henry, Brian, *Dublin hanged: crime, law enforcement and punishment in late eighteenth-century Dublin* (Dublin, 1994)

Herlihy, Jim, *The Dublin Metropolitan Police: a short history and genealogical guide* (Dublin, 2001)

——, *The Royal Irish Constabulary: a complete alphabetical list of officers and men, 1816–1922* (Dublin, 1999)

——, *The Royal Irish Constabulary: a short history and genealogical guide* (Dublin, 1997)

Hezlet, Arthur, *The 'B' Specials: a history of the Ulster Special Constabulary* (London, 1972)

Hirst, Catherine, *Religion, politics and violence in nineteenth-century Belfast: the Pound and Sandy Row* (Dublin, 2002)

Hogan, Dáire, *The legal profession in Ireland, 1798–1922* (Dublin, 1986)

Hoppen, K.T., *Elections, politics and society in Ireland, 1832–85* (Oxford, 1984)

Horgan, John, *Noël Browne: passionate outsider* (Dublin, 2000)

Horne, Edward, *A job well done: a history of the Palestine Police Force, 1920–48* (Leigh-on-Sea, Essex, 1982)

Hout, Michael, *Following in father's footsteps: social mobility in Ireland* (Cambridge, MS, and London, 1989)

Jeffery, Keith, *Ireland and the Great War* (Cambridge, 2000)

——, 'Police and government in Northern Ireland, 1922–69' in Mark Mazower (ed.), *The policing of politics in the twentieth-century: historical perspectives* (Providence, RI, and Oxford, 1997), pp 151–66

Jeffries, Charles, *The colonial police* (London, 1952)

Johnson, D.R., *Policing the urban underworld: the impact of crime on the development of the American police, 1800–87* (Philadelphia, 1979)

Kelly, Fergus, *A guide to early Irish law* (Dublin, 1988)

Kennedy, Jr, R.E., *The Irish: emigration, marriage and fertility* (Berkeley, CA, 1973)

Leonard, Jane, 'Getting them at last: the I.R.A. and ex-servicemen' in David Fitzpatrick (ed.) *Revolution? Ireland 1917–23* (Dublin, 1990), pp 118–29

Leonard, Paul, '"Spies in our midst": the boycott of the Royal Irish Constabulary, 1916–21', in Philip Bull, Frances Devlin-Glass and Helen Doyle (eds), *Ireland and Australia, 1798–1998: studies in culture, identity and migration* (Sydney, 2000), pp 313–20

——, 'The necessity for de-anglicising the Irish nation: boycotting and the Irish War of Independence', unpublished PhD thesis, University of Melbourne, 1999

Lowe, W.J., 'The Constabulary agitation of 1882', *Irish Historical Studies*, xxxi, 121 (May 1998), pp 37–59

——, 'The Irish Constabulary in the Great Famine', *History Ireland*, 5, 4 (winter 1997), pp 32–7

——, 'Irish Constabulary officers: profile of a profession', *Irish Economic and Social History*, xxii (2005), pp 19–46

——, 'Policing the Famine', *Éire-Ireland*, xxix, 4 (winter 1994), pp 47–67

——, 'The war against the RIC, 1919–21', *Eire-Ireland*, xxxvii (fall–winter 2002), pp 1–20

——, 'Who were the Black and Tans?', *History Ireland*, 12, 3 (autumn 2004), pp 47–51

—— and Malcolm, E.L., 'The domestication of the Royal Irish Constabulary, 1836–1922', *Irish Economic and Social History*, xix (1992), pp 27–48

Lydon, James (ed.), *Law and disorder in thirteenth-century Ireland: the Dublin parliament of 1297* (Dublin, 1997)

Macardle, Dorothy, *The Irish Republic* (4th ed., London, 1951)

McBride, Ian (ed.), *History and memory in modern Ireland* (Cambridge, 2001)

McBride, Lawrence, *The greening of Dublin Castle: the transformation of bureaucratic and judicial personnel in Ireland, 1892–1922* (Washington, DC, 1991)

McEldowney, John, 'Policing and the administration of justice in nineteenth-century Ireland' in Clive Emsley and Barbara Weinberger (eds) *Policing Western Europe: politics, professionalism and public order, 1850–1940* (London, 1991), pp 18–35

——, and O'Higgins, Paul (eds), *The common law tradition: essays in Irish legal history* (Dublin, 1990)

McElligott, T.J., *Secondary education in Ireland, 1870–1921* (Dublin, 1981)

MacEoin, Uinseann (ed.), *Survivors: the story of Ireland's struggle as told through some of her outstanding living people* (Dublin, 1980)

McGoff-McCann, Michelle, *Melancholy madness: a coroner's casebook* (Cork, 2003)

McHugh, John, 'The Belfast labour dispute and riots of 1907', *International Review of Social History*, 11 (1977), pp 1–20

McLeod, Neil, 'The blood-feud in medieval Ireland' in Pamela O'Neill (ed.), *Between intrusions: Britain and Ireland between the Romans and the Normans* (Sydney, 2004), pp 114–33

McNiffe, Liam, *A history of the Garda Síochána* (Dublin, 1997)

Malcolm, Elizabeth, 'From light infantry to constabulary: the military origins of the Irish police, 1798–1850', *Irish Sword*, xxi, 84 (winter 1998), pp 163–75

——, 'Investigating the "machinery of murder": Irish detectives and agrarian outrage, 1847–70', *New Hibernia Review*, 6, 3 (fall 2002), pp 73–91

——, '*Ireland sober, Ireland free*': drink and temperance in nineteenth-century Ireland* (Dublin, 1986)

——, 'Popular recreation in nineteenth–century Ireland' in Oliver MacDonagh, W.F. Mandle and Pauric Travers (eds), *Irish culture and nationalism, 1750–1950* (London and Canberra, 1983), pp 40–55

——, '"The reign of terror in Carlow": the politics of policing Ireland in the late 1830s', *Irish Historical Studies*, xxxii, 125 (May 2000), pp 59–74

——, 'The rise of the pub: a study in the disciplining of popular culture' in J.S. Donnelly Jr and Kerby Miller (eds), *Irish popular culture, 1650–1850* (Dublin, 1998), pp 50–27

——, 'Sir Andrew Reed' in C.S. Nicholls (ed.) *The Dictionary of National Biography: missing persons* (Oxford, 1993), pp 549–50

——, '"Troops of largely diseased women": VD, the Contagious Diseases Acts and moral policing in late nineteenth-century Ireland', *Irish Economic and Social History*, xxvi (1999), pp 1–14

——, '"What would people say if I became a policeman?" (Ned Kelly) The Irish policeman abroad' in Oonagh Walsh (ed.), *Ireland abroad: politics and professions in the nineteenth-century* (Dublin, 2003), pp 95–107

——, and Jones, Greta (eds), *Medicine, disease and the state in Ireland, 1650–1940* (Cork, 1999)

Mandle, W.F., 'Sir Antony MacDonnell and Crime Branch Special' in Oliver MacDonagh and W.F. Mandle (eds), *Ireland and Irish-Australia: studies in cultural and political history* (London and Sydney, 1986), pp 175–94

Marcus, David, *A land in flames* (London, 1987)

Martin, David, *The road to Ballyshannon* (London, 1981)

Maume, Patrick *The long gestation: Irish nationalist life, 1891–1918* (Dublin, 1999)

Mawby, R.I., *Comparative policing issues: the British and American experience in international perspective* (London, 1990)

Memmi, Albert, *The colonizer and the colonized*, trans. by Howard Greenfield (London, 1974)

Mitchell, Arthur, *Revolutionary government in Ireland: Dáil Éireann, 1919–22* (Dublin, 1995)

Moran, M.D., 'A force beleaguered: the Royal Irish Constabulary, 1900–22', unpublished MA thesis, University College, Galway, 1989

Muenger, E.A., *The British military dilemma in Ireland: occupation politics, 1886–1914* (Lawrence, KS, 1991)

Murtagh, Ann, *Portrait of a Westmeath tenant community, 1879–85: the Barbaville murder* (Maynooth Studies in Local History 25, Dublin, 1999)

O'Brien, Gerard, 'The missing personnel records of the R.I.C.', *Irish Historical Studies*, xxxi, 124 (Nov. 1999), pp 505–12

Ó Brion, Leon, *Fenian fever: an Anglo-American dilemma* (New York, 1971)

——, *The prime informer: a suppressed sandal* (London, 1971)

O'Callaghan, Margaret, *British high politics and a nationalist Ireland: criminality, land and the law under Forster and Balfour* (Cork, 1994)

——, 'New ways of loking at the state apparatus and the state archive in nineteenth-century Ireland: "curiosities from the phonetic museum" – Royal Irish Constabulary reports and their political uses, 1879–91', *Proceedings of the Royal Irish Academy*, 104, C, 2 (2004), pp 2–56

Ó Ceallaigh, Tadhg, 'Peel and police reform in Ireland, 1814–18', *Studia Hibernica*, 6 (1966), pp 25–48

O'Donnell, Ian, 'Lethal violence in Ireland', *British Journal of Criminology*, 45 (2005), pp 671–95

O'Halpin, Eunan, 'British intelligence in Ireland, 1914–21' in C. Andrews and D. Dilks (eds), *The missing dimension: governments and intelligence communities in the twentieth-century* (Basingstoke, Hampshire, 1984), pp 55–77

——, *The decline of the union: British government in Ireland, 1892–1920* (Dublin, 1988)

——, 'Historical revisit: Dorothy Macardle, *The Irish republic* (1937)', *Irish Historical Studies*, xxxi, 123 (May 1999), pp 389–94

O'Hegarty, P.S., *A history of Ireland under the Union, 1801–1922* (London, 1952)

Ó Maitiú, Séamas, *The humours of Donnybrook: Dublin's famous fair and its suppression* (Maynooth Studies in Local History 4, Dublin, 1995)

Orr, Philip, *The road to the Somme: men of the Ulster Division tell their story* (Belfast, 1987)

O'Sullivan, Donal J., *The Irish constabularies, 1822–1922: a century of policing in Ireland* (Dingle, Co. Kerry, 1999)

Ó Tuathaigh, M.A.G., *Thomas Drummond and the government of Ireland, 1835–41* (O'Donnell Lecture, Galway, 1977)

Otway-Ruthven, A.J., 'The native Irish and English law in medieval Ireland', *Irish Historical Studies*, vii, 25 (March 1950), pp 1–16

Owens, Garry, 'The Carrickshock incident, 1831: social memory and an Irish *cause célèbre*', *Cultural and Social History*, i, 1 (2004), pp 36–64

Palmer, Stanley, 'The Irish police experiment: the beginnings of modern police in the British Isles, 1785–95' in Ian O'Donnell and Finbarr McAuley (eds), *Criminal justice history: themes and controversies from pre-independence Ireland* (Dublin, 2003), pp 98–112

——, *Police and protest in England and Ireland, 1780–1850* (Cambridge, 1988)

Philips, David and Storch, R.D., *Policing provincial England, 1829–56: the politics of reform* (London and New York, 1999)

Philpin, C.H.E. (ed.), *Nationalism and popular unrest in Ireland* (Cambridge, 1987)

Radford, Mark, 'A trial of strength: the policing of Belfast, 1870–1914', unpublished PhD thesis, University of Liverpool, 2002

——, 'The borough policemen of Londonderry, c.1832–70', *Proceedings of the Royal Ulster Constabulary Historical Society* (winter, 1998), pp 6–7

——, '"Closely akin to actual warfare": the Belfast riots of 1886 and the RIC', *History Ireland*, 7, 4 (winter 1999), pp 27–31

Reiner, Robert, *The politics of the police* (New York and London, 1985)

Reith, Charles, *A short history of the British police* (London and New York, 1948)

Ryder, Chris, *The fateful split: Catholics and the Royal Ulster Constabulary* (London, 2004)

——, *The RUC: a force under fire* (rev. ed., London, 1997)

Seedorf, Martin F., 'Defending reprisals: Sir Hamar Greenwood and the "Troubles", 1920–1', *Éire-Ireland*, xxv, 4 (winter 1990), pp 77–92

Short, K.R.M., *The dynamite war: Irish-American bombers in Victorian Britain* (Dublin, 1979)

Sinclair, R.J.K. and Scully, F.J.M., *Arresting memories: captured moments in constabulary life* (Belfast, 1982)

Skelley, A.R., *The Victorian army at home* (London and Montreal, 1977)

Smith, Brendan, 'The concept of the march in medieval Ireland: the case of Uriel', *Proceedings of the Royal Irish Academy*, 88 C, 8 (1988), pp 257–69

Spiers, E.M., *The army and society, 1815–1914* (London, 1980)

——, *The late Victorian army, 1868–1902* (Manchester, 1992)

Stead, P.J., *The police of Paris* (London, 1957)

Steedman, Carolyn, *Policing the Victorian community: the formation of English provincial police forces, 1856–80* (London, 1984)

——, *The radical soldier's tale: John Pearman, 1819–1908* (London and New York, 1988)

Storch, R.D., 'The plague of blue locusts: police reform and popular resistance in northern England, 1840–57', *International Review of Social History*, xx (1975), pp 61–90

——, 'The policeman as domestic missionary: urban discipline and popular culture in northern England, 1850–80', *Journal of Social History*, ix, 4 (summer 1976), pp 481–509

Sweeney, Frank, *The murder of Conell Boyle, County Donegal, 1898* (Maynooth Studies in Local History 46, Dublin, 2002)

Taylor, David, *Crime, policing and punishment in England, 1750–1914* (London and New York, 1998)

Thompson, E.P., *Customs in common* (London, 1991)

Townshend, Charles, *The British campaign in Ireland, 1919–21: the development of political and military policies* (London, 1975)

——, *Political violence in Ireland: government and resistance since 1848* (Oxford, 1983)

Trustram, Myna, *Women of the regiment: marriage and the Victorian army* (Cambridge, 1984)

Vaughan, W.E. and Fitzpatrick, A.J. (eds), *Irish historical statistics: population, 1821–1971* (Dublin, 1978)

Index